Dolor y Alegría

Life Course Studies
David L. Featherman
David I. Kertzer
    General Editors

Nancy W. Denney
Thomas J. Espenshade
Dennis P. Hogan
Jennie Keith
Maris A. Vinovskis
    Associate General Editors

Dolor y Alegría

Women and Social Change in Urban Mexico

Sarah LeVine

In collaboration with
Clara Sunderland Correa

The University of Wisconsin Press

The University of Wisconsin Press
114 North Murray Street
Madison, Wisconsin 53715

3 Henrietta Street
London WC2E 8LU, England

Library of Congress Cataloging-in-Publication Data
LeVine, Sarah (Sarah E.)
Dolor y alegría: women and social change in urban Mexico / Sarah
LeVine in collaboration with Clara Sunderland Correa.
254 p.   cm. — (Life course studies)
Includes bibliographical references and index.
ISBN 0-299-13790-2   ISBN 0-299-13794-5 (pbk.)
1. Women—Mexico—Cuernavaca—Social conditions. 2. Women—
Mexico—Cuernavaca—Economic conditions. 3. Poor women—Mexico—
Cuernavaca. 4. Family—Mexico—Cuernavaca. I. Sunderland Correa,
Clara. II. Title. III. Series.
HQ1465.C84L48   1993
305.42′0972′49—dc20   92-39037

*This book is for Bea and John
and Nan and Vogtie*

Contents

Illustrations

Acknowledgments

This book reflects the support and encouragement of many people. In Mexico, I would like to thank Medardo Tapia Uribe who first led me into the labyrinths of Mexican culture and has been guiding me through them ever since. Solange Guzman Durán introduced me to many of the women on whose experiences this book is based and, during my absences from the community, kept in touch with them on my behalf. She and her family have been generous to and tolerant of me over many years. Marjory Urquidi and Kent Gardien housed me for months on end. In addition to providing me with hospitality, Tomás and Eva Frejka, María Correa, Porfirio and Yvonne Flores, Shigeko and Stanley Watson, and Charles and Chita Wicke all came to my aid at different times. In Cambridge, Aurora SanFeliz and Natania Remba helped me with library research. Terry Tivnan excavated the manuscript from an archaic computer program, Judy Singer was often called on to rescue sections of it, and Joy Sobeck provided editorial help.

My son, Alex LeVine, took the photographs.

My cousin, Ernie Greppin, provided a darkroom.

My husband, who was with me at the outset of fieldwork and later cheerfully kept house and walked the dog for long stretches while I returned to the field, encouraged me to write this book and read draft after draft of the manuscript.

The field research was supported by grants from the Population Council (International Fertility Determinants Awards Program, Subordinate Agreement CP 82.74A), The Rockefeller Foundation (Population Sciences Division), and the Ford Foundation (Child Survival and Urban Poverty Programs). Writing was supported by the Population Council and the Spencer Foundation. The study was carried out in association with El Colegio de México (Centro de Studios Demográficos y Desarollo Urbano) and the Universidad Autónoma de Morelos.

Last, I wish to thank my collaborator, Clara Sunderland Correa, most resourceful and reflective of companions on a compelling journey, and the women of Los Robles who shared their hopes, achievements, disappointments, and wisdom with us.

Dolor y Alegría

Introduction: The Mexican Woman in Historical Perspective

Our purpose is to examine some of the ways in which urbanization and rapid social change have affected Mexican women at each stage in the life course from childhood to old age. Our focus is on women belonging to different generational cohorts who came to adulthood, married, and raised children between the 1920s and the 1980s, under markedly different socioeconomic conditions. We began the research on which this book is based in 1984, a generation after the publication of Oscar Lewis's ground-breaking work, *The Children of Sánchez: The Autobiography of a Mexican Family*. Whereas anthropologists had previously concentrated on rural Mexico, Lewis, who himself had first worked in the countryside, followed migrants into the slums of Mexico City. There, in families such as the one Manuel, Roberto, Consuelo, and Marta Sánchez each in turn described, roles were strictly divided by gender. Males were superior, females subordinate. Husbands dominated their wives and brothers their sisters. Typically, fathers spent very little time with their children, who even so were deeply affected by them, at once fearing and resenting them and longing for their affection and regard. Though family life was characterized by loyalty and concern for one another, at the same time, heavy drinking, male promiscuity, and domestic violence were commonplace.

Introduction

While Lewis noted that the Sánchez family were not among the poorest inhabitants of Mexico City, he nevertheless saw them as belonging to a culture of poverty that, he suggested, was shared by poor people throughout the world. By "culture of poverty," a concept he first presented in *Five Families*[1] and developed in later publications,[2] he meant a "design for living" that is passed from generation to generation by people who form a virtually autonomous self-perpetuating subculture at the bottom of the socioeconomic scale.[3] He asserted that members of this subculture, which, in Mexico of the 1950s, he estimated to include one-third of the population, were not psychologically equipped to take advantage of new opportunities for advancement.

His contentions were greeted by a storm of criticism. The social life of the poor was determined not by personal incompetence as Lewis implied but by the structure of society as a whole, his critics argued.[4] Far from rejecting the values of the dominant society, the poor shared them but were prevented by poverty from approximating them. Furthermore, many of the personality traits that Lewis deemed characteristic of poor people—apathy and an inability to delay gratification or to plan for the future, in particular—were responses to an economic system that by turn exploited and excluded them, depriving them of a sense of control over their own destinies. Again, far from constituting a uniform "culture," the values, attitudes, and behavior of the poor, whether of Rio de Janeiro, Lagos, New York, or Mexico City, were extremely varied. If individual families appeared to exemplify Lewis's "traits," they were embedded in a large majority who, despite great odds, were working for a better future.[5]

In the 1960s and 1970s, a plethora of studies of the family life of the poor were carried out both in Latin America and the United States, where, even though the government had "declared war" on poverty, hitherto the life of poor people had been sketchily documented. Noteworthy among American studies was Joseph Howell's *Hard Living on Clay Street*.[6] In this account of white working-class family life in Washington, D.C., the author makes the distinction between "settled" and "hard" livers. The first group included families who, with male heads in steady employment, had clearly defined goals and strong ties to the community. The second group, whose male heads had work only intermittently, were characterized by poor health, alcoholism, rootlessness, and marital violence and instability. Lillian Rubin's *Worlds of Pain*[7] also focused on white working-class families, living in the San Francisco Bay area of California. The majority were living settled lives as opposed to the hard lives they remembered from their childhoods, but although most husbands enjoyed some job security, money was constantly in short supply, and anxiety levels were high. The most frequently voiced hope of parents was that their children would do better economically than they had, just as they had done better than their own parents. But if, as Rubin concluded, a belief in upward mobility provided a vital rationale and integrity to working-class life, at the same time, her subjects admitted to confusion at a more personal level. Perceiving their parents' marriages as primarily financial arrangements that allowed for little emotional communication or sharing of responsibilities, they wanted something different and better for themselves but lacked models for how to go about achieving this.[8] In Mexico, meanwhile, most researchers on the poor urban family were concentrating on household structure and economic survival strategies. Like Lewis, they portrayed family members as fiercely loyal and supportive of one another and, at the same time, male-female and parent-child relations as hierarchical and authoritarian.[9]

But Mexican society had been changing very rapidly, especially in the 1970s, which saw massive increases in educational opportunities and improvements in health care as well as the inception of a nationwide family planning campaign. How had these radical innovations affected family life and relations between husbands and wives and parents and children? Most especially, how had they affected women as social beings—as daughters, sweethearts, wives, mothers, and widows as well as workers and wage earners? These were some of the questions to which we hoped to find answers.

Many researchers in Latin America have focused their attention on the so-called *marginados* (marginalized ones), who live in slums in the inner city or shantytowns on its periphery, excluded from the mainstream of society by lack of urban skills.[10] The women whom we came to know in the central Mexican city of Cuernavaca, however, were ordinary working-class women, raising children or watching adult children raise *their* children. Not long before, "Los Robles," the neighborhood in which we conducted our fieldwork, had been a beachhead for new arrivals from the countryside; but by the 1980s, newcomers were settling elsewhere in the city, and, as it shed its rough reputation, Los Robles—particularly the upper residential section—was becoming a desirable place to live. Most of the women we knew described themselves as poor, but even those whose husbands were unemployed in the depths of the worst economic recession Mexico has experienced in modern times did not consider themselves and their families farmer, or craftsman's family of its economic function and give rise to a mass society in which work was performed in industrial and institutional settings or on their periphery. Until Mexico began to industrialize under President Porfirio Díaz at the turn of the century, economic activity there, too, had been family based; and there, too, industrialization signaled the end of the old order.

In its early stages, Mexican urbanization, as elsewhere in Latin America, occurred in response to the mechanization of agriculture and to industrial development. Migrants to the city were likely to come from small towns rather than villages and to have better than average levels of education.[16] But increasingly, as urbanization progressed, migrants started coming directly from the countryside, equipped only with rural skills.[17] For the most part, they left the countryside because population pressures on limited land resources forced them out, rather than because the city offered enticing opportunities. As Víctor Urquidi observed,[18] urbanization took place largely in response to rural stagnation rather than to industrialization. Unlike England, where well into the industrial era factories had still largely been manned by the unschooled, by the time industrialization on a major scale occurred in Mexico (in the 1950s and 1960s), the processes involved required a literate work force.[19] By importing capital and complex technology from outside, Mexico, like other Latin American countries, developed an industrial system capable of producing a large volume of goods with few workers.[20] Unskilled rural migrants provided the labor to build new factories, but, except in heavy industry, which employed manual laborers at very low wages to work with raw materials, once construction had been completed, they were shut out.[21] Thus a large proportion of the inhabitants of urban areas, excluded from many of the benefits of development, constituted a surplus population at the economic margins.[22]

Far from being deterred by limited employment possibilities in the city, rural people, often faced with the need to support impoverished parents and siblings as well as their own families, viewed migration to the urban area as their only option. Joining kinsmen and *paisanos* (people from their home communities), they settled in inner-city tenements and low-income developments and squatter settlements on the city's edge.[23] As Lisa Peattie[24] observed of the rural immigrants with whom she worked in La Laja, a shantytown in Ciudad Guayana, Venezuela, although in most cases they had never been in town before, on arrival they were already "proto proletarians," prepared for urban living by the media and by friends and relatives who had preceded them. The men worked as day laborers and in low-wage service occupations or were self-employed as lottery ticket sellers, shoeshine boys, and the like; the women worked as tortilla and snack food sellers and domestic servants.[25] Given that female employment opportunities were almost entirely lacking in the countryside, by the 1960s, young single women were pouring into the city and, having made the move, were likely to remain, marry, and raise their children there.[26] Though life was hard in the urban area, at least some services were available, in contrast to the countryside where health and educational facilities were often nonexistent, mortality rates could be double and triple those in town, and, even among the young, illiteracy was still widespread. Thus, while some men might work in the city during the dry season, returning to plant their *milpas* when the rains came, according to Humberto Muñoz and his colleagues, the majority of rural migrants left their home with scarcely a backward glance. Though they themselves lacked the skills to enter the urban mainstream, they hoped their children would stand a better chance. Thus they might continue to visit their birthplaces for funerals and annual fiestas, but ties would gradually loosen until, for most, they broke.[27]

During the boom years, though the majority of new arrivals to the city worked with their hands, they did not form a homogeneous group. As Andrew Whiteford showed in his study of Querétaro in the 1950s, the poor were stratified according to the type of work they did, the amount of money they earned, and how they spent it.[28] Jobs that required special skills (*oficios*) were ranked higher than those that did not. Thus, carpenters, truck drivers, plumbers, and bakers regarded themselves as superior in status to masons, porters, and laundresses; but given the instability of the labor market, they had little more security than those who had no skills. Rural-urban migration on the scale that Mexico experienced at midcentury created an immense reserve of cheap labor. This served to increase already dramatic inequalities as employers and their upper-echelon employees protected their privileges—and the economic conditions of the larger population fell farther and farther behind.[29]

A generation after Whiteford's study, low-income urban dwellers defined their status not so much in terms of skills as, following the formalization of some sectors of the economy, by whether they received a regular wage and their employment was registered with the government, enabling them to receive fringe benefits, notably, health insurance, through their place of work. Small-scale entrepreneurs, though excluded from the formal sector and its benefits, might do as well financially as those who were included and by hard work and useful connections might even pull themselves up into the middle class. But as Douglas Butterworth has pointed out, since educational qualifications rather than work experience were required for advancement, working-class people with little education had meager prospects of occupational mobility within the formal sector.

From its inception in the 1930s, the ruling political party, the Partido Revolucionario Institutional (PRI), developed and expanded health, education, and social services in an effort both to improve the lot of the poor and to ensure political stability in an economy that, despite spectacular growth after World War II, habitually failed to provide enough jobs or to prevent widening disparities of wealth. Acting on the principle, first championed by President Benito Juárez in the 1860s and enshrined in the 1917 Constitution, that education should be available to all who sought it, successive administrations placed great emphasis on the development of a public education system (Secretaría de Educación Pública, known as the SEP). From the 1940s on, however, the SEP—and every other social welfare program, as well as sources of employment—was in constant danger of being swamped by an exploding population. Thus in 1960, only 60 percent of children aged 6 to 14 were in primary school, and only 10.8 percent of those aged 15 to 19 were in junior high school.[30] By 1970, the proportion of children aged 6 to 14 attending primary school had increased to 79 percent and of those aged 15 to 19 attending junior high school, to 30 percent; but it was not until the late 1970s, when huge oil and natural gas reserves were discovered, producing additional revenues for government programs, that places could be provided for close to all Mexican children of primary school age. By the end of that decade, with the population still growing at around 3 percent, primary school enrollment was rising at an unprecedented 10 percent each year; secondary and postsecondary enrollment increases were comparable, although at the cost of a serious drop in standards. By 1982, 89 percent of Mexican women in their childbearing years (15–49) had attended school, and 57 percent had completed primary school;[31] however, since educational facilities were concentrated in the urban areas, large urban-rural differences still remained.

Neither the long years of economic growth nor governmental intervention had prevented the accentuation of social inequalities. In Britain, a country whose rate of urbanization in the nineteenth century had been comparable to Mexico's in the twentieth century, the working class's chronic fear of poverty had only been eliminated by the social revolution of the 1940s that had created the "safety net" of the welfare state.[32] In contrast, when Mexico, which had undergone no such social revolution, came to the end of its boom, most poor Mexicans still lacked any form of safety net other than what kinship and fictive kinship (*compadrazgo*) provided.

In August 1982, the Mexican government signaled the end of forty years of uninterrupted economic growth with the suspension of principal payments on the foreign debt, followed on September 1, 1982, by the nationalization of the banks. The crisis into which these events plunged the country was rooted in the inefficiencies of a policy of import substitution and protective tariffs, massive flights of capital, and the accumulation of a huge burden of indebtedness to foreign banks during the late 1970s and early 1980s by using Mexico's recently discovered oil reserves as collateral. An additional cause of the crisis was the PRI's longstanding practice of co-opting opposition at every level by providing employment, an approach that ultimately produced a bureaucracy larger and more expensive than the country could afford. In short order, *la crisis*—triple-digit inflation, widespread unemployment, and the termination of price controls on hundreds of staple items—imposed extraordinary levels of hardship on the urban poor who had had difficulty enough making ends meet during the years of prosperity. Between the latter part of 1982 and early 1986, consumer prices rose 981 percent while the minimum wage rose only 573 percent.[33] Typically, poor people blamed the collapse of the economy on corrupt politicians who, after robbing them, had left them to survive as best they could. This they struggled to do by forgoing even small luxuries, by simplifying their diets, and by sending more family members into the work force, which meant school-age boys looking for after-school employment and housewives looking for work that could be done at home. Young people, especially the better educated, delayed getting married and once married, like more and more couples, sharply reduced their expectations with regard to family size.

Throughout most of the boom period, large families had been regarded as desirable by the government as much as by the general population. In a society in which advancement came through personal connections as much as through merit, it was to the advantage of everyone at every social level to have as wide a kinship network as possible. Thus, when Urquidi wrote in 1967 that "as each day passes, birth control appears more essential to the social and economic development of Mexico,"[34] he was voicing the opinion of a very small minority of professionals and intellectuals. Indeed, in 1970, with the annual population growth rate at 3.5 percent, Luis Echeverría campaigned successfully for the presidency with the slogan, "To populate is to govern." Nevertheless, within two years, recognizing both the economy's failure to absorb a rapidly expanding work force and his administration's inability to provide solutions to multiple social problems, Echeverría reversed his position. In 1974, he sponsored the General Law of Population that created the Consejo Nacional de Población (CONAPO), which, working through already existing health care and social service institutions, launched a nationwide family planning campaign. After taking office in 1976, his successor, José López Portillo, earmarked more resources for the campaign, whose stated goal now was to decrease the population growth rate to 2.5 percent by 1982 and to 1.0 percent by the end of the century.

In rural areas where health care services were still sparse, the campaign proceeded slowly and met with widespread resistance.[35] But in urban areas, where more than two-thirds of the population lived and a complex health care structure was already in place, there was an immediate and positive response. By 1981, the birthrate had dropped from 44 per thousand in 1970 to 34 per thousand, and the average Mexican woman, who in 1970 had had 6.7 children by the time she reached the end of her childbearing years, had only 4.4 children.[36] As Viviane de Márquez noted,[37] the family planning campaign did not by itself provide the conditions necessary for bringing about fertility decline; even without government sponsorship, the likelihood is that birth control would have caught on in Mexico, just as it did in some other Latin American countries, notably, Colombia and Brazil. But the process would have occurred even later and proceeded more slowly.

The Study Setting

Cuernavaca is an old town that only recently grew into a city. The administrative center of the Tlahuica region of the Aztec empire in the fifteenth century, it attracted the emperor Mochtezuma I and his court, who would travel down from Tenochtitlán in the high, cold Valley of Mexico to enjoy the year-round warmth of Cuanahuac. In 1521, Hernán Cortés and his invading forces engaged in a skirmish there, and after his destruction of Tenochtitlán, signaling the collapse of the Aztec empire, he returned to take up residence. Called Cuernavaca by the Spanish, the town, which lies

Street scene, Los Robles

House construction

Jacal (hut) built beside the ravine

Apartment building

Vecindad (tenement)

only fifty miles south of modern Mexico City, became the capital of the Oaxaca Valley Marquisate with which the Spanish Crown rewarded Cortés for his role in the conquest. During the colonial period, the ruling elite of New Spain frequented Cuernavaca, a tradition that has continued through Mexican independence to the present day. Sugarcane, introduced from Cuba into the area soon after colonization, gave rise to an industry that went through several long cycles of expansion and retrenchment before reaching its peak during the regime of Porfirio Díaz at the end of the nineteenth and beginning of the twentieth centuries when Morelos became the country's primary sugar-producing region.[38] The peasantry, whose lands had been alienated and absorbed by the great sugar haciendas of Morelos, coalesced around Emiliano Zapata, who led the guerilla army of the south into the Revolution of 1910.[39] Over the next decade, Cuernavaca, which at the outbreak of hostilities had been a prosperous commercial center and a fashionable resort for the upper class from Mexico City as well as the capital of the state of Morelos, was a battleground for federal and revolutionary forces on several occasions. By the time peace was restored in 1920, only 7,000 inhabitants remained, about one-third of its prewar population.

Recovery was slow. By 1940, the population of Cuernavaca had scarcely returned to the size it had been in 1910. But between 1940 and 1960, it doubled, and by 1970, it had increased to an astonishing 160,000, as population pressures on land resources and economic stagnation in the rural hinterland combined with a federal policy encouraging industrial development in the provinces to bring migrants to Cuernavaca from all over central Mexico. According to census figures for that year, only a little more than half (57%) of the city's inhabitants were native to the state of Morelos. By 1980, the population of the city of Cuernavaca stood at 232,000; together with five contiguous semiurban municipalities, it numbered over half a million inhabitants.

Until the late 1960s, the poor of Cuernavaca were concentrated in an inner ring of neighborhoods where they lived in tenements (*vecindades*) and shacks built on the slopes of the ravines that cut through the city north to south. One such neighborhood was Los Robles, formerly a small (approximately thirty acres) sugar plantation that lay about two kilometers north of the central plaza within sight of Tlaltenango where Cortés had begun planting sugarcane in 1529. In the aftermath of the Revolution, in anticipation of government appropriation, the owner abandoned her property to her former *peones* who, with a handful of outsiders, organized themselves into a union of settlers and obtained titles to their plots.[40] In 1938, when Los Robles formally became a *colonia* (an official neighborhood of Cuernavaca), the municipal authorities divided the remaining unoccupied plots and sold them off. When a slaughterhouse was built, tenements to house its workers sprung up around it, and, as bars and brothels followed, Los Robles, with its poorly constructed dwellings and unpaved and unlighted lanes, soon became known as the toughest neighborhood in the city. It was there that many new arrivals—the majority from rural Morelos and the neighboring state of Guerrero—got their first taste of urban life.

In the late 1960s, Cuernavaca, weekend resort for residents of the Federal District and winter haven for Europeans and Americans, started to industrialize, and Los Robles, too, began its own transformation. Because there and in other inner-city neighborhoods building land was growing scarcer and increasingly expensive, new arrivals from the rural area began heading for squatter settlements (*colonias populares*) on the edge of town.

There the poor in large numbers were invading both private property and communal agricultural *(ejido)* land, building shacks and claiming title to the plots they had appropriated. In the meantime, Los Robles was "upgrading." The slaughterhouse was closed and relocated on the outskirts of Cuernavaca; a municipal ordinance shut the bars, whereupon the brothels went out of business. Schools were built, streets were paved, and piped water, followed by electricity, was introduced. Behind the new pink-washed parish church, the municipal authorities built a covered market, one of very few in the city. Shops offering a wide variety of merchandise soon lined the streets leading up to it, giving a bustle and an air of prosperity to the neighborhood. *Tortillerías* (tortilla shops) and *abarrotes* (small general stores) selling everything from candles to matches, from tomatoes and dried chili peppers to laundry detergent and packaged cakes, opened at intersections, and ironmongeries and mechanics workshops arose along side streets. When we began working there, besides vecindades and modest single-story houses, the neighborhood included a number of apartment buildings and on the northern and western edges, some quite elaborate houses boasting flower-filled patios, garages, and even the odd swimming pool.

But although Los Robles was going up in the world, its approximately 10,000 inhabitants were still predominately working class, with the men employed in semiskilled and unskilled occupations. While some of the poorer residents continued to occupy huts perched on the slopes of ravines, most families lived in iron-roofed tenement units, consisting of one room, fronted by a narrow kitchen. Of brick and cement, these units were built around washing-festooned courtyards in which as many as twenty families shared laundry, bathing, and toilet facilities. Within, fifteen-foot-square rooms were crammed with furniture, appliances, and children's toys. Photographs—studio portraits in heavy frames as well as snapshots of family members at every age and life stage—were everywhere. Almost every family had a television and a cassette recorder; refrigerators, too, were common.

Rents were about U.S. $15 a month (with the legal minimum wage at $3 a day, this represented almost a week's wages) and did not include electricity. When the *dueño* (owner-developer) of the tenement was living on the premises, conditions might be reasonable, but more often, the owner lived elsewhere, and, with management delegated, maintenance was neglected. Efforts by tenants to organize so as to obtain improvements from the owners were likely to lead to eviction. Everyone who lived in the vecindades complained about the crowded conditions and even more about paying rent that they viewed as throwing money away. They daydreamed about buying a lot in a low-income development or joining a squatter invasion of private or ejido land and then building a house of their own, but to do so one needed savings, and so long as one was paying rent, it was almost impossible to save. Apart from large commercial tenements, there were many similar but smaller developments housing three-generational families, that is, several nuclear households living in separate units in a single vecindad that belonged to the senior couple. Additional units might be occupied by rent-paying nonkin. As these family vecindades were owner occupied, maintenance was usually better than in the commercial establishments. Life was a good deal more pleasant, too, when toilets were cleaned, garbage was collected regularly, patios were paved and swept and shaded by fruit trees, bougainvillea climbed up walls and over trellises, and herbs and flowers grew on windowsills in recycled cans and terra-cotta pots. Like the single-family homes, many of the smaller vecindades had telephones.

In a city whose water system was designed to supply 40,000 people but was now being called on to supply a population six times that size, water was a major problem, and nowhere was it more acute than in the vecindades of Los Robles. All year long throughout the city, water was rationed to a few hours each day, but whereas private residences had roof tanks and underground cisterns in which to store water, the commercial vecindades lacked such amenities. Tenants were obliged to line up their pails and plastic containers near the faucet and return to their rooms to wait for water to flow; and when it did—often before the sun rose—a cry would go up and women would jump out of bed and go running to fill their containers and haul them back to their rooms. Water had to be used with great frugality, especially toward the end of the dry season when it was common for Los Robles to be without water for weeks, a lack that the municipal authorities tried to address by sending out tanker trucks at irregular intervals.

The Study

The research on which this book is based was part of a study, "Women's Schooling, Fertility and Maternal Behavior," conducted by Robert A. LeVine, myself, and our colleagues in Cuernavaca between 1983 and 1986.[41] Although an extensive literature based on censuses and national surveys conducted in developing countries had shown maternal schooling to be a highly consistent predictor of reduced fertility and child mortality, the intervening processes whereby education in childhood affects a woman's reproductive and health behavior in adulthood were not clear.[42] To shed light on the role of formal education in the demographic transition (i.e., the decline of birthrates and death rates), the medicalization of maternal and child health care, and the family as an interactive environment for raising children, we chose to work in urban Mexico where birthrates and death rates were already rapidly declining.

Some of the questions we hoped to answer in Cuernavaca were:

1. Is there direct evidence that schooling has an educational or psychosocial effect on women's health and reproductive behavior, apart from its effect on their social position and their access to resources, as a result of marrying better-educated and more upwardly mobile men?

2. What kind of educational experience do girls have in school which might influence their behavior as mothers years later? Can a few years' attendance at low-quality schools and the acquisition there of health information, cognitive and language skills, and social attitudes account for fertility and child mortality declines?

3. To what extent do declines in fertility and child mortality reflect school-influenced changes in parental investments of time, energy, and economic resources in their children's upbringing?

To a multidisciplinary study that included health and attitudinal surveys of over three hundred mothers of varying levels of education, naturalistic observations of mothers with their infants and toddlers in the home setting, standard cognitive and language tests, participant observation and ethnographic interviews, we added an autobiographical inquiry designed to provide a historical perspective in which to set our quantitative findings.

Following a pilot study, conducted in the late winter and spring of 1983 in two rural communities in the state of Querétaro, we moved to Cuernavaca, where in the early months of fieldwork we noted mothers and grandmothers who, impressing us with their openness, we hoped would be willing to participate in an intensive study of family life and female social development. The larger study was being carried out in both Los Robles and "El Coyote," a squatter settlement on the western edge of Cuernavaca. Recently incorporated into the city, El Coyote was undergoing a process of upgrading similar to that which Los Robles had experienced in the 1970s. We decided, however, to confine our life course research to Los Robles, where the focus would be on families who were already fairly established in the urban area, as opposed to more recently arrived from the countryside.

Ultimately, fifteen women agreed to participate. Native Spanish speakers of mixed *(mestizo)* Indian and Spanish descent, they ranged in age from 19 to 73 and in level of education from unschooled to 9 years. Only three had been born in Cuernavaca, the others, in rural Morelos and nearby states. Ten were currently married or living in consensual union with the father of their youngest child; the rest were widowed and, in one case each, separated and never married.

Though the nuclear household, consisting of a couple and their unmarried children living together, is much the most common living arrangement in Mexico, families expand and retract in response to the domestic cycle and the labor market. Brígida García and her colleagues[43] estimated that in low-income communities of Mexico City, between one-fifth and one-fourth of the population were living in extended households, that is, including parents, married children and their families, and other not necessarily related people. Only three of the women in the study lived in nuclear households. Four others lived in three-generational households composed of an older couple and their married children and their families. In one case, everyone lived under a single roof; in the rest, each nuclear unit lived in their own quarters but side by side. Though each unit had their own domestic budget, they cooperated in several ways, including child care, house maintenance, and minor economic exchanges. Eight of our informants lived in female-headed households: five were headed by widows; two were headed by married women who, because their husbands worked and lived outside the city, were in day-to-day charge of their families; and one was headed by a single mother who lived with her only daughter, two grandchildren, and a sister.

Though most of the older women in the study had started married life with little more than the clothes they stood up in, by the time we got to know them, some were fairly comfortable, their husbands having had oficios or small businesses and having thus prospered to a modest degree. Several of them had adult children living—and doing well—in the United States. The younger women, meanwhile, were much less comfortable economically. A few husbands worked in government agencies, commercial enterprises, or factories that provided some social welfare benefits; but given a lack of formal schooling and the intensification of credentialism in Mexico, their long-term prospects for advancement into managerial positions were not good. Others who worked where and when they could as laborers on construction sites, earning the legal minimum wage, lived hand-to-mouth.

Introduction

Interviews with the women of childbearing age were conducted in the home by Clara Sunderland Correa, who is Mexican. I, British by birth and upbringing, conducted interviews with the older women. Before coming to Harvard University as a graduate student, my collaborator had worked as a psychologist with mothers and children in shantytowns in Mexico City. My own previous fieldwork in tropical Africa had focused on the social development and enculturation of young children. In this instance, our stated purpose was to learn about how family life, and the lives of women in particular, had changed over the previous half century.

The younger women who, typically, were raising small children with little practical help, welcomed the opportunity to focus on themselves and to feel, if only for an hour at a time, that they were "more than just house-wives." They often used interviews to unburden themselves and to discuss options. To avoid interruptions by children, relatives, and neighbors and to ensure a modicum of privacy, they would sometimes suggest taking a walk. Interviews with the older women, who tended to be somewhat less busy, were more private. If, initially, they were shier and more reluctant to talk about themselves than were the younger women, as they grew accustomed to looking back to events that had occurred much earlier, they became more forthcoming. They tended to use their interviews to try to resolve to their own satisfaction certain issues that sometimes had troubled them for years. At first, they might describe their younger selves as tossed by the wind (or largely subject to the whims of others), but with time they began to sound more decisive and self-assured.

That our informants rarely asked me personal questions may have reflected both good manners and a lack of curiosity. After all, though I was a foreigner, I was, like them, married with a family. My collaborator, who at the time was still single, lived alone, and enjoyed a degree of freedom they marveled at, was the object of considerably more curiosity.

We decided against using tape recorders, which were generally regarded with suspicion, and instead took brief notes during sessions, followed immediately afterward by more extensive notes that we expanded and typed up at the end of the day. The training we had both received in psychotherapy had stressed the commitment of dialogue to memory for recording later, a method that we had both used extensively before coming to the field. Each of us read the other's notes, and throughout the period of fieldwork, we met weekly to discuss our material.

We visited the women, eight of whom were mothers and seven of whom were grandmothers and great-grandmothers, on a semiweekly basis between March 1984 and June 1985 to interview them about life course issues. Though we each had a long list of topics through which we gradually worked our way, much of the time we spent with our informants was unstructured. We had many conversations with members of their immediate and extended families, and we were regularly included at meals, on ritual occasions such as first communions and weddings, and on trips to pilgrimage centers and places of origin in the countryside. We were both charmed and delighted by the warmth with which we were received. Unfortunately, we found it difficult to engage husbands or adult sons. As researchers whose interest was the growth and development of their young children, nephews, and nieces, they, like their wives and mothers, welcomed us. But because we were women, they tended to keep us at arm's length with superficial if humorous conversation. During the summer of 1984, however, some agreed to be interviewed by a male member of our research team, a Morelos native. Thus this book is informed by their experiences, too.

The "ethnographic present" is 1984 and 1985, the period during which we regularly conducted interviews. After concluding the "Women's Schooling, Fertility and Maternal Behavior" project, however, our team carried out further studies in Tilzapotla, a rural town thirty miles south of Cuernavaca; this enabled me to stay in touch with many of our Los Robles informants, their families, and kin through 1991. By then, the Mexican economy, which in 1984–85 had been crippled by foreign debt and "structural adjustment" measures imposed by the International Monetary Fund, was on the road to recovery.

Women and Social Change in Urban Mexico

In chapter 1, we introduce the women our study focuses on, most of whom were born and raised in villages and rural towns and came to the city after childhood. The older women grew up during the Revolution and the long period of social disorganization that followed in which threats of hunger, plunder, and physical danger and displacement provided a background to familial disorganization. The younger women were raised in a politically more stable period; but typically their childhoods, too, were disrupted by parental conflict, desertion, and death.

In chapter 2, which focuses on adolescence and courtship, we discuss the code of honor and the seclusion of daughters that rural and urban parents alike rigorously enforced until midcentury. Although marriage was by personal choice, not arrangement, traditional restrictions kept courtship secret until the young man asked for the girl's hand in marriage. Elopement, whether or not it was followed by formal marriage, was common. By the 1980s, though adolescent girls were still being closely supervised in the Morelos hinterland, in town, where educational opportunities were steadily increasing, most girls were continuing their education well into adolescence and then going out to work. In consequence, age at marriage was rising. Again, with parents having to allow their daughters a considerable degree of independence, courtship was more in the open, and engagements were lasting longer as young couples saved to set up an independent household and their parents saved for the wedding festivities.

In chapter 3, part 1, we look at the marital relationship. We show that though women married in the hope of finding trust, understanding, and companionship, men expected to be free to do as they pleased. The city was a harsh place for the unskilled rural immigrant, even harsher perhaps for his poorly educated, city-born son. Adopting conventional *machista* responses, men were likely to drown their sense of inefficacy in alcohol and to bolster self-esteem with extramarital affairs. Domestic violence, too, was common in many of these households. In the past, lacking an alternative, women with many mouths to feed put up with abuse and neglect, withdrew emotionally from their husbands, and focused on their offspring. By contrast, in the 1980s, young wives were likelier to stand up to their husbands physically and to demand that their emotional needs be met. Moreover, they were determined that their daughters should get enough education to be economically independent if necessary and so be ensured against suffering "at the hands of a man" as they had suffered.

In chapter 3, part 2, we note that although within the household, young women were beginning to stand up for themselves, outside they were less assertive. Traditionally, sex roles were clearly defined: responsibility for providing for the family fell on the husband, and responsibility for running the household and raising the children fell on his wife, a division that in the main had persisted into the 1980s. Much has been written about the energy that rural migrants to Mexico City—women as well as men—invest in the construction and maintenance of social networks, but we found that working-class women in the much smaller and more manageable city of Cuernavaca had a less urgent need for support and tended to associate closely only with immediate kin. It was from among immediate kin also that they generally chose their children's godparents. If, despite firmly entrenched sex roles, the economic crisis was forcing women elsewhere in urban Mexico out of the house to earn money to supplement their husband's wages, in Los Robles spouses' opposition still combined with their own ambivalence and lack of credentials to keep women at home or in the immediate vicinity performing domestic chores for better-off neighbors for very little money. To our informants, feminism meant equal pay for equal work; but since theirs was essentially *women's* work, it did not apply to them. In their view, Women's Liberation was for rich women who were economically independent of their husbands, not for poor women like themselves, struggling to make ends meet during la crisis.

In chapter 4, we look at childbearing and child rearing and the effects that the medicalization of health care and mass education have had on both. Modern medicine and a whole range of public health measures have reduced risks to the survival of mother and offspring. At the same time, in preparation for adult economic roles, children today require much more intensive investments of parental time and resources than they did in the past. Young mothers, aware of—and often daunted by—the demands of modern parenting, want fathers to be more involved in the day-to-day business of child rearing, a departure from their traditional role on which men are still reluctant to embark.

In chapter 5, we note that Mexicans are living longer and that women are living considerably longer than men; furthermore, without government old age pensions or social security benefits, most continue to look to adult children for economic support. Knowing how financially stressed their children already are, elderly women in Los Robles do all they can in the way of household chores to make—and keep—themselves indispensable to children and grandchildren. Younger women, perceiving that as parents they might not be able to command their children's loyalty and support, often anticipate an old age in which they might have to fend for themselves.

Chapters 1 through 5 include an ethnographic overview of the life stage under discussion, a review of the relevant anthropological literature, case material illustrative of how female experience has altered over time, and a concluding summary.

In chapter 6, we look at family relationships in urban Mexico in the 1990s, with a focus on women as wives, mothers, and wage earners, which, as la crisis wanes, many have become. A postscript provides some more recent information about the fifteen women of Los Robles on whose experiences this book is based.

To preserve confidentiality, we have changed the names of the neighborhood in which we worked as well as of our informants and their relatives.

Fifteen Women of Los Robles

MARGARITA (73), born in 1911 in Malinalco, state of Mexico. Her father was a peasant farmer. She had two years of schooling. She married *Edmundo*, the son of a cattle rancher, in 1931 and had eleven children, eight of whom survive. In 1940, she and her husband came to Cuernavaca, where they opened a store with a loan from Edmundo's father. She was widowed in 1955. Her income is derived from two taxis and a vecindad where she lives by herself in a four-room house; a daughter and her family live in one of her rental units. She has health insurance through one of her children.

ESTELA (71), born 1931 in Parandino, state of Michoacán. Her father was a carpenter. After completing primary school in Mexico, she moved to Los Angeles with her family and graduated from junior high school there. Married *Julio* in Los Angeles in 1929 and had four daughters. In 1940, she and Julio came to Cuernavaca where Julio opened a mechanic's workshop; later they opened a student boardinghouse that they continue to operate. Estela suffers from Parkinson's disease. She has health insurance through one of her children.

INÉS (64), Estela's sister, born in Parandino, Michoacán, in 1920. She attended primary school for five years in Los Angeles and three years back in Mexico. She married *Antonio* in 1940 and had ten children, eight of whom survive. She first came to Cuernavaca in 1942 but lived in many other places before settling permanently in the city in 1962. Antonio, who works for a transportation company, is a labor union leader. Inés owns a large house that contains four separate apartments, two of which are occupied by adult children and their families. She has health insurance through her husband.

LOURDES (62), born in 1922 in Emiliano Zapata, Morelos. Her father was a janitor. In 1927, at age six, she came to Cuernavaca, where she completed primary school. She married *Amando*, a musician, in 1938 and was widowed in 1945; she married *Luis*, a silversmith, in 1946. She had eight children with him, six of whom survive. Widowed a second time in 1971, she lives with her only daughter, Rocío, and infant granddaughter in a vecindad. She is financially dependent on her children. In poor health, she has medical insurance through one of her sons.

INOCENCIA (60), born in 1924 in Mexico City. Her father was a mortician. After completing primary school, she took a dressmaking course and supported herself as a seamstress. She has never married. She settled permanently in Cuernavaca in 1961, just before giving birth to her daughter. She now lives with her daughter, two grandchildren, and a sister in a spacious if dilapidated house inherited from her parents. Her daughter, a secretary, and her sister, a lawyer, support her economically. In poor health, she has medical insurance through her daughter.

CATALINA (55), born in rural Morelos in 1929. Her father owned a general store. She had two years of schooling. She came to live with a cousin in Cuernavaca at age sixteen in 1945. The following year she married *Joaquín*, who was in business. They had six children, all of whom survive. Widowed in 1983, Catalina lives with three unmarried adult children in a spacious apartment on the second floor of a building that she owns. Two of her children help her financially. She has health insurance through one of them.

SOLEDAD (49), born in 1935 in a small village in the state of Hidalgo. Her father was a peasant farmer. She received no schooling. She came to Cuernavaca at age thirteen in 1948. At fifteen she married *Jorge*, a charcoal maker, by whom she had twelve children, nine of whom survive. She lives in her own house, which she built herself, with three adult children and their families, three teenage children, and four out-of-wedlock grandchildren. Jorge lives elsewhere. Soledad receives some economic support from him and one unmarried son. She suffers from high blood pressure and *nervios*. She has no health insurance.

MATILDE (34), born in 1950 on a farm in the state of Guerrero. Her father was a peasant farmer. She had two years of schooling. At nineteen she married *Pedro*, by whom she has four children ranging in age from two to fourteen. She and her family came to Cuernavaca in the mid-1970s and now live in a large commercial vecindad. Matilde supplements her husband's earnings as a carpenter by working as a laundress. No health insurance.

IRENE (29), born in 1954 in Cuernavaca but spent her early childhood elsewhere. Her parents separated when she was about four, and her mother remarried when she was thirteen. Irene had nine years of education and some training as a practical nurse. At sixteen she became pregnant by and married *Víctor*, a mechanic, by whom she has four children aged two to fifteen. Although she has been separated from her husband for several years, he continues to visit her to claim his conjugal "rights." She lives with her widowed mother in a house that her mother owns. She is supported economically by her mother. No health insurance.

VERÓNICA (29), born in 1955 near Cuautla, Morelos. Her father died when she was an infant; her mother remarried a businessman. Veronica had nine years of education. After getting married and being deserted at seventeen, she eloped to Cuernavaca with *Rubén*. She lives in a vecindad with her five children aged one to eight by Rubén and a daughter aged twelve by her first husband. Rubén, who works in another city as a driver, comes home on alternate weekends. The family has health insurance through him.

JULIA (28), born in 1956 in Altamirano, Guerrero. Her father deserted her mother when she was nine. Two years of schooling. She married at eighteen and had a daughter. After three years of marriage, her husband deserted her. She got a divorce and now lives in consensual union with *Pancho*, a taxi driver, by whom she has three sons aged one to five. She and Pancho moved to Cuernavaca, where they live in the same vecindad as Julia's mother, sister, and brother-in-law. No health insurance.

ROSA (27), born on a farm in the state of Michoacán in 1957. Her father, a rancher, died when she was nine. Her mother has remarried. Rosa had two years of schooling. At about age seventeen, she eloped to Cuernavaca with *Hugo*, a truck driver, by whom she has two sons. They were not formally married until 1984. They occupy a unit in a small vecindad owned by Hugo's parents. Rosa's younger sister and her husband live there, too. As

Hugo is unemployed, the family lives on Rosa's wages as an aerobics teacher and loans from relatives. The family has health insurance through her work.

ELOISA (24), born in Cuernavaca in 1960. Her father was a soldier. Her parents separated when she was six, and both remarried. She completed primary school and a year of secretarial school. At sixteen she married *Marco*, by whom she has two sons. She and her family live in a vecindad belonging to her maternal grandmother. Her mother and married sister and their husbands and families live there also. As Marco is unemployed, the family subsists on Eloisa's earnings as a seamstress. She pays their health insurance premiums herself.

OFELIA (23), born in a remote village in the state of Oaxaca in 1961. Her father was a peasant farmer. She had three years of schooling. After giving birth out of wedlock at fourteen, Ofelia left home to work in Mexico City, where she eloped with *Arturo*. In 1980, they came to Cuernavaca where Arturo works as a cook in a restaurant. They live with their four children in a commercial vecindad. They have health insurance through Arturo's place of work.

LUZ MARÍA (19), born out of wedlock in Cuernavaca in 1965. She never knew her father. After eight years of schooling, Luz María eloped and later married *Octavio*, by whom she has a young son. She and her family live in a vecindad belonging to her parents-in-law. Octavio is intermittently employed as a manual laborer. No health insurance.

· 1 ·

Niñez: Childhood from the 1920s to the 1970s

"In those days I knew nothing. It's the troubles I've encountered since I married that have made me what I am today."

Few of the women dwell on memories of childhood, which they view as a hurried prelude to "real" life. Preoccupied with the demands of marriage, motherhood, and economic survival in widowhood, they need encouragement to talk about early experiences. Though they may also have warm memories of childhood, uncertainty and disruption come more readily to mind. Caught in a whirlwind of social change, war, migration, and the stresses of integration into urban life, in addition, their young lives were often drastically disrupted by paternal death or abandonment. Of fifteen women, only six grew to adolescence with both parents, and only five lived their first twelve years in the same place. Small wonder that they prefer to focus on the present, on immediate concerns and challenges. These, as adults, they have some confidence in meeting, whereas too often, as children, they were helpless in the face of events.

All but four of the women were born in the countryside or small market towns in central Mexico, the daughters of peasant farmers, laborers, and artisans. Their mothers were *amas de casa* (housewives) concerned exclusively with childbearing, child rearing, and the domestic routine—unless their husbands died or deserted or failed to support them, in which case they worked long hours for low wages as laundresses, seamstresses, street vendors, and domestic servants. When families moved to the city in the hope of a better life—meaning steady employment for the father and schooling for the children—it could take several decades to get established. "We were poor, it was very hard for my parents to provide for us," they say repeatedly.

Some women came to Cuernavaca as children; others came later. One woman was in her forties when, after several short stays, she and her husband finally settled there for good. Lourdes, a widow of sixty-three, recalls her arrival in Cuernavaca in 1927 at age six when her family moved from her birthplace, a village a few miles away. "In those days, our vecindad was on the very edge of town. We looked across the ravine to the fields on the other side, and when they started selling off that land, papá would talk about how he was going to buy one of the plots and build a house for us." In the country he had earned his living playing the fiddle, but after he brought his family into town, he gave up fiddling except on special occasions and became the caretaker of some buildings belonging to the electricity company. "He never had enough money to build that house he dreamed about," Lourdes adds. "He and mamá lived in the same vecindad on Morrow Street till they died."

Estela was born in Parandino, a market town in the state of Michoacán in 1913, three years after the Revolution began; her sister, Inés, was born there in 1920, just months before hostilities came to an end. During the Revolution, their father, a cabinetmaker, had shunted his family back and forth between town and countryside as he looked for work and avoided the fighting. One of Estela's earliest memories is of riding in a farm cart through an orchard where she saw corpses hanging from the trees. "I can't tell you if they were Federalists or Revolutionaries, only that they were soldiers—their uniforms were torn and mud-stained—and they were dead." Even after peace was established, economic recovery was slow and work as hard to come by as it had been during the war years. In 1924, the family moved to Acámbaro, in the neighboring state of Guanajuato, but things were no better there. So, with eight children to feed, Estela and Inés's father and their oldest brother went north to work in the orchards of Orange County, California. The following year, having established themselves and found a place to live, they came back to fetch the family and found Mexico once more on the verge of war.

Niñez

The 1917 Constitution had included measures subordinating the Catholic church to the state, but enforcement had varied widely in its vigor, and in some areas the law had not be enforced at all.[1] On becoming president in 1924, however, Plutarco Elias Calles began to enforce the law in earnest, thereby provoking militant opposition in the Bajío, the most Catholic part of the country. In August 1926, Calles responded by closing all the churches. Within days, fighting broke out in the Bajío city of Guadalajara between government and conservative forces who, calling themselves the Cristeros— an echo of their battle cry, "*Viva Cristo Rey!*" (Long live Christ the King)— took the Virgin of Guadalupe as their patron saint and her blue and gold image as their symbol. Fighting rapidly spread to smaller towns and into the countryside, and Estela's last memory before leaving for the United States with her family was of federal troops stabling their horses in the church across the street. "They rode their horses right through the door without dismounting," she recalls, still incredulous sixty years later.

Inés, who had just turned six, vividly remembers the journey north, in particular, the border crossing at El Paso, where all Mexican passengers were ordered off the train. "Before the gringos let us into their country they had to disinfect us." With a wry smile she continues, "They had all of us— even my grandmother—strip and bathe. The first thing I learned about North Americans was that they believed we Mexicans had fleas and lice and skin diseases!" From Texas, the family traveled to Los Angeles, where the children were enrolled in a special school for Mexican refugees. "They'd fine us a penny each time we spoke Spanish," Inés recalls. "The big kids monitored the little ones, and that way we learned English fast." The family lived in a house that was light and airy and more spacious than their house in Mexico. Each morning, they attended mass conducted by a Mexican priest, an exile like themselves, from the Bajío. On summer Sundays, they rode to the beach and into the countryside in a battered car. Before long Estela and Inés had begun thinking of themselves as Los Angelenos.

But in January 1931, with the United States plunged into the Depression, the family headed home to Mexico where, now that the Cristero war was petering out, things looked somewhat brighter. "Papá bought a truck," Inés recalls, "and off we went, with papá driving and mamá, the baby, and our grandmother sitting up front with him and the rest of us sitting on benches papá had built in the back." Estela, who by this time was married, also made the trip with her husband, Julio, and their baby daughter, but after a few months in Acámbaro, they decided that Depression or no

Depression, their prospects were better in the United States and they returned to Los Angeles. It would be almost ten years before they moved back to live in Mexico.

Catalina, a widow in her fifties, who first arrived in Cuernavaca as a teenager, recalls her native village, five hours on horseback from the nearest town. "The rainfall was very sparse in our place, and nothing much grew there except cactus. The mountains all around were full of *guerrilleros*, Zapatistas, Cristeros, and just plain bandits." Indeed, in the long period of violence and disorder that followed the Revolution, life in much of rural Mexico was hardly more secure than it had been during the Revolution itself.[2] Nevertheless, protected by her youth from political and economic realities, Catalina recalls happy times when she and her siblings went swimming in the nearby hot springs, ate watermelon in the short melon season, and watched silent movies that a man brought out from Cuernavaca and showed in the plaza twice a year. Unlike her own children, who grew up in town and spent much of their childhood worrying about homework and examinations, she says with a smile that she never had to worry about those things. "A lot of the time the school was shut because our place was so far away that teachers didn't like to stay there. They'd come for a week or two and quit."

Soledad, who, like Catalina, came to Cuernavaca as a teenager, was born in a small Hidalgo village in 1935 but spent most of her childhood in the thickly forested mountain range that divides Morelos from the state of Mexico. Her mother and stepfather—her real father had died when she was an infant and her mother had remarried soon afterward—made charcoal that they sold in villages in the valley below. When she was six or seven, Soledad recalls that her stepfather suddenly collapsed. "He didn't have any symptoms. No cough, nothing. He just lay down and didn't get up any more. . . . And then one day he died—from nerves, is what people said. . . . He was tall and nice looking, and he didn't smoke or drink or fight with mamá, and he'd always been kind to me." She adds, "For a long time after he died I felt very sad."

Within three months, his widow had found a new man. "Trinidad was our neighbor and a charcoal maker, too," Soledad recalls. "He was a young fellow, younger than mamá, and a drunkard, but with four young children, she would have accepted any man who was willing to help feed us. She couldn't afford to be particular." The family lived in a *jacal de pura paja* (straw hut); they had only rags to cover themselves at night. In the mountains there was often frost, and in the winter there was snow. "We had no land of our own, nowhere to plant crops. Mamá would go gleaning after the harvest in other people's fields, but the maize she collected was never enough. When we had money from the charcoal, we'd buy maize; but mostly we didn't have money." After a moment's reflection, Soledad adds, "But poor as we were, life was more normal in the mountains than it is in town. In the mountains the children had so much space to run, whereas here you're never alone. There's always a heap of people bothering you or else you're bothering them."

Matilde, one of the younger women, lives hand-to-mouth with her husband and four children in a tenement room. Recalling her childhood in rural Guerrero, she echoes Soledad. "In the *campo*, even if you didn't have money in your pocket or shoes to put on your feet, provided you had maize and beans to eat and a few animals, you didn't think of yourself as poor." Indeed, most of the country-bred women are nostalgic for their rural homes. Ofelia's eyes shine as she describes the rainy-season green of the hills surrounding the Oaxacan hamlet where she was born. "Papá was much admired because he worked so hard and his farm was so productive," she says with pride, adding regretfully that he lives in Mexico City now. Her brothers, too, have left for the city where, even as unskilled laborers, they make better money for less work than they did at home. "Papá has told me and my husband that if we want the farm we can have it." She continues after a moment, "The trouble is, my kids are used to water coming from the tap and going to school half a block away from where we live. They wouldn't be happy fetching water from the river or walking several kilometers to school. They're city kids. They couldn't adjust to the country, and the truth is, I wouldn't either. I was ten when I left our *ranchería*, and although I've been back, I've never stayed there long." She realizes that in her remote Altiplano home, accessible in the rainy season only by fording three rivers, life would be as difficult for her now as it would be for her city-bred children.

The other women who were born and raised in town recall a catch-as-catch-can life as their parents, recent arrivals from the countryside, struggled to gain a foothold. Inocencia, the only woman who was born in Mexico City, also recalls childhood hardship, but unlike the others, whose parents viewed migration to the city as the first step on the road leading to a better life, Inocencia's parents were on their way down in the world. Her father, scion of an old landowning family and a graduate of the Colegio Militar, had fought with the Federal forces during the Revolution. His wife, the daughter of a judge, was also from a family of *hacendados,* but they, too, had fallen on hard times, and as a newly married man right after the Revolution, he needed a job. "Unlike many of his friends who'd become poor, just as he had, he wasn't afraid of hard work. He did what he had to do," Inocencia says proudly. He became an undertaker ("There's always plenty of work in that business!"), and though he never became rich, he managed to feed and educate five children, three of them for the professions. The family lived in an apartment near the Alameda Park in the center of Mexico City. They kept a maid in their city apartment, across the street from the Teatro de las Bellas Artes; they made trips to visit relatives in other parts of the country and took occasional vacations on the Caribbean coast. In the thirties, in lieu of payment on a longstanding debt, her father accepted a plot of land in Los Robles. There, room by room, he built the weekend house in which Inocencia and her sister, Judith, still live today. In a word, the family lived a bourgeois life; and although Inocencia insists that they were poor, she is comparing their circumstances with those of friends and relatives in Mexico City who had managed to continue a semblance of the old privileged life rather than with those of their working-class neighbors in Los Robles.

For Inocencia, as for the women who were born and raised in the city, rural life, which they learned about from parents or saw for themselves on occasional visits to country kin, holds little attraction. Referring to her parents' native village, one young woman declares, "*La vida tranquila* [the quiet life] is for my grandparents, not for me!" Competitive and expensive as urban life may be, she wouldn't trade it for what she perceives as the tedium, restrictions, and hardships of the countryside.

Family Relations

Large families were looked on as a blessing by parents and children alike. "Though we didn't have much materially," one middle-aged woman remarks, "we had each other, so we never lacked companions. I wanted a big family, too, and I had one, and my kids enjoyed the same companionship I did; but the most children any of them has is three. They say they can't afford to have more. They're sorry about that, and I'm sorry for them." Children with many brothers and sisters are kinder, warmer, more affectionate, and less self-centered, she insists, than those from small families. Infant-caretaker sibling pairs tend to be especially close and to remain so throughout life. She herself still pays weekly visits to her "baby" sister, whom she carried on her hip more than five decades ago.

Parents, whom as children most of our informants addressed as *usted* rather than the intimate *tú*, were regarded as *jefes* (bosses) rather than *amigos* (friends). Apart from an occasional command or rebuke, fathers, whose authority was almost never challenged, spoke little to their children. "Papá's word was law to all of us," Inés remembers. "When he was angry, mamá would stay very quiet. She didn't see the point of arguing; that would only have made things worse. Instead, she'd smile and try to soothe him, and usually she succeeded! Years later, when I began having problems with my husband, I'd remember how mamá used to behave with papá, and I'd try to do the same." Nobody argued with Inocencia's father, either. "He had his own views on everything," she recalls. "He was very strict when we were children, and after we grew up, his attitude didn't change. Mamá had been a teacher in the school her father had established on his hacienda for the children of his *peones*. She was very intelligent and had plenty of strong views of her own; even so, she'd back up papá on everything. A wife should do so always, that's what she believed." In those (rare) instances when daughters recall parental compatibility and contentment, they ascribe that state of affairs to maternal endurance, self-effacement, and tact.

Mothers were sometimes almost as remote as fathers. They had "so many worries" and they worked all the time, so these women recall many years after childhood. Indeed, one very important concern is that as mothers they be closer to their daughters than their own mothers were to them. In large families, the main source of adult affection was often a grandmother rather than an overburdened mother. "As soon as mamá weaned a child, she'd hand him over to our grandmother," says Estela. "It was she who looked out for us, not mamá."

There were exceptions, however. Lourdes, for one, remembers both her parents as very affectionate. "They were always hugging and kissing us and holding us on their laps," she recalls. Ofelia remembers her father "as *bien jugetón* (full of fun). My brothers and sisters and I would tease him, and instead of getting angry, he'd just tease us back." Again, Matilde describes her parents, her father in particular, as *muy cariñoso*. "On fair days he'd take us into town to the bullfights. He'd buy us candy and show us off to his friends, and mamá used to complain that he spoiled us. I suppose he did, too. He used to carry me and my sisters—two in his arms and one on his back. . . . When we got older, he'd tell us that after we grew up and got married, we'd spend the rest of our lives working, and so as long as we were under *his* roof, he wouldn't have us work too hard. Although he showed us how to plant maize and beans in case we should ever need to, usually he let us stay in the house with mamá." There, too, they had to work, but domestic chores were less onerous than the backbreaking labor of the fields.

Heavy drinking and the physical violence that followed binges were common in many homes. "My mother suffered a lot," these women often grimly recall. Infidelity and fights over *la otra* (the other woman) were common also. Ofelia admits that her father, whom she loved very much, was *borracho y bien canijo en la calle* (a drunkard and womanizer) and that he made her mother's life a misery. "One night, papá came home spoiling for a fight and beat mamá so badly that she ended up in hospital in Oaxaca City. My oldest sister, who by then was married and living in the capital, came down and fetched her, but within a month," Ofelia recalls, "Papá showed up at my sister's house. And despite all mamá had been through—years of him drinking and running around and beating her—she took him in, and they've been living together ever since. These days papá's old, and he doesn't run after women. He's stopped drinking, too, so he doesn't beat mamá any more. But she had to wait till he was an old man for him to learn to treat her properly."

Like Ofelia's mother, most women of that generation put up with things (*aguantaron*) because, with many mouths to feed and no independent resources, they saw no alternative. As John Ingham[3] noted in Tlayacapan, a rural town thirty miles from Cuernavaca, philandering and physical abuse were considered male prerogatives; the first, because in the postpartum period, a husband should avoid having intercourse with his wife lest she become pregnant again too soon; and the second, because a wife's insubordination was thought to fully deserve punishment. Lourdes's mother may have been one of the few who stood up to her husband. "Papá carried on an affair for many years," Lourdes recalls, "and whenever mamá complained, he'd tell her, 'What are you complaining about? She's not costing me any money.' This was because la otra owned a store and could support herself, and besides that, she was infertile, she couldn't have children. Even so, papá and mamá fought a lot about the woman. 'I'm the mother of your children,' mamá would yell. Though he was always beating her—to get her to shut up—she kept on. Eventually he *did* give up his lover, and after that, there was no more fighting in our house, and we were all much happier."

Niñez

Family Disruption

If families of ten and twelve children were common, so was child death. Lourdes, for example, saw four siblings die in infancy and childhood. Paternal death or desertion were very common also, and unless a mother remarried quickly, the economic consequences for the family were little short of catastrophic. "It wasn't until papá died that I knew poverty and hunger," Catalina recalls. Her father, who owned the only store in the village, was a very heavy drinker. "As time went on he got worse and worse until he couldn't work any more, and then my uncles took over his business. But instead of investing the profits in new stock, they spent them. When one day papá fell down dead in the field behind our house, some people said that the woman with whom he'd lived before mamá had bewitched him. But as I see it, it was alcohol, not witchcraft, that killed him." Shortly after his death, the store failed. Abruptly reduced to poverty, Catalina's mother found herself providing for five children and her own widowed mother on a few hectares of rain-fed land.

The nightmare of her parents' separation is still very real to Eloisa who was six years old at the time. Told they must choose between them, her older brother and sister stayed with their mother. Eloisa and her younger sister, Juanita, elected to live with their father. "At that time I suppose I must have loved him," Eloisa says, sounding bemused. First her father took the little girls to live with his mother and then with his new woman. "We had a terrible time there. Her kids were bigger than we were, and they'd persecute us, beginning the moment papá left for work in the morning. They'd beat us and threaten that if we told papá, they'd kill Juanita. And I believed them! My worst fear was that they'd lock me up, and without me there to protect her, those kids would actually kill my little sister."

She goes on, "After a year papá took us to live with our aunt, who raised dogs. She made us clean out the stable where she kept them. She beat us, too, though not as often as our stepmother had." But here in their aunt's house there were new terrors. "One night I awoke to find my cousin on top of me," Eloisa recalls. "He was much older, almost a man, and afterward he threatened to hurt Juanita if I told my aunt what he'd done. That was how he kept on forcing me to have sex with him. When finally mamá came to fetch us and we'd packed up our belongings and were ready to leave, I went to the toilet, and to get my revenge for all I'd endured in that house, I smeared the place with feces." Since that day many years ago, Eloisa has seen her father, who caused her so much suffering, only twice. "Thinking about him still depresses me terribly."

Household Responsibilities

Writing about working-class parents in a small town in the state of Puebla in the 1950s, Robert Hunt[4] noted that they looked on their children virtually as personal property, from whom they expected to receive a rapid economic return—to begin with, in the form of domestic labor and later, in the case of males, in wages. By four or five, both boys and girls were performing simple household chores (*quehaceres*). They fetched and carried, swept floors, took messages to neighbors, and distracted younger siblings, and as girls—this was less true of boys—grew older, their work loads steadily increased. Soledad reports that at age six she was grinding maize from sunrise until early afternoon. "Mamá always kept one eye on me. 'Do this, do that. That's not right, do it this way.' She was after me constantly, and if I slowed down, she'd slap me. Even if I didn't slow down, she'd slap me! After I'd ground the maize I made tortillas for dinner, and when we'd eaten, I'd go to help my stepfather make charcoal in the forest until dark. I had only half an hour in the whole day to play." Inocencia, too, was doing her share of housework before she entered primary school, even though her mother employed a maid. By age nine, Catalina was already an experienced baby-minder and laundress. "I used to help my grandmother do the wash on flat rocks at the river." Rosa, growing up on a farm in Michoacán in the 1960s, describes herself as *muy machorra* (a tomboy). "What I liked was riding horses and taking the cows out to graze," she recalls, and, as she had no brothers, she was soon working as a vaquero.

When girls who lived in town were not busy doing housework, they were confined to the patio and expected to play quietly with their siblings. One woman recalls, "Mamá never let us bring a friend home. She would tell us that a child mightn't look like a thief, but looks don't tell you everything." "Papá disliked *chismes* (gossip)," another reports. "He was afraid visitors would spread rumors about us, and so we never were allowed to have any." Typically, country girls were less confined than those who grew up in conventional urban families. Matilde, for example, remembers playing in the farmyard and running freely with her sisters in the fields. "I was *bien chiva* [willful], always getting into scrapes," she recalls with a smile. Nevertheless, they rarely had playmates other than siblings, for their parents, too, strongly discouraged friendships outside the family. Meanwhile, girls whose mothers went out to work did pretty much as they liked. One young woman reports that although her mother forbade her to do so, she frequently brought friends home after school. Instead of doing housework, she would play all afternoon, and then just before her mother returned from work, her friends would leave and she would tidy up. "Mamá knew perfectly well what I was doing, and she didn't like it, but she was never there."

Schooling

By the mid-nineteenth century, there was widespread agreement among people in public life in Mexico that "the most effective way to better the moral condition of the land is to educate women."[5] The kind of schooling they had in mind would make women "good daughters, excellent mothers, and the best and most solid support of the goals of society." In reality, however, few girls except those from the most privileged families had the opportunity to get an education. Furthermore, although the 1917 Constitution gave all children the right to go to school, until well into the second half of the twentieth century, this "right" remained a fiction for a broad segment of the population. Indeed, since it was believed that, in a society that was starting to industrialize, an educated work force would greatly inflate labor costs, there was considerable opposition to mass education.[6] But even while decade after decade the central government failed to fulfill its educational mandate, nevertheless, some parents were managing to provide daughters as well as sons with the rudiments of literacy and numeration, so that they would be able to make their own way in the world (*defenderse*), that is, read and write letters and hold their own in commercial transactions.

Becoming literate required considerable determination, especially in the countryside. There, such schools as existed were financed by the community and, hence, fee paying; they routinely lacked books, desks, and chairs, not to mention teachers; and at most, they went only to fourth grade. Furthermore, parental requirements for domestic and agricultural labor often interfered with the academic schedule. After wintering in the village, in spring, many peasant families would leave for distant fields to plant their crops and pasture their cattle, returning to the village only after the harvest. A few better-off parents would hire a señorita to go with them to teach the children, but as most could not afford to do so, many children would be taken out of school in April and kept out until October. As school was closed between November and February, in any given year they would rarely be in class more than three months, and once they had learned to read a little, they would be withdrawn for good. A shame-faced Catalina, who dropped out of school when she was nine, admits that she only learned *"un poco."* "It wasn't till I was forty years old that I learned to read easily, and that was in Bible class. Even now, I'd never dare read aloud. I'd make too many mistakes." Her writing was even worse than her reading, she confesses. "Many parents didn't want their daughters learning to write," she adds, "because they were afraid they'd start writing letters to their sweethearts, and the next thing, they'd be running away!"

Before the onset of the economic boom in the 1940s, most urban parents, too, would withdraw their children from school once they had learned to read "un poco." In this respect, Lourdes's parents, raising a family in Cuernavaca in the 1930s, were unusual. "They made sure my sisters and I finished *primaria*," Lourdes recalls, "and after that, in my case, my teachers told my father I was bright and had promise, and he agreed to let me go to the *normal* (teacher training college). I was very happy because I loved to study." Her happiness did not last long, however. It was 1934, the year in which President Lázaro Cárdenas imposed a "socialist" education program on the schools. Under Article 3 of the 1917 Constitution, the program was designed to exclude "all religious doctrine and combat fanaticism and prejudices in the schools by organizing instruction and activities in a way that shall permit the creation in youth of an exact and rational concept of the universe."[7] Lourdes recalls sadly, "Papá didn't like those Communist ideas at all, and he withdrew me from the college." Inés's father, too, was deeply disturbed by the new curriculum. "If he could have afforded it, he would have transferred me to a private school," Inés reports, "but he couldn't. By then I was fourteen, and I'd attended school for five years in Los Angeles and three in Mexico. Papá said eight years was enough for a girl anyway, and so he took me out." As Cárdenas shifted his focus from an attack on the church to social and agrarian reform, anticlericalism gradually diminished, until finally, in 1942, the remnants of the socialist education program were scrapped by his successor, Manuel Avila Camacho. Notes Lourdes, "At that point, papá let my youngest sister study to become a teacher, but it was too late for me. By then I was married, so I never became a teacher as I'd hoped."

In the countryside, parental attitudes toward education were slow to

Mother and small daughter

Junior high school girls

Older brothers and younger sister

change. When Matilde was a child in Guerrero in the 1960s, schooling was still considered a luxury. In the view of most parents, a smattering of literacy and numeracy was all any child required. Although the SEP had assumed control of community schools and schooling itself was now free, there were uniforms and supplies to pay for, and as before, absenteeism among teachers was a major problem. Parents continued to take their children out of school for the growing season, and the expectations even of those who let their children study all year were not high. Thus, Matilde, aged eleven, finding herself pressured by a boy in her class to become his girlfriend and scared that he might beat her up if she rejected him, had no difficulty in persuading her parents to let her drop out of school. "There was plenty for me to do at home," she explains.

Meanwhile in town, where there were fewer chores to be done than in the countryside, parents were less likely to view a daughter's schooling in terms of loss of domestic labor. A grounding in reading, writing, and arithmetic had become an essential attribute of being "modern." Furthermore, as parents began to realize that her education might lead to paid employment and an additional source of income, they were often a good deal keener that she continue studying than the girl was herself. One woman who attended primaria in the 1960s, recalls, "I didn't want to go to *secundaria*, but my parents insisted." With a self-deprecating smile, she adds, "Once I was there, my head was filled with other things, and all I did was fool around." Acknowledging that she did not make good use of her opportunities as a girl, another woman urges her daughter not to make the same mistake but to study, study, study, pass all her exams, and enter a profession. "Don't do what I did," she pleads. "Make something of yourself!"

Two Women's Childhood Experiences

MARGARITA, a diminutive white-haired widow and, at seventy-three, the oldest woman in our study, lives in a two-bedroom house at the entrance of the vecindad that she owns. Rose bushes grow in handsome clay pots beside her front steps; a patch of lawn in which more roses grow stretches off to one side. Her rather commodious house is furnished with living and dining room sets; there is a red carpet on the living room floor, books on the shelves, pictures of lakes and mountains on the walls, and plastic flowers in vases on the sideboard. The refrigerator is ample; the color television and large print Spanish Bible are both gifts from her sons who live in the United States.

Though today she may be the most financially comfortable of all our informants, her childhood was probably the most hazardous. "*Nací con hambre* (I was born hungry)," she says. Born in 1911, the year after the Revolution began, she was the fifth and first surviving child of her parents who, at the outbreak of hostilities, like much of the rural population, had abandoned their village and fled to the mountains. The first "home" that Margarita remembers was a mountain cave in which she and her family subsisted on whatever they could gather and catch: berries, roots, birds, rabbits.

"Mamá was *una güerita*, fair-skinned, with blue eyes and light brown hair," Margarita recalls. "She wore long skirts and blouses with high necks and long sleeves, as women did in those days. She was graceful—and always so worried and sad. During the Revolution she was suffering a lot," adds Margarita seventy years later, with tears in her eyes. "But even so, she never ceased to work and struggle and push on. She had a very strong character."

In 1913, another child—a son, Arturo—was born, and not long afterward, because Margarita's father got sick, the family left the *cerro* (mountains) and went north to Tenango del Valle where they had relatives. But there, Margarita's father died, and a week or two later, her mother gave birth to a baby girl who also died. "Because of grief and worry, mamá gave birth too soon, and then she had no milk to give the baby," Margarita explains. As soon as she had recovered from childbirth, the new widow took her two young children south again, over high mountains to Miacatlán del Río, Morelos, where an uncle of hers lived. But there, life was hardly any easier than it had been in Tenango del Valle or the cerro. "Mamá would get up at three in the morning to grind maize and make tortillas," Margarita recalls. "She'd keep back one each for my brother and me and one for herself. The rest she had to sell. . . . We were always hungry."

Soldiers frequently raided the village for food and women. "It didn't matter which side they were fighting on. Both sides were equally bad." Margarita's older female cousins would have to hide in the granary, buried under maize cobs, until the soldiers left. "I was just a little girl so they weren't interested in me, but they caught and raped one of my cousins. She was so shocked by the experience that ever after she was afraid of men. She never married."

From Miacatlán, they fled once again into the mountains. When things quieted down enough, they came down to Tetecala in the valley and thence to San Andrés where they had heard there was land to plant; there they spent a growing season. Only in 1919 was it safe at last for Margarita and her mother and brother to go home. They found the village of Palpan, deserted nine years earlier, in ruins. Margarita, aged eight, remembers her mother pointing out their house. What house? All she saw was a heap of charred stones, overgrown with morning glory vines. Her mother, whose parents and siblings were now dead, set about rebuilding her house with the help of those few of her husband's relatives who had survived the Revolution. "Never a day went by that I didn't see her weep. From her return to Palpan until her death twelve years later she lived a solitary life. It wasn't acceptable for widows to marry again. Though some did take lovers, mamá never did. 'I married for life,' she used to tell me. Never once did I see a man in our house."

Margarita's mother had been taught to read and write by her Spanish-born parents, and education was very important to her. "Poor as she was, she hired a señorita to teach me and my brother," Margarita recalls. "Each day we went to her house. I couldn't wait to go, as I loved my lessons, though Arturo was too restless, and he never did apply himself. When I was ten they opened a school in the village, and from then on, we went there instead of to the señorita's house." At school, too, Margarita enjoyed her lessons and did well. She had a good singing voice and a gift for mimicry and would put on dramatic performances for her classmates. However, the school drew its teachers from outside the community. As was the case in so many other rural schools, they were hard to recruit and came irregularly, and after Margarita had been attending for two years, her mother withdrew her. "'Why should I pay good money if the teacher doesn't come?' mamá said. I would like to have continued. I'd like to have had a profession like teaching or nursing, but in those days girls from Palpan didn't study. . . . My grandnieces are going to the *preparatoria* now. They stay in town in the week to attend school and go home on weekends, but in those days parents said, 'What's the point of education for a girl when all she'll do is marry?' Mamá didn't say that, mind you. She'd have let me continue studying. It was because we were poor that I had to stop." By then Margarita could read fairly well, and she could add, subtract, and multiply. She never found division easy, she admits, even after many years in business, although—and her face lights up—since one of her sons gave her a calculator, that's no longer a problem.

For eight years, between leaving school and getting married, she stayed at home, taking care of the house while her mother made and sold tortillas, just as she had during the war, and cheeses, which she also made herself, and hawked vegetables that she brought in from Malinalco, the nearest market town. With Arturo's help, Margarita's mother also worked her land. Meanwhile, Margarita was alone in the house all day, washing, cleaning, sewing, cooking, and feeding the animals. If time allowed, she was permitted to visit a girl cousin, roughly her own age, who lived down the street, but she had to be back home by three o'clock to start preparing dinner. Her only outings were to mass once a month when the priest came to Palpan. There were no fairs in those days, and her mother would not permit her to attend dances.

Looking back, she remarks with a shrug that her childhood lasted only four years. Before age eight, she was a refugee and after age twelve, a housekeeper.

LUZ MARÍA, at nineteen, is the youngest mother in our study. She lives with her husband, Octavio, twenty-two, and her two-year-old son, Héctor, next door to her parents-in-law and upstairs from two brothers-in-law and their families. A few weeks before we met her, a baby son had died of congenital complications at age one month. A turbulent young woman, Luz María is at once immature and unusually reflective for her years. Memories of her childhood, which she escaped by eloping with Octavio, are still exceedingly painful.

Luz María was born out of wedlock in 1965 when her mother, Ema, was fifteen. Ema and her widowed mother, Luz María's grandmother, had recently arrived from rural Michoacán. The 1960s saw a tide of female migrants sweep into the rapidly expanding cities. Primarily young girls and widows or abandoned wives, they came in search of employment as maids in middle-class households, from which they sent home their wages to support siblings or offspring left behind in the countryside. In this case, mother and daughter lived together and went out to work by day, and on the street going to and from the house in which she was employed, Ema met a much older man, who soon became her lover.

"My papá was married and had a family," says Luz María, "and I suppose he took up with mamá, *una chamaquita* [a little girl] who knew nothing about men, to show her a thing or two. He was a *judicial* [member of the secret police], and he was killed in a shoot-out with drug dealers when I was nine months old and mamá was pregnant with my sister. That's all I know, because mamá has refused to tell me anything more. My grandmother says he was tall and fair-skinned—that must be why my son Héctor has green eyes. And my godmother says he was handsome. She even has a photo of him, but she won't show it to me. She says I should forget about him—just put him out of my head." Luz María is bitter than she does not know where her father is buried and also that she has never had the chance to meet her paternal relatives. "I think I have a right to know them, don't you?" she asks.

When she was four years old and her sister, Lucrecia, three, her mother became involved with Alfredo, a traveling salesman who came to her door selling notebooks. They have since had eight children together, the youngest of whom is younger than Luz María's son, Héctor. "Mamá has no interest in birth control," says Luz María impatiently. "Once two social workers came to the house to talk to her about family planning, and she told them to mind their own business and slammed the door in their faces. She won't listen to anything I say about it, either." Luz María suspects that Alfredo has never married her mother because he has a legal wife elsewhere. "Or it could be that because she's *floja* [lazy], he doesn't want to! Alfredo has never really lived with mamá either. He'll come for a day or two and then he'll go off, attending to his business. Really, I can see why, with her braids, her dirty apron, her unwashed face. Who would want to live with *una flojita* like her?" Luz María adds with a grimace of distaste.

When Alfredo asked Ema to become his *novia*, he assured her that having two children by another man made no difference to him. But although at first he was kind to his stepdaughters, he soon began mistreating them. "Mamá didn't interfere, either," Luz María recalls. "He'd tell her, 'These *escuincles* [puppies] aren't going to eat what we're eating.' And she'd do as he said. We never got enough to eat or decent clothes." Indeed, in photographs taken when they were in elementary school, Luz María and Lucrecia, dressed in ill-fitting, unattractive clothes, look wan and scrawny. "Everything we owned was secondhand," Luz María comments.

"My stepfather often beat us for no good reason," she continues. "Once—for supposedly losing a chair—he hit me so hard with his belt that the buckle gashed open my thigh. The chair was found right afterward. A child in our vecindad had hidden it. Another time, I don't know why, he flew into a rage and dragged Creci and me off to the barber and got our heads shaved. Everyone at school laughed at us—they said we'd been shaved because we had lice." Although Alfredo was a heavy drinker, Luz María insists, "He knew perfectly well what he was doing. He wasn't cruel because he was drunk. He took a sadistic pleasure in our suffering. Once, he burned my hangnails with the sun's rays through a magnifying glass. And he got a big charge out of telling ghost stories and murder stories, too, just to scare us." Yet, for all his bullying, Luz María says she is thankful for one thing: he never sexually molested either her or her sister. "As our room was so small, the neighbors all assumed he did. In fact, they used to ask us straight out, and we'd deny it. Even so, they didn't believe us. We'd overhear them saying, 'Poor little things. When they get married their husbands won't love them,' meaning that we'd already lost our virginity with our stepfather."

Luz María spent as much time as she could with her maternal grandmother, who at that point was living in the same vecindad. "She looked out for me," Luz María remembers, "and I thought of her as being my real mother. When mamá refused to give me food, I would eat at my *abuelita*'s. She'd get up to make me breakfast before I went to school, whereas mamá never did."

Ema was often physically abusive. Luz María recalls one incident in particular when her mother threw a tin of powdered milk at her, gashing open the side of her head. "The blood came pouring into my eyes, and mamá said that if anyone asked what had happened I'd better say I'd fallen off the bed, because if I told the truth, they'd put her in prison.

"When we were small," she continues, "Creci and I both thought we must have been given to mamá, that she'd been forced against her will to take us, and that was why she didn't love us. Not that she loves her children by my stepfather, it's just that she prefers them to us. . . . She's not capable of making any of her children love *her* either," Luz María adds bitterly. From her entire childhood, she has only one memory of Ema treating her as a mother ought to treat a daughter, with concern and generosity: when Luz María pierced her ears (herself), Ema gave her a pair of her own earrings to wear.

Most new mothers learn from their own mothers how to care for babies, but Luz María claims Ema never taught her anything. Rather, from a very early age, *she* was the one taking care of the little ones. "From the time my brother—mamá's first child with my stepfather—was born, I had to take care of him. I was only five, and that's too young for a kid to have so much responsibility." Once she had been broken in as a baby-sitter, that was Luz María's principal function in the household. She recalls having an especially difficult time with an infant half-brother who would not sleep at night. Her job was to walk up and down with him, with the result that the next day, in school, she would be exhausted. "By age seven I was already *harta de tanto chamaquito* [sick of children]. I'd get so angry with those kids that I'd pinch them. I used to ask mamá, 'Why do I have to do this? They aren't my kids—they're yours!' " But her complaints fell on deaf ears. "Because I was taking care of babies so much, I couldn't study. Even if the kids were quiet, our room was horrible—so small and full of my stepfather's merchandise. I used to climb a tree in the patio and study there; it was the only place I could find peace and quiet."

Lucrecia, too, was required to shoulder a great deal of responsibility from a very young age. "Mamá began sending her downtown on errands all alone. She couldn't have been more than six when that started, and once she got lost. . . . It was terrible for her. . . . Mamá had so many children, and they came so close together, that she never gave any of us the attention she should have. It was her fault that Creci had a baby when she was fourteen. She never supervised my sister at all!"

School offered Luz María an escape from emotional neglect and the drudgery of household chores. Although even before Alfredo's arrival on the scene, Ema had taken the trouble to teach Luz María the alphabet, she doubts it would have occurred to her mother to send her to school—though by law she was obliged to do so—had a neighbor not intervened. But after that first year, it was up to Luz María to register herself and her sister also at the beginning of each school year. Ema never attended parent meetings or met with any of her daughter's teachers. "She used to say to me, 'You're studying because you want to, not because I tell you to, so why should I talk to those people?'"

Luz María had little time to do her homework because in addition to having to care for her siblings, her stepfather insisted on turning out the light at eight in the evening, on the grounds that everyone was tired and needed to sleep. "The truth was, he wanted to stop me from studying," Luz María exclaims. "*He* hadn't had much chance to study, and he was jealous that I could and that I got good grades as well!"

From early on in her school career, Luz María was obliged to earn the money to pay her own expenses. Though in primaria this did not take too much time, once she entered secundaria her expenses increased sharply, and as a result, she had to spend many hours a week cleaning houses. Too often, instead of researching a paper, she would have to invent the contents. "Once I was supposed to interview someone about their life and work and write it up," she recalls. "But I didn't have time, so I made up an interview with a priest. I got an excellent grade, too," she adds with a small smile.

Even though it drastically reduced her study time, Luz María derived a great deal of satisfaction from working, because having her own money gave her a sense of independence and of future possibilities. "I used to love eating eggs," she remembers, "but in my house I hardly ever ate them, and so I'd say to myself, when I'm older and I earn more money, I'm going to eat a lot of eggs!"

Throughout her school years, Luz María suffered from fainting spells, which often prevented her from participating in physical education. When she was still in primaria, the authorities sent a note to Ema saying that they would not allow her daughter back in school unless she took her to a doctor. "'Why don't you quit school?' mamá said to me. 'You've studied long enough.' Mamá couldn't understand why I wanted to go on learning. She'd quit in the third grade herself, and Creci had quit in the third grade, too." At first, Ema had no intention of taking her daughter to a doctor, but Luz María begged and begged and finally got her way. "I had to pay for the visit myself, though," she recalls wryly. "It cost 110 pesos, and as I was only earning 10 pesos a day in those days, I didn't have enough money left over to fill the prescription." She is convinced that her fainting spells were due to the inadequacy of her diet. "All my stepfather would let mamá give me to eat was tortilla and salsa, salsa and tortilla."

Though she studied as much as she could and did well, exams never ceased to be a torment. "I'd get so anxious. It took a lot of self-control to stop my hands from shaking so that I could hold a pen," she recalls. "I think my stepfather must have been at the root of my nervous condition. I was so terribly afraid of him!"

At school she was a loner. Owing to a pervasive feeling of weakness as well as her fainting spells, she could not participate in sports, while her classmates, who were not interested in war or the future or the end of the world as she was but only in boyfriends and makeup, found her too serious. Her only long-term relationship was with her aunt, Isabel, two years her senior, and even that was hardly a friendship. "We were very competitive," Luz María admits. "Each was always trying to do better than the other at school." Isabel's mother—Luz María's grandmother—would take the girls swimming in the hot springs that abound in the region. She spent the little free time she had swimming and reading.

When Luz María was twelve, at her stepfather's insistence—"I was answering him back and giving him *mucha lata* [a lot of trouble]"—Ema put her in a Catholic boarding school. There she began to write poetry. When one of the nuns read a poem Luz María had written, however, she pronounced it sacrilegious. "And another nun who read it said I must have been smoking marijuana; otherwise how could I write like that? After I'd been there a month, they told mamá they couldn't do anything with me because I was crazy, so she'd better take me out."

Back home, Luz María continued to write poetry, and she began to receive a favorable response from her teachers. Asked to write and recite a poem for the graduation exercises, she did so, to much praise. Even so, she could not forget the nuns had said she was crazy. Maybe they were right. Maybe writing poetry and worrying about war and the future and the end of the world instead of boys and makeup *did* mean she was crazy. "I used to ask myself, 'Why am I so different? Why can't I be like other girls?' "

Summary

Initially the women in this study were reluctant to dwell on childhood experience, which they dismissed as unimportant and irrelevant to their current lives. Over time, however, as they began to speak more freely, it became evident that for many, childhood had been socially and emotionally turbulent.

Margarita and Estela vividly recalled their fear of soldiers—Zapatistas, Federales, Cristeros, all equally menacing. Inocencia, whose parents had lost everything in the Revolution, grew up in a household in which the atmosphere, long after the hostilities were over, was pervaded by incredulity and shock. Catalina recalled the dread that parents and neighbors had of the guerillas who in the 1930s lived in the surrounding mountains and preyed on the defenseless peasantry. Younger women, meanwhile, rather than ordering their memories by political events, did so in accordance with the abrupt discontinuities occurring in their own lives: "Before we moved into town." "Before papá died." "Before papá left us." "Before mamá remarried." "And afterward." Unlike the children of Sánchez, whose mother died when they were two, four, six, and eight, respectively, none of our informants lost her mother in childhood. Hard as their young lives were, they readily conceded that to lose one's mother very young would be the hardest blow of all.

In many families *la otra* (the other woman) posed a constant threat. Although Lourdes was fortunate because her father stayed, other fathers did not. Often children had to contend with a stepfather who was much more likely to resent their presence than to accept and love them as his own. Strongly discouraged by parents from forming "outside" friendships, some women were lucky to find a best friend among their siblings, a source of mutual protection and consolation in childhood and beyond; but others, restricted to the house and patio, waited vainly for a soulmate.

A handful who recalled doing very well in class admitted that no praise they had received since sounded as sweet as their teachers', and they deeply regretted not having had the chance to study longer. Others remembered school as tedious, a situation they got out of as soon as they could. For most, however, whether to drop out or continue was not their choice. As soon as a girl of the generation born before 1940 could read a street sign or a familiar biblical passage, her parents were likely to withdraw her because there was work to be done at home. As a rule, the younger women who grew up in town did manage to finish primary school, but education was a privilege denied those whose mothers were bringing children up alone. Whether or not they had learned to read already, daughters had to drop out to help support younger siblings.

Though these women might insist that it was the tests and trials of marriage and motherhood that had made them what they were, the emotional pain and physical dislocations of childhood had undoubtedly left their mark, making them the more determined to provide their own children with a better start in life than they had had themselves. But while some took an obvious pride and pleasure in the offspring to whose care and upbringing they devoted themselves, others were harder to satisfy. One young mother said bitterly to her daughter who had just brought home indifferent grades, "Don't you know how lucky you are to have a mother behind you? When I was a kid, my mother didn't care! You're getting so much more attention than I did. You ought to be doing a whole lot better than this!" Nothing less than a perfect performance by her daughter could make up for the deprivations she herself had suffered as a child.

· 2 ·

Ya Soy Señorita:
Adolescence and Courtship

"Mamá never spoke to me about *la regla* (menstruation)," says Margarita, "and when it started I had no idea what was happening. I thought I'd been wounded while I was asleep, so I went and stood in the river, hoping to staunch the blood, but no, the bleeding continued as before."

In Margarita's girlhood sixty years ago, the facts of life were a taboo topic between mothers and daughters and frequently between sisters as well. Furthermore, adolescent girls were often so carefully secluded that they spent little time with agemates or friends from whom they might have gleaned information. From the reactions of adult female relatives, however, they grasped that the onset of la regla had dangerous implications.

"They told me, 'Now you're a young lady and you must take care of yourself [*Ya eres señorita y tienes que cuidarte*],'" Inés recalls, "though what they meant by that, really, I didn't know, and I had nobody to ask. By then, Estela had already been married for a long time and my next oldest sister, Lupita, had entered the convent." While the workings of her body remained deeply mysterious, she was given to understand that a very significant change had occurred and that male passions (*los deseos de los hombres*) would henceforth constitute a grave threat. Lacking both will and physical strength to resist his advances, the likelihood was that if she found herself alone with a man she would be dishonored, bringing shame on her family as much as herself. To protect her from this dire fate, she needed to be supervised at all times. Her parents withdrew her from school and thereafter kept her at home under the watchful eyes of her mother and grandmother until she married in virginal white (*de blanco*) several years later.

Recalling her conventionally confined girlhood in the 1930s, Inés reports, "In the morning my sisters and I did housework and in the afternoon, embroidery—tablecloths, pillow slips, towels for our trousseaux. So many we embroidered, and when they were finished, we folded them away in boxes we kept under our beds. Papá worked at his carpenter's bench at the entrance to our patio, and there was no getting past him! Our only outings were to church. After we came out of mass my parents would chat with their friends for a few moments, and that was the one chance my sisters and I had to see boys, let alone talk to them. Our lives were very dull. We had no distractions except daydreams." Parents who could not afford to seclude their daughters sent them out to earn a living with regret, and the girls themselves viewed their "freedom" ambivalently. "It was because my mother wasn't able to protect me [i.e., let her stay at home] that I married so young," one middle-aged woman explains. Out on the streets and in the houses of her employers, she was frequently harassed by men. Better to elope, she decided; if she "belonged" to one man, the rest might leave her alone.

In discussing the rationale for the seclusion of daughters in Latin America, J. M. Stycos[1] suggested that the "ideology" of the sacrosanctness of virginity combines with a general distrust of men—including male relatives—and the belief that a girl is endangered by innocence and physical weakness to make the seclusion of daughters mandatory. In addition to affording her protection, parents are enjoined to teach a daughter to behave in such a way as to avoid provoking men sexually, in other words, to behave with modesty on all occasions. But seclusion, Stycos argued, encourages the development in a young girl of those very characteristics— innocence, unworldliness, and an incapacity to take care of herself—that it is designed to protect. In a discussion of the Code of Honor in peninsular Spain, Carrie Douglas[2] suggests that while young girls in Spain, and throughout the Spanish-speaking world, are being taught that *male* passion is the greatest threat to their well-being, at a deeper level of consciousness, *female* passion is conceived of as posing the greater threat. It is female passion, furthermore, that the ideology of the sacrosanctness of virginity aims to control. Douglas notes that as a precondition to proving himself in the public sphere, a man must be able to guarantee the virtue (i.e., virginity before marriage and fidelity afterward) of the females in his family. This is no easy task, given that seductiveness—and the social disorder it engenders—is regarded as the very essence of womanhood. Passion puts not only the honor of women at risk but that of their male relatives also. In order, then, to control female sexual impulses, it is essential that, as father, husband, brother, and son, a man keep his women secluded and subordinated at home.[3]

If, as it appears, for at least a generation virgin brides have probably been rather rare in urban Mexico, nevertheless, there, just as in Spain, virginity at marriage is the ideal and continues to generate considerable concern, particularly among men. As Octavio Giraldo (1972) noted, no blow to the self-esteem of a working-class man is greater than the discovery that his *novia* has deceived him and that, contrary to what he believed, he is not the "first." Not that he feels constrained to wait until the wedding night to make his discovery. As one middle-aged woman said with annoyance, "Men are such hypocrites! For all their talk about wanting purity, they'll dirty yours the moment they get the chance!"

Though Mexican popular culture, always highly romantic, became increasingly eroticized as urbanization and consumerism progressed, within the family, traditional norms of modesty and respect between generations were still widely observed.[4] By the same token, communication between working-class mothers and daughters on sensitive topics like sex and reproduction was scarcely more open in Luz María's adolescence in the city in the 1970s than it had been in Margarita's in the country fifty years before. None of the younger women recalls her mother telling her about menstruation, and only one remembers being informed by an older sister. In contrast with the older generation, however, most were not withdrawn from school at puberty and so had the chance to learn about "those things" from classmates.

"My girlfriends had warned me about la regla," one woman recalls, "and when it happened, though I was scared, I also felt important. I felt like a woman." She adds wryly, "I told mamá, thinking she would be excited like I was, but all she said was *muy bien*, very good." Instead of being gratified by her daughter's confidence, her mother felt embarrassed.

As a teenager in the 1960s, Verónica, too, learned the facts of life from her friends. "When I began menstruating, I was happy, but I didn't tell mamá. The second time I had a period, mamá spotted a bloody rag, and that's how she discovered. I didn't tell her anything." By contrast, as a mother in the 1980s, she has taken care to prepare her eleven-year-old daughter for la regla. "But I'm más abierta [more open] with Beatriz than mamá ever was with me," she adds in explanation.

Most of the younger women report that after la regla began, parents attempted to restrict their activities, without much success. Verónica, forbidden by her mother and stepfather to use cosmetics or go out with boys, did both. "My friends and I began experimenting with makeup when we were thirteen. We'd just go off some way away from my house so my parents wouldn't see us, and I'd wash my face before I went home." She had novios (boyfriends), too, on the sly. "If my parents spotted me talking to a boy, they'd thrash me when I got home. Sometimes, my stepfather wouldn't even wait, he'd thrash me then and there in front of the boy! They never give me permission to go to fiestas, either, but of course I'd sneak off."

Girls employed outside the home, meanwhile, were virtually free of supervision. They had plenty of opportunity to see their boyfriends on their way to and from the houses where they were employed as domestic servants. Luz María, who paid her school expenses by working as a maid, reports, "I could have done whatever I wanted and no one would have known." In fact, she adds that what she wanted was to concentrate on her schoolwork, not to fool around with boys. If one asked her out to the movies, she would accept—because she did not want to antagonize him—and then "forget" their date. When Octavio, whom she would eventually marry, began waiting for her outside the school gates, she would hide from him and jump on the first bus that passed by. When she eventually agreed to go out with him, she insisted that her aunt, Isabel, accompany them on dates. "Octavio knew that if he wanted to see me, he'd have to invite Isabel, too." This was Luz María's stipulation, not her mother's. "If I'd gone out alone with Octavio, mamá wouldn't have noticed."

Courtship before 1940

In the older generation, the only legitimate adult role open to working-class girls—apart from entering a religious order—was that of wife and mother. Though marital choice was supposedly free, given the seclusion of adolescent girls, the opportunities for young people to meet were extremely limited, and the decision to marry was often made on the basis of quite superficial acquaintance. As one woman puts it, "Our parents were more concerned with our purity than our happiness. So long as we married *de blanco* (as virgins), they felt they'd fulfilled their responsibilities. They didn't seem to worry too much about what happened to us later on."

After a typically clandestine courtship, the young man would propose—usually by letter—and, if accepted, would come with his father and his *padrino de boda* (wedding godfather) to his novia's parents to ask formally for her hand. Following an engagement *(compromiso)* lasting between two and six months, the couple would be married. Two forms of marriage, one religious, the other civil, existed. These were simple ceremonies, requiring minimal expenditure, and optimally, one underwent both. *El contrato civil matrimonial,* originally introduced in 1859 for non-Christians, was the only form of marriage that the government recognized as legal after 1929.[5] But because it required documents that the poor often did not possess, they continued either to marry in church, which common folk regarded with greater respect than the secular authorities, or, despite intermittent government campaigns to get people to marry legally, to live in consensual union *(unión libre).* Margarita's husband was her father's cousin by marriage; he lived a mere hundred meters down the street, and she had known him since childhood, yet their two-year courtship took place entirely by surreptitious exchange of letters. "Mamá confined me to the house because, years before, one of her sisters had been abducted by a man she didn't love," Margarita explains. "Having seen my aunt in the street, this man had taken a fancy to her, but, figuring that if he asked for her hand in the usual fashion, she'd refuse him, he broke into her parents' house and stole her away. After that my aunt was no longer señorita, and she had to remain with him as his wife because no one else would have wanted her. Marriage *por robo* [by abduction, against one's will] happened to a lot of girls in those days, and mamá was afraid of it happening to me. Men could do whatever they wanted in the countryside and get away with it. If the boy and girl were novios, if they liked each other, it wasn't as bad, but often that wasn't so. The boy wanted the girl, but as for her, she had no interest in him."

Margarita continues, "When Edmundo began courting me in secret, I was happy because I liked him very much. At the same time, I was worried, because mamá was often sick and I didn't want to marry and leave her. After a year and a half, Edmundo said he'd waited long enough, so he came openly with his father and his padrino de boda. Six months later, in January 1931, at the feast of the Three Kings we got married. We were both twenty years old. We had the civil ceremony on the Friday, and on the Sunday we were married in church." As there was no priest in their village, they had to ride a considerable distance to find one. "Then we turned right around and rode back again to Edmundo's father's house. We didn't have a party or anything. I didn't even have a new dress." Margarita and Edmundo were fortunate to find a priest to marry them, for at that time, in the aftermath of the Cristero War, much of rural Mexico was still without clergy.

Estela and Inés's father had had several good reasons for moving his family to Los Angeles: a decent job and freedom of worship and religious instruction for his children *and* protection for his daughters from abduction, a practice that, given the almost total expulsion of the clergy by Calles's government, had become epidemic in his native region. His anxiety focused on his oldest daughter, Estela, who was just thirteen when the family moved north. She had already completed primary school and had she remained in Mexico, would have gone no farther. But California law required that she stay in school until her sixteenth birthday, and in Los Angeles her father was obliged to agree to her attending an all-girl junior high school. Thus, instead of staying at home under close parental supervision, each morning she was escorted through the streets to school by a younger sister, who returned in the afternoon to fetch her and escort her home. Forbidden by her father to wear cosmetics, Estela nevertheless experimented with her girlfriends' makeup during recess. When her father ran into her one afternoon just as she was coming out of school, he was shocked to see that she was wearing "ashes" on her face, as he called face powder. Taking out his handkerchief, he grabbed her and wiped her cheeks. She wanted to wear short flapper skirts like her classmates, but her father insisted on long Mexican-style clothing. Nor, with the single exception of her classmate, Elsa, whose family came from the same town in Michoacán, would he allow her to bring any of her school friends to the house. "He wanted me to remain a child as long as possible," says Estela. "He couldn't admit to the inevitable—that I was growing up."

Estela was in the eighth grade when she and Julio, a garage mechanic whom she had seen in church, began their courtship. After two years of communicating exclusively by letters that they would leave for each other in a bush down the hill from Estela's house, Julio came with his padrino de boda to ask for her hand. Her father was very much taken aback by his proposal. At sixteen, Estela was too young to be married, he protested. Better that she wait until she was older and had more "sense." But he had known Julio's family back home and had even been Julio's father's padrino de boda, so after some reflection, he relented and agreed that the wedding could take place three months hence. "We got engaged without ever having spoken to each other—just imagine!" Estela exclaims. "One month before the wedding, Julio came back again, and after first making sure that papá was out, mamá let me see him in the patio. Five minutes—that was the only time we were ever alone together before we got married, and even that meeting had to be kept secret from papá! Perhaps the main reason I wanted to marry was to get away from papá," Estela adds slowly. "He was terribly strict. . . . He refused to see that life in the United States was different from Mexico. Really, I married in order to have a girlhood."

Estela graduated from junior high school on June 10, 1929, and got married a week later. Although her father had given his consent, neither he nor her mother participated in the preparations; nor did they attend the wedding itself. All the arrangements were made by her classmates. Her friend, Elsa, was her *madrina de boda*, and her brother, Enrique, one year her senior, gave her away. After the wedding mass they had dinner in a restaurant, and from there Julio brought her back to her parents' home. "No, that wasn't the custom at all, but papá insisted," Estela explains. "It was because I was the oldest daughter and he loved me so much and didn't want to lose me that he put so many obstacles in Julio's way. Well," she adds with a chuckle, "at least I wasn't abducted. We were properly married by a priest!" The following week, Julio came to the house for dinner, after which he was permitted to take his bride to the apartment he had rented. "From that time onward he was very well received by papá." Not surprisingly, at first Estela did not find married life easy. "Julio was eight years older than I, and before our wedding day, we'd never so much as held hands. I wasn't used to men; I preferred being with my girlfriends. I was the first in my group to get married. The others had graduated, too, and were at home with time on their hands, and so right after Julio left for work in the morning, they'd arrive at the house and stay all day. We'd have a great time chatting and dancing to the radio. . . . It was only after I got married that I finally had a girlhood."

When her father objected to the marriage on the grounds that Estela was not old enough, it seems he had good reason. "I'd been married a year before I had my first period. When it happened, I was all alone in the house and I thought I was dying, until Julio came back from work and told me what was happening was natural." With a wry smile, Estela adds, "I'd been wondering why I'd been married so long and still wasn't pregnant!"

Women of the older generation recall—often with bemusement—the romantic daze of their courtship: surreptitious glances across the aisle during mass on Sunday morning; scribbled notes and the anxious wait for a reply; stolen moments during fiestas while the chaperone's back was turned. Inés first saw Antonio in church where he sang in the choir. "What a sweet voice he had!" she recalls. One day he slipped her a note asking her to be his novia, and after a two-year secret courtship, he came with his parish priest—his parents lived in another town—to ask her father for her hand. As both were still only seventeen, they were obliged to wait another two years before getting married. "Though papá insisted we wait, in some respects he'd mellowed since Estela and Julio's courtship. Now that our engagement was official, he allowed us to meet at the patio gate." There they would exchange besitos (quick kisses) in the shadows, where Inés's grandmother, their chaperone, could not quite see them. When in 1940 they finally got married, Inés's parents gave a party for them. "There wasn't any alcohol, as papá didn't drink alcohol," she recalls, "but there were lemonade and cookies, . . . just a simple party, but a party nevertheless. It showed papá approved, and Antonio's mother bought him a new suit and Antonio bought me a dress." In their wedding photograph, flanked by parents and siblings, both look handsome, reserved, and a good deal older than nineteen. "That night we began our married life in a shack Antonio had built in the yard of the lumber company where he was working. I was very happy in that little place. The truth is, I'd have been happy anywhere because I was very much in love."

Courtship after 1940

Working-class parents who were edging up the socioeconomic ladder were beginning to see the education of daughters in a more favorable light. Completion of primary school was not sufficient now; they wanted daughters to pursue further studies in secundaria, teacher's college, or a private technical school in the hope that this training would lead to employment as store clerks, teachers, nurses, or secretaries. But though boys were licensed to sow their wild oats (with prostitutes or deserted wives), girls—as ever—were expected to remain virgins until marriage. Now that they were studying longer, ensuring this was becoming more difficult, for even though schools continued to be segregated by sex, girls had plenty of opportunity to get to know boys in the street on their way back and forth. Thus, when Margarita and Edmundo came to Cuernavaca and opened a store, they were convinced that Margarita, who managed it, did not have the time to supervise their daughters properly; and so as each one approached adolescence, they placed her in a convent boarding school in Mexico City. On Saturdays Edmundo would mind the store while Margarita took the bus to the capital to visit their daughters. The girls would come home for school vacations, but even then, their parents would confine them to the house while their younger (prepubescent) sisters or a maid ran errands. Only after they had completed junior high school (at 15 or 16) did Margarita consider them mature enough to go out on the streets unchaperoned. "By then I felt we understood each other and I could trust them. Nowadays," she adds, "mothers send their girls out alone before they know how to handle themselves, and look what happens! One of my own granddaughters had a *fracaso* [failure, i.e., out-of-wedlock pregnancy], and in my opinion, it was her mother's fault."

Rising affluence, a refection of the economic "miracle" that Mexico experienced in these years, was bringing new pleasures and entertainments, as well as opportunities for advancement, within reach of ordinary people. Wanting daughters as well as sons to enjoy youth (*disfrutar la juventud*), mothers were advising them to take their time about settling down and getting married. Though teenage boys and girls were still forbidden to go out in couples unchaperoned, it was becoming acceptable for siblings and cousins to go out in groups to movies and fiestas. Girls whose families could not afford to seclude them had long gone out to work, and now daughters of respectable families were going out to work as well. Though they gave half or more of their wages to their parents in compensation for the expenses of their upbringing, they still had money to spend on themselves, according to their own developing tastes.

Traditionally, on her fifteenth birthday a Mexican upper-class girl would be presented to society at a *quinceaños*, a coming-out party signaling that she had reached marriageable age, a custom that was adopted by the middle class in the years following the Revolution. By the 1950s, working-class parents, too, were beginning to give their daughters fifteenth birthday parties, though rather than indicating a girl's readiness for marriage, they now signaled only that childhood was over and she was entering the world of adults.

The *quinceañera* (birthday girl), wearing a white ball gown (often rented), would be escorted by parents and relatives to a mass in her honor. Afterward came the dinner in the girl's own home if there was room enough, otherwise in a godparent's house or a restaurant. When Catalina's oldest daughter, Gloria, turned fifteen, her parents held her party in the patio behind the family store. "She started off the dancing with her father," her mother recalls. "The first dance was a waltz. The next one, a rumba, she danced with her uncle. We ate pozole [a traditional pork dish] and a beautiful cake, and there was beer to drink, and brandy, and dozens of relatives attended. . . . We gave a quinceaños for my second daughter, too, but the other girls were shy, they didn't want all that attention and we didn't force them. We said it was their choice."

Growing up in the 1960s, Irene, whose parents were divorced, describes herself as having been a troubled—and troublesome—teenager by the standards of the day. "I insisted on my freedom, on doing what I wanted, and as mamá was working during the day, she couldn't stop me!" Irene frequently played truant from school, and though she managed to graduate from primaria, she refused to go to secundaria, opting instead for nurse's training, which in short order she abandoned. When she turned fifteen, she demanded a quinceaños. "I made such a fuss," she recalls, "that mamá agreed to let me have one. Really, she couldn't afford it, but she gave in, to keep me quiet." Not long afterward, while her mother was out of town on a visit to relatives, Irene began having sexual relations with Víctor, a boy from her own neighborhood. "He was handsome, and I suppose I was looking for the affection I didn't get at home." Only after she realized she was pregnant did she discover Víctor was officially engaged to another girl. He did not love her, and she did not love him either; nevertheless, believing that having made her bed she had to lie in it, she persuaded him to break his engagement and marry her. His parents, who were fond of his other girlfriend, were very much opposed to the marriage. His mother wept throughout the ceremony, which his father refused to attend. In contrast, Irene's mother wholeheartedly supported her daughter's decision. "She told me it was better to marry an unemployed sixteen-year-old than be left with a child on the shelf," says Irene with a shrug.

In the countryside, too, girls were starting to have more freedom to get into trouble. At fourteen, Ofelia went walking in the fields with a boy her own age, "and what had to happen, happened [*y sucedió lo que tenía que suceder*]." When her parents learned of her pregnancy, they did not pressure her to get married. Rather, after giving birth at home, she stayed with her son until she had weaned him and then, leaving him with her mother, went to the capital to work. Meanwhile, Matilde, who claims that as a young teenager she had welcomed parental supervision, began to chafe at it as she got older. Pedro started coming to the house while her mother was out, and soon he was pressuring her to go "away" with him. "One day, just to see what happens when a woman goes with a man," says Matilde, "I ran off with him. A week later, papá came to fetch me back from my in-laws'. Though he knew I wasn't a señorita any longer, still he wanted me at home." But to Matilde, as to Irene and indeed to most girls of her generation, engaging in sexual relations was no trivial matter. Having done so with Pedro, she felt committed to him, and so she persuaded her parents to let her get married. "Papá was sad to lose me and afraid of what my life might be like in the future, and at my wedding he got drunk out of his mind," she recalls.

Contemporary Adolescence and Young Adulthood

Fueled by bountiful oil revenues, in the 1970s Mexico's public education system was able to expand to include children from sectors of the population who had hitherto been excluded. Many working-class parents, perceiving that their own economic futures were dependent on their children's ability to acquire the formal qualifications needed for employment in an increasingly competitive market, were becoming more willing to make the financial sacrifices necessary to provide them with an education. Lau (1987:67)[6] reports that although Mexican middle- and lower-middle-class parents, clinging to the bourgeois conception of the provider husband and the secluded wife, may encourage sons more than daughters in their school careers, working-class parents, by contrast, are likely to encourage daughters more than sons. Literate or not, a boy can usually find work as a manual laborer at the government-legislated minimum wage, whereas if a girl wants anything other than domestic work—at even less than the minimum wage—she must have a junior high school certificate. Thus, though all but two women in our study had left school before sixteen, their daughters and granddaughters are continuing their education well beyond that age. A daughter, Los Robles mothers say, should be educated so that she can contribute to the parental household before marriage and to the marital household afterward. Most important of all, if her marriage does not work out, instead of "putting up with things," she should be in a position to leave her husband and support herself and her children at a decent standard of living. Again, as parents often perceive daughters as being more emotionally attached to them than sons, who tend, after marriage, to be drawn away to the wife's family, an investment in a daughter's education has a better chance of providing a return to themselves in their old age. But if they want their daughters to do well in school, they have to allow them time to do their homework. In the past, a teenage girl might routinely have spent the evening hours doing household chores, whereas today, she is likely to be studying—in other words, to be concentrating on her own development rather than on her family's needs.

A generation ago it was almost universally believed that an adolescent girl, being innocent and physically fragile, needed protection against *los deseos de los hombres*. Today's parents, though still very much concerned with their daughters' sexual conduct, assume that, within certain limits, they are able to protect themselves. As one mother comments, "My daughters are much more self-confident around boys and much less likely to be taken advantage of than my sister and I were at their age." As all public and most fee-paying educational institutions have shifted from a single-sex to a coeducational model, teenage girls now spend many hours each weekday with boys on the "neutral" ground of the classroom. The same mother continues, "My daughters are far more used to boys than my sisters and I were at their age. They make *friends* with boys in a way we never could. We were only sweethearts." If girls are more self-confident than their mothers were, in part this springs from the more egalitarian relationship that has come about between parents and children, in particular, between mothers and daughters. Today's mother is more likely to trust her daughter's judgment where boys are concerned, believing that she will stay out of harm's way because her own future—not just the family's honor—is at stake.

Though working-class parents may still be stricter with oldest than with later-born daughters, by and large they let their fifteen- and sixteen-year-olds go out with boys, provided they say where they are going and they return by the stipulated hour. Typically, parents welcome the boyfriend into the house, for as one woman explains, "If you don't, a girl becomes *callejera* [she's always in the street], and then you really have reason to worry. This way, if the boy's in your living room, watching your television, your daughter will be sitting beside him, so at least you'll know where she is!"

Farther down the socioeconomic ladder, however, parents tend to be more restrictive, forcing girls to keep their romantic lives a secret. Discovering that her daughter is courting, a mother may simply throw up her hands, but the father's likely response is to impose further restrictions on her liberty. That fathers are so suspicious of and punitive toward their daughters and yet do nothing to restrict their sons is a major source of complaint for teenage girls. "If I get home one minute after seven in the evening," one remarks, "my father whips off his belt and comes at me." Eyes flashing with indignation, she continues, "If he knew I had a boyfriend, he'd kill me. Two of my sisters eloped, just to get away from his bullying. But my brothers are girl-chasers, and if they come home after midnight or if they don't even come home at all, papá doesn't punish them. He just doesn't care!"

The quinceaños, now universal among all but the very poor, has become little more than an occasion for conspicuous consumption after which the girl continues her education. It is not unusual for a hundred guests to attend the dinner, and the record player of a generation ago is replaced by a live band. To pay for the clothes, the food, the drink, and the music, many parents go into debt, something that most do willingly, for they regard a daughter's quinceaños as the fulfillment of an essential social responsibility. Meanwhile, not only does the birthday girl invite her boyfriend if she has one but he stands beside her during the mass and may even open the dancing with her at the party afterward.

Today's adolescent girl expects that after finishing her education she will find a job and work for several years. Though she continues to live with her parents or close relatives, who exercise a degree of supervision over her, she has considerably more social and economic independence than her mother, or even her older sister, did. She expects to go out with several men before deciding who she wants to marry and, once she is officially engaged, to continue working for a year or two to save money for a home—even if it is only a room in a vecindad—separate from parents and in-laws. Following the massive expansion of public education facilities in the 1970s, age at marriage has risen steadily for both sexes.[7] Census figures for 1970 gave the mean age of marriage nationally as 20 for girls (considerably higher in urban areas, especially Mexico City and the border region; considerably lower in rural areas). Only six years later, the World Fertility Study found the age had risen to 21.7 years nationally. In Cuernavaca, our figures for 333 married couples—who had married over the previous twenty years— show 18.5 years as the mean age of marriage for women and 21 years for men. However, almost all sixth-, ninth-, and twelfth-grade boys and girls surveyed in Los Robles and contiguous neighborhoods in 1983 said they wanted to get married but not until they were old enough to shoulder the necessary responsibilities. For girls, this meant age 22 on average and for boys, age 23. Almost all wanted to have children; typically, the girls wanted "two, no more than three," the boys "three or four." Though most girls said they intended to work after marriage, few anticipated continuing their careers after their first child was born except out of "dire necessity." Only a handful suggested they might continue out of an interest in the work itself.

In several important respects, the female adolescent experience has changed dramatically in recent years, but provocative clothing, makeup, and air of worldliness notwithstanding, most teenage girls in Mexico, as in most of the developing world, have scant opportunity to learn about the workings of their bodies. Though today's mothers appear to be more comfortable about preparing their pubescent daughters for menstruation than their own mothers were, they still find talking about sexual behavior per se no easier. Some admit they "know" they should be talking with their daughters about "those things" but add regretfully that they "can't." Soledad's sixteen-year-old, Josefina, goes to school in the morning and works in the market to earn money for school expenses in the afternoon. The market shuts at seven, but despite her mother's threats and beatings, Josefina is rarely home before ten. Soledad assumes she is spending those hours with her boyfriend; she also assumes that they are having sexual relations. Eyebrows knitted with anxiety, she says, "I've told Josefina, 'You're only a señorita once. When you are no longer, there's no turning back the clock.' But contraception? No, I haven't told her anything about that. It would make me too ashamed."

In compliance with the 1974 Law of Population, sex education is mandatory beginning in the sixth grade.[8] This is the second attempt on the part of the SEP to introduce sex education, the first being in 1934 when, along with their "socialist" education program, the government of President Cárdenas tried to introduce "sexual" education into the secondary school curriculum. This program, a response to what the administration considered to be a high incidence of unwanted births and venereal disease among girls of poor family, consisted of instruction in elementary physiology and hygiene based on contemporary North American high school texts. Greeted by street demonstrations and an order by the archbishop of Mexico to parents to keep their children out of school, the program's name was hastily changed from "sexual" to "social" education. As Jim Tuck reports, the name change made it no more acceptable to parents, and it was abandoned by teachers, many of whom literally feared for their lives.

The sex education curriculum of the 1980s does not seem to have proved a great deal more successful than that of the 1930s. In Los Robles, students and teachers alike agreed that the authorized texts explained the facts of life *muy oscuramente* (very unclearly). As a male teacher in the neighborhood junior secondary school told us, "Parents don't want teachers telling their kids about sex. They say that to do so would invite promiscuity. So then what do we have? A passage in which a husband and wife are talking about wanting to have children. Next comes a picture of a fetus growing in the mother's stomach, and then we have the parents rejoicing over their new baby. But the book doesn't tell how the mother got the baby in the first place or how the baby was born. And believe me, I'm not going to be the one to tell these kids how, either. As for contraception, there'd be a riot if we said anything about that!"

Luz María, who was in the eighth grade when she started going out with Octavio, recalls that after the first night she spent with him, her friends assumed they had had sexual relations. At the time she agreed, even though, despite three years of so-called sex education, she was still too ignorant of her own anatomy to be sure whether in fact this was so. Now, after five years of marriage, she looks back on that night and realizes that they did not! In this same vein, Esther Corona,[9] writing about young women employed as domestics in the capital, comments on their abysmal ignorance concerning the structure and functioning of their own bodies in general and of their sexual organs in particular—which puts them at great risk for unwanted pregnancy.

In the 1980s, health clinics offered contraceptive services only to women who had already given birth, and though contraceptives were widely available for sale in pharmacies, information about how to use them correctly was hard to come by. Thus, instead of working and enjoying themselves and marrying when they were "ready for responsibility" as they had planned, some teenagers found themselves pregnant. As they tended to deny their condition for as long as possible, by the time they accepted their situation, the pregnancy was usually far advanced. While some Los Robles adolescents did get abortions—which were illegal and expensive as well as dangerous—we were told that, compared with married women, they were few in number. Rather, once the parents became aware of the situation, they made every effort to get the girl and her baby's father married.[10] Again, far from being deprived or disadvantaged, because of their youth and perceived inexperience, adolescent mothers received more support from relatives than older mothers did. In the rather rare event that the father refused to marry her, the young mother would leave her baby with her mother or grandmother and get whatever work she could by which to support the two of them. In Los Robles, it was very unusual for an unwed mother—whether a teenager or older—to surrender her child for adoption.

Getting Married

The normative process by which working-class couples marry is as ritualized today as it was a generation ago. Even if the girl's parents have known the boy for a long time and approve of him, he is still expected to come with his father and godfather to make a formal request for her hand. The civil marriage ceremony is brief and inexpensive, and many couples are content with only that. The religious ceremony—which involves a much more serious commitment, as it is almost impossible to obtain a religious divorce—can also be extremely simple; indeed, a couple can be married along with several others following Sunday mass. But for the most part, working-class couples who choose to have a religious wedding want an elaborate affair. Parents try to reduce expenses by spreading them among relatives and friends, who in return become "godparents" of the couple.[11] For one, the madrina de boda, who is the bride's "sponsor" or adviser about married life and the counterpart to the groom's padrino de boda, is expected to contribute heavily to the wedding costs. A second woman will be invited to be godmother of the dress (*madrina de vestido*), a third, godmother of the cake (*madrina de pastel*), and so on. In return for their financial contributions, each receives the status of special guest. But for all the help they may get with expenses, the bride's parents are likely to "hurt" for a long while afterward. Nevertheless, we were assured that the joy they experience at seeing their daughter marry in a white dress—a symbol of parental obligations successfully met—fully compensates for the debts they have incurred. As noted earlier, these days young couples are more than likely to have sexual relations before marriage. Tracy Ehlers reports[12] that in San Pedro Sacatepequez, San Marcos, the ladinoized town where she worked in highland Guatemala, sex during courtship is more often an expression of male dominance than of mutual desire, observing that "despite amorous teenage

"Ya eres señorita"

Teenagers

High school girl

flirtations, girls are utterly unprepared for the marital bed" (1990:135). In Los Robles, too, premarital sex seems to occur, at least initially and sometimes throughout the courtship period because the boy "insists." While today's young woman may have a good deal more opportunity to engage in premarital sexual relations than her mother did, she may be no less conflicted. Having rigid prohibitions imposed on you by your parents may be irksome, but having your novio impose *his* wishes may hardly be an improvement. Should pregnancy occur, the bride will still wear white at her wedding, however. Nor, even if the pregnancy is far advanced, does she appear to suffer social stigma, for as one mother explained with a shrug, "It happens so often these days."

With la crisis, a couple may put off the expense of a church wedding until "later," which they know might mean a year or two, and in the meantime marry according to the civil ceremony alone. By the time their parents are in a position to provide for the religious ceremony and the party afterward, the young couple may well be parents, too.

Ya Soy Señorita

Two Women's Adolescent Experiences

CATALINA, the oldest of five, was born in a small Morelos village in 1929. "Papá and mamá never got along," she recalls sadly. "Papá used to say that mamá only came to live with him because he had a shop and because in those hard years he was a little better off than other people. The bargain she struck was that my grandmother and my two uncles would move in as well. Mamá was only eighteen at the time she and papá got together, and he was over forty. . . . When he realized he was very sick and likely to die, he'd get drunk and weep about mamá's not loving him. Some people said his old lover, a barren woman with whom he'd lived before mamá, had bewitched him and that was why he was dying. *He* used to say mamá was killing him with her coldness. As for me, I think he died of drink."

Soon after his death his business failed, and, as Catalina recalls, her mother, who had been accustomed to sending out her laundry, had to start making a living by doing other people's wash. "My grandmother and I were doing all the housework, and when the rains began, we were going out to plant the fields. If I asked for a new dress, mamá would tell me, 'If that's what you want, then buy the cloth yourself!' "

Catalina had her first period when she was fourteen. "Mamá hadn't told me anything, and my friends hadn't either. Anyway," she adds softly, "I wouldn't have understood even if they had, because my mind was closed [*mi cabeza estaba cerrada*]." Though she told her grandmother, who gave her some rags and showed her how to fix them with safety pins, she did not say a word about it to her mother.

Boys were beginning to pay her a lot of attention. They would follow her along the village street and down to the river, teasing her and, on coming closer, whispering compliments. Indeed, in photographs dating from that period, she is very pretty. One day she received a letter from a boy, saying that he was planning to abduct her. "That's how many girls got married in those days," she explains. "It had already happened to one of my cousins. Those country boys, they'd come to the house at night, all armed, and what could you do? My *pretendiente* [suitor] was a boy of seventeen called Blás. He was *muy grosero* [very crude]. I knew I couldn't stand to live the rest of my life with him, but my father was dead and my brothers were still very young. On her own, mamá couldn't protect me."

Catalina confided in her grandmother, who arranged that very night for one of her uncles to take her away. "At every sound I heard as we rode through the countryside I thought, 'It's Blás, he's caught up with me!' But we got away all right and in the dawn, arrived at my cousin's house in Tilzapotla, papá's birthplace. After that, I never lived in my home again."

With tears in her eyes, Catalina continues, "It's very hard to talk about those years. . . . Once I'd left home it seemed that no one cared what happened to me. Really, I was on my own." She went to work earning thirty pesos a month, half of which she sent to her mother and the other half of which she kept. "In those days [1943], fifteen pesos seemed like a lot of money. It bought you a dress or a set of underwear." The cousin she lived with was kind enough, but a problem soon arose with her daughter, who was about Catalina's own age. "She became so jealous of me that after three months I knew I couldn't stay in that house any longer. When I went home for my saint's day I told mamá how bad things had gotten with that girl, and she arranged for me to go to Acapulco to another cousin who was expecting a baby and needed help. But as soon as I arrived, her husband was after me. I know what he thought—'Catalina's father's dead and she has no one to look out for her, so I can do what I like.' I didn't tell my cousin what her husband was doing—I was *muy tímida* in those days—but when I went home I told mamá."

Instead of going back to Acapulco after her visit, Catalina went to a third set of relatives in Zacatepec, a rural town not far from her home. "In that house," she recalls, "the whole family slept in a single room, and now the oldest son was the problem. He'd wriggle over to where I lay and try to force himself on me. So I couldn't stay there either. . . . Next, I went to my aunt, but her husband would come after me the instant she left the house. Once—and I wasn't even alone with him, there was a younger child with me—he tore off my pants, and I dashed into the street and stayed there till my aunt came back. I told her what her husband had done, and guess what she said? It was all my fault—I'd enticed him!"

By now Catalina had lived with so many different relatives that she could not face asking her mother to find another place for her. Instead, she decided to elope. "I had a novio of whom my aunt disapproved because he drank a lot. I didn't love him, but I couldn't think of anything else to do except run away with him. Luckily my aunt discovered my plan and packed me off to Cuernavaca to live with my cousin Vera who'd recently been widowed. That's how I happened to come here." First, Catalina worked in a factory and later, as a maid. "My employers didn't try to seduce me," she remarks wryly. "Only my relatives did that!" Soon she met Joaquín who came from her father's birthplace, Tilzapotla, and worked as a clerk in his uncle's store in the center of town. Cousin Vera, meanwhile, was not letting the grass grow under her feet. "Already she had a lover," Catalina recalls, "and she often didn't come home at night. I had much more freedom than most sixteen-year-olds. Vera let me go to the movies and out dancing whenever I wanted. She didn't care." But rather than enjoying her freedom, Catalina felt unprotected and scared.

Meanwhile, her new novio, Joaquín, was pressuring her to have sexual relations. "If that's what you want, then first we get married, I told him," she recalls, adding, "I married him because it was the only thing to do [*porque no había ningún otro remedio*]." Once or twice she tried to tell Joaquín about her experiences with her male relatives. "But he didn't want to hear those stories. He didn't want to know anything about my life before we met. He wanted me to be entirely pure." She shrugs. "That's what men are like—they want to have sex with you before they marry you and at the same time, they want to marry a virgin!"

As Joaquín's father was dead, it was his paternal uncle who traveled with him to Catalina's home to ask for her hand, and when they were married six months later, the same uncle hosted the dinner following the wedding ceremony. "In those days, it was the groom's family who paid the wedding expenses. Joaquín even paid for my dress! This custom of the bride's family having to pay was brought here by the gringos later on."

Their honeymoon trip was to Morelia. During the train journey, Joaquín developed stomach cramps, and on arrival, instead of going to a hotel as planned, they went immediately to the house of a relative who sent Joaquín to bed with a hot water bottle to hold over his stomach. Next day when he was feeling better, they went to a hotel. "We were only in Morelia three days," Catalina says, "but still, for poor people like us it was something, it was a honeymoon."

Despite a succession of experiences with men, at marriage Catalina was still profoundly ignorant about sexual relations. "I'd realized what it was those men had wanted," she says, "but I didn't know exactly how they'd go about getting it, and when I got married I was very scared. It could be that Joaquín was, too, and his stomach pains were from nerves, not from the soup he'd eaten at our wedding dinner, as he claimed!" she adds, smiling. "Still, he certainly knew much more about sex than I did, and yet he didn't tell me anything. He didn't say, 'Now I'm going to do this and this.' He just went ahead and did it! I'd never been hurt in that place before, and I was very shocked. It took me a month to get used to having sexual relations, but then I began to enjoy it." She pauses. "Really, getting married was a shock in many ways. Though we'd known each other for a year before the wedding, I'd only known one side of Joaquín. While we'd been courting he was very affectionate, but almost as soon as we got home from our trip he changed. He started turning inward. . . . When I asked him, 'What are you thinking?' he'd say, 'Nothing.' He refused to share his thoughts. I got pregnant right away, so perhaps it was the prospect of having a family so soon, with all the responsibility, that made him like that. But for me, it was very painful."

Remembering her own confusion as a girl, as her oldest daughter, Gloria, approached puberty, Catalina wanted to prepare her for the onset of menstruation, and though she found it very difficult, *más o menos* (after a fashion), she managed to do so. "I assumed she would tell her sister Yolanda for me, but she didn't! Poor Yolanda. When her period started, she was terribly worried! I didn't tell my younger daughters either. I knew this was wrong, but I was very shy and I told myself, 'Well, they're in the secundaria so they must know much more about everything than I do. I only went to school for two years!'"

Catalina admits to having been overly strict with Gloria, perhaps because, as a girl, she herself had suffered so much from lack of supervision. She recalls that in the 1960s when Gloria reached adolescence, she and Joaquín didn't let her go to fiestas, let alone go out with boys. "We believed she should have the chance to make something of herself before she started thinking about boyfriends. In my own case, I'd married at seventeen and had six babies in nine years. I never had a girlhood, and after I got married I was so busy with the children and doing what my husband wanted. He was *muy exigente* [demanding]. I think most husbands are that way. No, I didn't want Gloria to marry young as I had. I wanted her to have time for herself."

After graduating from secundaria, Gloria went to work for the telephone company, where she met Chucho, who is now her husband. As she knew her parents did not want her to have a boyfriend, they courted secretly. "The first time we laid eyes on Chucho was when he came to ask for Gloria's hand, and by then they'd been novios for six years!" says Catalina. "We were a bit less strict with her sisters. . . . We assumed they had boyfriends, and we weren't about to try to stop them. All the same, we didn't want to know about them until they'd made up their minds to get married. 'Once their engagement is official, their novios are welcome in the house, but not before,' that's what Joaquín used to say when he was still alive, and I agreed with him. . . . If Gloria had brought Chucho home any sooner, I'd have been so sad, thinking, she's fallen in love, she's going to leave us. . . . I couldn't have stood having that sadness drawn out for six years!"

ELOISA, a vivacious young woman of twenty-five, lives with her husband, Marco, and her two sons in the same vecindad where, as a schoolgirl, she lived with her grandmother. Her mother, meanwhile, was living next door with her new husband, Eloisa's stepfather. "I'd see mamá several times a day," Eloisa recalls, "but it was always my abuelita who looked out for me. Mamá and I weren't close at all. She seemed to care only about my step-father and their new baby."

Eloisa learned nothing from her grandmother about the facts of life. "You'd have thought I'd have known more than I did," she says ruefully, "seeing what had happened to me as a little girl [she had been sexually abused by a much older cousin], but I'd pulled a curtain over the whole experience and I remembered nothing. I had an idea about sexual relations because I'd sometimes seen lovers together in the countryside, and boys at school would show me pictures of nude women in magazines. Even so, at thirteen, when my period began [*me bajó la regla*] I was shocked. I must've heard other girls talking about Kotex, but I hadn't taken in what they were saying, or else I'd told myself, what's happening to them isn't going to happen to me!" One day she was playing basketball at school when she had a stomach pain, something she had experienced often before, and it had passed. This time, however, just as she realized her shorts were wet with blood, a classmate whispered, 'You've got your period, that's what's the matter! Here, put this on,' and she lent her her sweater to cover herself.

Asking to be excused from school, Eloisa ran home and dashed into the shower to wash off the blood, but it only seemed to flow faster. When he heard her weeping in the shower, her brother went to fetch her mother and grandmother. "Mamá just laughed and gave me a cloth to pin on, but my grandmother was very moved. 'You're a big girl now,' she told me."

Eloisa continued her tomboy behavior until one day it dawned on her that boys found her attractive. She grins. "In other words, I had sex appeal, and I began to take advantage of it!" After finishing primary school, she began a secretarial course and in the *academia* she began to note how her female classmates dressed and did their hair and to imitate them.

Her grandmother, meanwhile, had started supervising her more closely.

She told her not to talk to boys, but then as now, Eloisa was extremely sociable *(sumamente sociable)*, and there was no holding her back. "When my abuelita went out, she used to lock me in the house, but I'd climb out the window. Sometimes she'd catch me and give me a thrashing, but more often, I'd be home again before she'd realized I'd been gone. I'm glad I don't have daughters. I wouldn't want the problems my abuelita had raising me!"

When she was fourteen, she met her future husband, Marco, in the street when she was going *por el pan* (to buy bread). Soon she was going to bakeries that were farther away so she would have more time to spend with him. Another way of evading her grandmother's surveillance was by saying she was returning to school in the afternoon to play basketball. Her budding romance with Marco did not stop her from having boyfriends among her classmates as well, however. "The truth is I was a real flirt. If I were to name all my boyfriends, it would be a very long list!" She would arrange her school day carefully so she could see a different boy in each break between classes. "They each got ten minutes of my time," she says, smiling. "I wanted to see if I liked anyone more than Marco, but I made them understand that the relationship was only for school, and once outside, if they met me in the street with Marco, I wouldn't acknowledge them. I don't know why I was so popular with boys," she continues. "I wasn't particularly pretty, though perhaps I attracted them because I was *relajienta* [lively]." Other girls were jealous of her success, and to this day she has few women friends.

"From the start I loved Marco very much, and I don't think I was doing anything wrong by having other boyfriends. If I'd stuck with him all the time, I'd have become resentful." Indeed, she remembers their courtship as a very happy time. She would wear shorts under her school uniform, and when she got out of school, she would take off her skirt and leave it and her books with a shopkeeper she knew and go off with Marco and his friend, Felipe. "We looked so much like three boys," she recalls, "that once a taxi driver, seeing Marco with his arms around me and Felipe, thought we were homosexuals and shouted obscenities at us!"

She loved going to the fiestas that took place in neighbors' patios, though her grandmother would often insist on coming along as her chaperone. Other girls her age were allowed to go out dancing with their sisters or even on their own, she would complain bitterly, but to no avail. Granny kept on coming!

"In those days," Eloisa continues, "fiestas were much 'quieter' than they are now. We went just for the pleasure of dancing. I suppose couples did neck in cars and in the backs of buses, but they didn't on the dance floor like they do today." Sometimes Marco would attend a fiesta also, but each would dance with other partners. This was Eloisa's idea. "Otherwise it would have been boring." She adored dancing, and would dance every dance with a different boy, until it was time to go home.

But, meanwhile, she was cutting classes, and even when she went to school, she spent so much time socializing that she flunked. After that, she stayed at home. To her chagrin, she found herself being watched much more closely by both grandmother and novio, and she had far fewer opportunities to meet boys. She explains that she did not have a quinceaños because when she turned fifteen she was not on good terms with her stepfather, who would have been responsible for paying for it. In addition to regarding him as an intruder, she detested him on account of the beatings he gave her mother when he was drunk. "When I tried to intervene to protect her, she'd tell me off instead of thanking me," Eloisa recalls. "She was so dependent on him that she couldn't stand up for herself, or let me stand up for her either. That's why, when I was a teenager, I hated my stepfather. Not that I was openly rebellious," she hastens to add. "I'd just refuse to meet his eyes, and the second he walked into the room I'd walk out." During her adolescence she resented him so much that rather than ask him for money to buy clothes, she would choose to go without.

Estela wanted to hold off having sex with Marco. "La regla, growing up—all that was scary to me, because of what had happened when I was a kid," she says. "But one day Marco convinced me to try it, and once I realized it was something so wonderful [*algo tan maravilloso*], I went on doing it!" Sometimes they had intercourse in the empty lots that dotted the neighborhood but more often, right there in the vecindad, *donde fuera* (any old where), behind the shower stall, next to the laundry sinks. "We called them *rapidines* [quickies]. Maybe we did it that way for the excitement. Will we get caught this time? But we never did!" They used no birth control, but they were lucky. Eloisa did not get pregnant, and after two years, when she was sixteen and Marco twenty-one, they decided to get married, "because that's all there was left to do." A decade later, Eloisa still has her wedding dress and veil—"everything," she adds, "except my bouquet of plastic flowers." (Those she presented to the Virgin of Guadalupe when her older son, Abram, was very sick, hoping that in return for such a precious gift, the Virgin would restore the boy to health.)

"My stepfather didn't come to the ceremony," she recalls. "At that point we still weren't getting along, so I refused to invite him." Their relationship improved, however, when she went into labor prematurely with her first child and her stepfather took her to the hospital. "Then I felt so bad because of the way I'd been treating him. Also, after I got married and found myself dependent on my husband, emotionally, economically—really, in every way—I began to understand my mother's position better, I mean, why she'd gotten mad at me when I'd tried to protect her from my stepfather when he was drunk."

"Marco and I had a great time when we were courting," she adds wistfully, "but after you get married, things change; they aren't ever quite the same."

Summary

Only recently did Mexican mothers begin to talk with their daughters about sexual development ("those things") or older sisters to inform younger sisters. Until a generation ago, once their schooling came to an end—usually well before menarche—girls had little contact with female peers from whom they might otherwise have obtained information (or misinformation). Thus, for our older informants, menstruation often came as a profound shock. Not surprisingly, at first many thought that they were dying. Told by female relatives that she was now a señorita, a cause for celebration, a girl felt reassured and proud. But she soon learned that her new status involved many restrictions, for her virginity, while greatly prized, could by the same token occasion great personal danger. It was assumed that any man could and would try to dishonor her should the least opportunity present itself, and as no unmarried girl had the emotional maturity or physical strength to defend herself, it was her family's responsibility to protect her at all times. As this required seclusion, after menarche, further schooling—and exposure to the streets—was out of the question. Social contact with would-be suitors was also out of the question. Thus, courtship was often conducted exclusively by letter, and although once the novios were officially engaged closely chaperoned meetings might be permitted, at marriage the young couple still barely knew each other.

Meanwhile, far from enjoying her freedom, an adolescent girl whose economic circumstances obliged her to go out to earn a living was likely to find running the gauntlet of male attention a daily humiliation; if she had to live away from parents and siblings, she felt uncared for; even in the houses of close kin she risked being sexually exploited. Thus, she was likely to see elopement as the only way out of her plight. Marriage—albeit to a boy with few prospects—offered her the protection that her own family could not provide.

Levels of education rose steadily during the period of the economic boom. Though in the countryside parents still terminated their daughters' education at puberty, if not before, by the early 1980s, 90 percent of girls between the ages of fifteen and nineteen in Cuernavaca were still attending school. Whereas as adolescents, their grandmothers had had no contact with boys other than brothers and cousins and their mothers, if permitted more exposure, had been carefully chaperoned, in the 1980s teenage girls were likely to spend a good deal of unsupervised time with boys. They knew that boys did no better academically than girls and often, because "they're distracted and don't apply themselves to their studies," not as well. As classmates and casual friends, they had an opportunity to learn how to *comportarse bien* (conduct themselves properly) with the opposite sex, an opportunity that their mothers never dreamed of having. Even so, as far as parents, teachers, and physicians were concerned, sexuality was still a taboo subject.

A girl's first responsibility was to herself, our informants insisted, and without "preparation"—the capacity to support herself economically—she put herself at risk. Mothers stressed that their own parents had believed education was wasted on a girl who would "only get married"; in contrast, they themselves were convinced that education was essential both for self-respect and for the economic opportunities it provided. They hoped that their daughters would acquire a professional qualification—followed by employment—that would allow them a period of freedom before they undertook marriage and motherhood and the self-sacrifice those roles required. Most important, *una mujer preparada* (an educated woman) could provide for her children should her husband desert her or, if his treatment of her became intolerable, she left him.

· 3 ·

La Vida de Casada:
Expectations and
Realities of Marriage

Part 1: The Marital Relationship

Much has been written about *machismo* (male dominance) and its counter-part, *hembrismo* (female submissiveness), in Latin America and in Mexico in particular. According to the stereotypes, the man is hard-drinking and easily angered, promiscuous, callous to all women except his mother, and domineering with his children. The woman meanwhile, is *abnegada* (self-denying), *ahorradora* (frugal), *dócil* (obedient), and *aguantadora* (capable of almost infinite emotional and physical endurance).[1] Taking a historical perspective, some commentators have ascribed Mediterranean roots to these character traits. Under the sixteenth century Iberian legal code, women were designated "imbeciles by nature",[2] a condition of inferiority that would be further emphasized in colonial Mexico where, with Spanish women in short supply in the first century following the conquest, Spanish men took Indian women as wives and concubines. These unions produced a *mestizo*—mixed—race. In contrast to indigenous societies, in which relations between the sexes appear to have been less hierarchical than in peninsular Spain,[3] machismo as it developed in mestizo culture took on a "distinctly aggressive element," reflecting the nature of the sexual relationship between male and female, conqueror and conquered.[4]

La Vida de Casada

Other commentators, adopting a more psychological viewpoint, have stressed the defensive violence inherent in machista behavior. Psychoanalyst Santiago Ramírez contended that for the mestizo male, sexual relationships, especially the marital relationship, give rise to a terrifying insecurity against which he protects himself by sadistic violence and an escape from intimacy into compulsive promiscuity. Erich Fromm and Michael Maccoby[5] interpreted the antagonism characteristic of male-female relationships that they observed in "Las Cuevas," a village near Cuernavaca, in terms of contempt on the woman's part and retaliation on the man's. The woman, who in childhood is likely to have lacked a father on whom she could rely emotionally or economically, distrusts and despises her husband and, albeit subtly, undermines him. In turn, the man reacts to the threat of psychological castration with physical violence and abandonment. According to Stycos, from earliest childhood sexual inequalities within the family encourage and reinforce male dominance and female submissiveness. As a *machito*, the small boy receives special privileges, in contrast to his sister, on whom restrictions—which both he and she take as indicative of her innate inferiority—are imposed. Hence, both grow up believing it is the male's natural right as a superior being to command and the obligation of the female, as his inferior, to obey. Henry Selby and his colleagues point out, meanwhile, that "macho" has another connotation. Though it commonly denotes a bully who tyrannizes his wife and family, it may also imply a quite different character type: a man who is *formal y respetoso*, proud but not arrogant, reflective, authoritative, and hardworking. Indeed, as Oscar Lewis portrays him, in most respects, Jesús Sánchez conformed to that ideal. A teetotaler, he worked tirelessly to support two families that together at times included more than twenty souls. He provided them with housing, food, clothing, schooling, and medical care, and if a son or daughter got into any kind of serious trouble, regardless of their age or life stage, he did his best to extricate them. Though his manner of relating to his dependents was distinctly authoritarian, his oldest son, Manuel, admitted that his straight behavior made him "an easy man to love."

Women in Los Robles told us that to a true macho, the fulfillment of family responsibilities is of primary importance; he drinks only in moderation and keeps his infidelities, if any, secret from his wife. Indeed, Margarita describes her husband, Edmundo, in just these terms. "After he died, people urged me to marry again," she says, "but I told them, 'My kids couldn't accept a stepfather.' The truth is, though, it was I who couldn't have accepted another man. From our wedding day, we'd been each other's best friend." Together, they had overcome many setbacks and losses: a fire that destroyed their first business; the deaths of two young children and the serious street accident of a third; fourteen years of caring for Edmundo's paralyzed father; and long periods of separation when Edmundo went to the United States as a bracero. "Six months out of every year he'd be gone," Margarita remembers, "and I'd be left here with the kids and the store and my sick father-in-law, whose temper was terrible." Every two weeks she would receive a postcard from Edmundo saying, "I love you, kiss the kids." and that kept her going. Where did he work? California, Michigan, she is not sure. What did he work at? She is not sure of that, either. How did he spend his free time? That was his affair, she says with a shrug, adding that what was important was the money he earned up there, the money with which she was able to build their vecindad and, after his death, raise and educate their children.

Estela frequently describes her husband, Julio, as *buena gente*, a good person. Other women talk about brothers and cousins and brothers-in-law who work tirelessly for their families' well-being (*el bienestar de la familia*). Recalling her oldest brother, Enrique, Inés says that he was so devoted to his wife and children that "he even managed to die in California, so that after his death, his widow could receive social security benefits from the American government. It's now twenty-five years, and my sister-in-law still gets her monthly check in the mail!" Lourdes talks about her brother-in-law, a heavy equipment operator, who managed to provide all nine of his children with a professional education and after forty years of marriage cannot bear to be parted from his wife for an afternoon. Soledad and Ofelia describe sisters and brothers-in-law building up businesses together. Another woman mentions that her *concuño* (her sister-in-law's husband) is so devoted to his children that he never misses a parent-teacher meeting. In short, all these women know good men, responsible men, who respect their wives and work tirelessly *para que salga adelante la familia* (so that the family gets ahead), but few use these words to describe their own husbands.

Whether they married because they were madly in love or to escape difficult home situations, they expected to be happy. "My head was full of fantasies," one young woman admits ruefully. *Comprensión* (understanding), *compañía* (companionship), and *confianza* (trust) are what she hoped for: the husband and wife making a future *juntos, unidos* (together, united). "But when the truth of how married life actually was hit me, it was horrible!"

La Vida de Casada

The Realities of Marriage

Living Arrangements and Household Economics

A newly married couple aspires to an independent household, even if only a living space physically separated from that of parents by a plywood or cardboard partition, in which the young wife can keep her own kitchen. Co-residence, with its inevitable conflicts, should be avoided.[6] But after marriage, most of the couples in our study lived with one or other set of parents, because finances did not allow for independence. The young wife had no choice but to share a kitchen with either her mother or her mother-in-law.

Husbands, who averaged only twenty years of age when they got married, had little formal education. None had studied beyond primary school, and two had never been to school at all. When they got married they were still in the process of making connections that might eventually lead to a steady job. Few had an *oficio*. Most worked as masons, porters, caretakers, or messengers or else were self-employed carpenters and house painters. As Selby observed,[7] lower-class men, excluded by lack of preparation and connections from the formal sector, suffer more from underemployment than unemployment: they can usually find work but rarely work that produces a living wage. Among the older generation, Estela and Catalina, both of whom married men several years their senior (one a mechanic and the other a small-scale entrepreneur), moved into their own places straightaway. Inés, too, briefly had her own place, until Antonio lost his job and they had to move in with his mother. Among the younger women, only Ofelia and Verónica, who eloped to different towns from those in which their parents were living, started married life apart from relatives. After several years on her in-laws' farm, Matilde and Pedro moved into town and life in a large commercial vecindad, a situation that Matilde regards as an improvement psychologically, though physically she is not so sure. In the country her children had space to play without interfering with anybody, but if they play ball in the vecindad, in no time they will have a neighbor screaming at them. Most women her age, however, are still living—rent-free or at nominal charge—in a vecindad belonging to one or the other set of parents.

"There's always jealousy when you're living with your husband's family," a woman remarks. "My *suegra* was accustomed to my husband giving her half his salary, and when she saw him giving almost all he earned to me, she didn't like it!" Wives prefer to live with their own parents, as they generally get on better with their mothers than their mothers-in-law, but that relationship, too, can have its problems. One young woman who has spent long stretches with both sets of parents reports, "My suegra was always interfering, and I hated that. She drove me crazy, the way she never let me alone. Now I'm living with mamá, and she's the opposite. She pays me almost no attention at all. If anything, being ignored is even worse than being ordered around."

Whether they live with parents or in a rented room, a young couple's most cherished dream is to get a plot and build a house on it and thereafter, *hacer lo que quiera* (do whatever one wants) with a minimum of interference from relatives and neighbors. By all accounts, during the boom they had a fair chance (provided the husband worked hard and did not drink excessively) of acquiring a house plot by purchase or *invasión*, the establishment of squatters' rights on farmland on the edge of town. As they could afford materials, they would build a house of *tabique* (sun-dried bricks and mortar) or cement blocks. Beginning with a kitchen/bedroom and expanding room by room, construction might take decades. Given hard times, however, few young couples are likely to realize their dream of a home of their own very soon, and so when relatives and neighbors interfere, young wives bite their tongues and put up with it.

Traditionally, a Mexican husband is expected to earn the family living while his wife takes care of the home.[8] He may give her most of his wages for *el gasto* (household expenses), reserving a small sum for his own pocket money, or the entire amount, out of which his wife gives him an allowance. In any event, failure on the husband's part to provide his wife with household expenses automatically, thereby forcing her to ask, is regarded as seriously reprehensible. Ideally, a husband should earn enough so that his wife does not need to undertake the *doble jornada* (double work load) of going out to work and running the house; just as important, she should be denied the opportunity to cuckold him with men she might meet at work. But, in reality, the majority of our informants have routinely been obliged to supplement their husbands' contributions by earning money as laundresses, seamstresses, and baby-sitters. By working at home, however, they have been able to maintain the fiction that the husband's support is adequate.

The city, never an easy place for the unskilled or semiskilled, became brutal with the onset of la crisis. "*Todo está muy caro* [everything is so expensive]," is the universal complaint in 1984, as, with the long years of economic expansion at an end, inflation soars and working-class people, who just a short while before believed in their future, see their hopes for advancement evaporate. While men who have steady work are threatened with layoffs, others scramble after casual laboring jobs that often pay less than the legal minimum wage. Soledad's sons consider themselves lucky if they work five days in the month. "If only they could go to California," their mother laments. In California there are jobs and the possibility of earning at six times the rate that a manual laborer earned in Mexico.[9] "But where will they get money for the trip? *El norte* is for those who have *conocidos y recursos* [contacts and the wherewithal to get there], not for people like us." Rosa, whose truck driver husband has hardly worked in a year, struggles to support her family on her salary as a part-time aerobics teacher. Eloisa begs her unemployed husband to go out of the house during the daytime so that they can pretend he has gone to work. "Wouldn't that be easier for both of us, instead of you sitting around all the time?" When she can find customers, Eloisa spends her days at her sewing machine. ("I can make a dress in two hours," she boasts), but, meanwhile, the plot on the edge of town she and her husband have their eye on is appropriated by another couple. Unless you build on your *terreno*, you lose it, and given the state of their finances, they haven't been able to buy a single brick.

Alcoholism and Domestic Violence

"I tell my daughters, 'Enjoy yourselves while you're young,' " says one woman, "because once you're married, you won't get the chance.' " She recalls that within weeks of establishing her with his mother, her husband went back to spending all his free time outside the house. Instead of the relationship in which they worked together and shared decisions that she had anticipated during their courtship, he left the day-to-day management of the household entirely to her, while retaining control of everything else: where they were to live, all major expenditures, whether she worked or not, and whether or not she should have another child. Though he allowed some discussion of these issues, he insisted on having the final word. Their lives were almost totally separate. Hers was *adentro* (inside) and his *afuera* (outside). As she says bitterly, "*Él está libre y yo, encerrada*" (He's free, and I'm trapped).

Afuera, with its excitements that encourage the development of *vicios* (bad habits), is the enemy women seem to battle interminably. "When you're courting, a man may be able handle himself so his *novia* doesn't know anything bad about him," says one woman, the wife of a government worker. "You walk around together, you go to the movies, you eat a taco in the plaza, and then you separate and go home. My husband and I were novios for six years without my even suspecting that he had a drinking problem. I only found out about it after we were married! At night, there I'd be all alone in the house, worried to death. Where was he? In the cantina! Now our roof leaks, and where d'you think the money to fix it went? The bar! It leaks so badly that when the rainy season comes, we'll have to move in with my mother."

Soledad admits that even when she and Jorge were courting, she already knew he drank a lot. "But I thought, it's because he's unhappy. Once we're married, he'll be happy, and then he'll give it up! I didn't realize how *duro* [rigid] he was, how set in his ways. Then after we got married, whatever he earned he'd spend on liquor—pulque, beer, brandy, mescal—anything he could lay his hands on. And then he'd come home and beat me. Even so, it took me a long, long time to accept his drinking for what it was—something permanent. Finally—by that point he'd knocked out most of my teeth—I did. I said to myself, 'This is his character, he isn't going to change.' I became very bitter, and I began to drink, too. I'd go to the cantinas. You know what kind of women go there? The worst kind. Or I'd buy a bottle and bring it home. . . . I became a drunkard, just like he was. . . . After a year of that, the children begged me to stop. 'Mamá, you're making us so ashamed!' So for their sakes I did stop. . . . I stopped going to fiestas, too, because I was afraid that if they offered alcohol, I'd take some and become a drunkard again, and in this family we can only afford one."

One young woman who eloped at sixteen hoping for affection and companionship admits she was soon disappointed. Her husband's absences from home were frequent and lengthy, and he often returned drunk and spoiling for a fight. Over the years, rather than getting better, things have only gotten worse. "The smart thing for me to do would be to walk out of the house the minute he walks in." But if it is the middle of the night and the children are sleeping, she does not dare leave them for fear he will harm them. "So I stay, and that's when the trouble begins."

Luz María recalls that as newlyweds in California, she and her husband, Octavio, were together all the time: they worked together cleaning houses; they went out together; they stayed home together; they were *juntos, unidos,* earning good money, making a decent life. But on their return to Cuernavaca, just as la crisis was starting, Octavio was discouraged by his failure to find steady work and began to drink heavily. Now, three years later, he will work for a few days as a laborer, quit, and go to drink. "In the evening I go looking for him in the streets and the vecindades, and if I find him drinking, I beg him for a few pesos for food before he spends all he has," Luz María says. "Often, when he comes home drunk, he fights with me and breaks my dishes and yells that he's punishing me for following him." Only after he has spent his last cent, sobered up, and experienced remorse does he look for work again. For a time, then, things are better. Husband and wife go hand in hand to the movies and the park, and Luz María is "safe" from Octavio's blows—until the next binge. "That's how it is," she says, "*altas y bajas* [highs and lows]." Alcoholics Anonymous, which has several groups in Los Robles, only accepts people who admit they have a problem. "Octavio claims he can give up drinking whenever he wants," says Luz María bitterly. "He says he drinks because he wants to, not because he must." Each time, fleeing his drunken blows, she runs across town to take refuge with her grandmother, Octavio comes after her and promises he will change, and she goes back home with him. "Luz is used to suffering," her aunt observes with a gesture of helplessness. "She's one of those people. . . . What d'you call them? *Masoquista.*" She was so often beaten in childhood that even though she detests it, violence is an integral part of her life.

As the economy stagnated, increasingly husbands vented their disappointments and frustrations on wives and children. Mercédes González de la Rocha, who carried out a study of women's participation in the labor force in Guadalajara in 1982–83 (the first year of la crisis), reported a high incidence of marital violence.[10] The large majority of wives stayed with their husbands, while the few who left returned in short order, in part because of pressure placed on them by female relatives—especially by mothers and mothers-in-law—who told them they should stay for the children's sakes. Children needed their father, they heard from all sides, both for the economic support he provided and the social status his presence in the household afforded. If a mother had no right to remove her children from the marital home, to leave them with their father was just as unacceptable. In hushed and horrified tones, our Los Robles informants spoke of wives who had left husbands just as they had come—"with nothing"—and of the tragic consequences to their abandoned "orphans."

On a busy street outside the central market in Cuernavaca, I once watched a man repeatedly punching a woman, who I estimated to be in her thirties, in the face. Ignored by passersby, the woman stood, arms at her sides, making no attempt to defend herself. When the man turned and walked away, the woman wiped her bruised and bleeding face with her apron, took a deep breath, and followed him. González de la Rocha pointed out that by defending herself, a woman risks provoking further brutality, and in working-class neighborhoods of Guadalajara, it was her observation that few women did.[11] As for Luz María, she excused her submission to Octavio by saying, "At least drinking and fighting isn't as bad as taking drugs. He knows if he starts on those, I'll leave him. Drinking and fighting's not as bad as running around with other women, either. I've told him, 'The day you try that, you'd better get out of this house!' "

Infidelity

In a national survey of family values carried out in Mexico in 1982, fidelity led all other factors believed to contribute to marital "success."[12] But fidelity on whose part? When two people in Los Robles fall in love and plan to marry, both take the wife's fidelity as a given. All the stories she has heard growing up about *mujeriegos* (womanizers) notwithstanding, the girl hopes that her young husband will prove an exception to the rule. But attentive as he may be at the outset of their marriage, his culture virtually demands he be unfaithful.

In a discussion of machismo as portrayed in Oscar Lewis's anthropological works, Giraldo argued that far from inhibiting its expression, marriage promotes it.[13] According to a popular saying, "It is the wife who marries." Indeed, to convince himself that he has not been "caught and tamed," the newly married man feels compelled to plunge into *la caza de otras mujeres* (the hunt for other women), leaving his wife in virtual imprisonment at home. In Los Robles, even teenage husbands bragged about extramarital adventures, real or imagined; their wives, meanwhile, were equally insistent on their sexual rectitude. Typical was one young woman, well aware of her physical attractions, who, after boasting about the many propositions she had received, in the next breath declared, "But I tell them all to go to hell. Just because my husband screws around, should I also?" Another claimed that during the three years separating her divorce from her first husband and her remarriage, she had several suitors but slept with none of them. Why not? As she was no longer a señorita, what did she have to lose? Her self-representation as a pure woman seems to be the answer.

Guillermo de la Peña in a 1984 article reported that among peasants and urban dwellers in southern Jalisco, philandering is disapproved of only if a man deserts the family; a wife's infidelity, meanwhile, is regarded as rebellion against (legitimate) male authority and unequivocally condemned. This double standard, noted in other Morelos communities by Lewis,[14] Lola Romanucci-Ross,[15] and Ingham,[16] is likewise entrenched in Los Robles: the woman as daughter, novia, wife, and mother must remain pure, while the man as son, novio, husband, and father has the right to seek his pleasure where he will. Husbands who feel under no obligation to explain their overnight absences from home, tightly restrict their wives' movements. Our informants complain bitterly about their husbands' suspiciousness. "Men are *sumamente celosos* [terribly jealous]," one says. "The smallest thing can make them angry." When they go out as a couple, men like their wives to dress in tight skirts and high-heeled shoes with plenty of makeup, so that other men will envy them. The same women continues, "But if they see you wearing lipstick or a pretty dress just to go to the market, or they find you talking to another man, even to your brother-in-law in the street, right away they'll think he's your lover and you'll never hear the end of it!" Irene and her husband, Víctor, who, while they lived together, was physically abusive, repeatedly unfaithful, and a very poor provider, have lived separately for several years. Irene has a male friend, Nacho, who has been vitally supportive of her efforts to continue her education and who regularly gives her money for household expenses. But Víctor is still so jealous of her that she does not dare go out with Nacho for fear that they will run into him and he will give her, not Nacho, a thrashing. Furthermore, Irene insists that Nacho is only her "amigo" (friend), not her "novio" (boyfriend). Víctor's behavior, outrageous as it has been and continues to be, does not give her license to take a lover. María Roldán reported that though working-class women in Mexico City wanted the same rights as men in terms of education and salary, they accepted the double standard of sexual behavior.[17] Of their husbands' infidelity, they said their only hope was that by accepting it, they would avoid physical violence. Again, Roldán found not only that husbands demanded fidelity of their wives but that the wives demanded it of themselves.

At fourteen, Eloisa discovered that sex was *algo maravilloso* (something wonderful). At twenty-four, aware that her husband, Marco, has no compunction about pursuing other women, decides that she, too, has the right to enjoy herself. She admits on occasion to having, however, "given way to desire." She could be unique in her neighborhood. Other women acknowledge that sexual relations are an important part of marriage—but largely for instrumental reasons. You let your husband "use" you to keep him involved with you and your children. María del Carmen Elu de Leñero reported that as many as half her female subjects in a study of family life regarded sexual relations as an unpleasant obligation.[18] Though our informants were not quite so negative, few volunteered that they found sex enjoyable. Even if your husband were flagrantly unfaithful or neglected you sexually, you would not go looking for another man. It appears that in large measure, a woman's self-respect depends on self-denial and levelheadedness in contrast to her husband's self-indulgence and irresponsibility.

Silvia Arrom noted that the double standard of sexual behavior, still almost universally accepted in contemporary Mexico, is rooted in Spanish law.[19] During the colonial period, married women and widows could be punished for adultery by forfeiture of property and even imprisonment, whereas, except under very exceptional circumstances, men got off scot-free. After independence from Spain in 1820, Mexicans began to modify their notions about the inequality of the sexes, signaling a gradual rise in the status of women. But midcentury saw the advent of Mary worship, or the Latin American version of the Victorian cult of motherhood for which Evelyn Stevens coined the word *marianismo*.[20] Women were now regarded as spiritually superior to men, but the price they paid for this increment in status was confinement to the home, where they were "placated" for the loss of any role in the public sphere with the exclusive charge of children. Stevens argued that rather than excluding women from influence, strict role differentiation empowers them. They accept the social domination, physical abuse, and economic support of men, secure in the conviction that their capacity for enduring male-inflicted indignities and, ultimately, for forgiving the perpetrator, lends them semidivine status in their children's eyes. In the same volume, Jane Jaquette asserted that Latin American women choose not to work outside the home because their position of unassailable moral supremacy gives them the emotional leverage they need to achieve worldly goals through the manipulation of husbands and sons.[21]

According to Stevens, machismo and marianismo are equally balanced, allowing both sexes the authority to reach their objectives, a notion that Susan Bourque and Kay Warren[22] challenged on the grounds that so long as men are in control in the outside world, women are by definition subordinate, however much their children might venerate them. Again, Tracy Ehlers[23] argued that the balance of power, such as it is, can only be maintained so long as women are socialized to avoid men and public visibility.

La Vida de Casada

When they enter the world of work, thereby challenging the dominance of both male co-workers and spouses, they are likely to provoke a defensive callousness—both in the workplace and the home—against which their capacity for self-abnegation and endurance is an inadequate defense. Spiritual superiority is an effective weapon only so long as men and women live separate lives; once they are in direct and daily competition, its power evaporates. In a recent article, Elhers asserts that while marianismo comes in different forms implying different degrees of subordination depending on class and personality, in every instance, it is no more than a strategy for psychological survival necessitated by women's exclusion from income-producing activities.[24] The women with whom she worked in the Guatemalan highlands put up with male callousness and neglect only because they had no alternative. If deserted, it was the money their husbands had previously brought in rather than the men themselves that they missed.

It was our observation that many Los Robles women—the younger women, in particular—were convinced of their moral and spiritual superiority in relation to their self-indulgent men and that this conviction was crucial to their emotional well-being. At the same time, unlike middle- and upper-class women who might indeed, as Stevens suggested, find marianismo—and the leverage it provides with male kin—sufficient compensation for social subordination and seclusion in the home, the working-class women we knew, most of whom were also confined to the home, found spiritual superiority a less than effective weapon, even in the domestic sphere. Too often, they reported that their strategies for keeping the family together and on track were undermined by husbands and adolescent and adult sons. Female kin—mothers, sisters, and most especially daughters—were regarded as far more dependable allies than males.

La Otra Mujer: The Double Standard in Los Robles

Extramarital relationships consist of three general types. The first is casual and may be pursued with any woman who is willing, often someone encountered in the workplace. In an earlier generation, women who worked outside the home were almost exclusively widows, abandoned wives, or girls from very poor families, but these days, young single women from all social backgrounds work in public situations where traditional norms of sexual conduct no longer have to be observed. A woman can have a relationship with a married man she meets at work without her family knowing anything about it. In a word, work and home lives may be kept quite separate, by women as much as by men. Los Robles women sometimes admitted that their husbands had never taken them to the factory in the industrial area where they had worked for years, let alone to one of the entertainments that the factory management periodically put on for employees. "He goes to the Christmas dance with his *compañeros*," one woman told us, "he doesn't invite me." If he is smart and does not want trouble, a married man does not take his wife to places where they might run into his girlfriends. Again, as these casual flirtations are unlikely to deprive his family financially, they may escape his wife's detection altogether.

A second type, in which a young married man has an affair with an older woman who is more sexually experienced than his wife, is likely to be longer term and quite disruptive to the man's own family. His overnight absences from home and reduced contributions to household expenses soon alert his wife to the fact that he has another woman. She has usually been deserted by her husband and may or may not be involved with more than one man, from each of whom she receives *ayuda* (help). If she bears a child, whoever she decides is the father may increase his financial support and even after his relationship with the mother comes to an end, may continue to give his child presents; but unless he acknowledges paternity, he bears no legal responsibility.

In a third type, the married man sets up a household with his lover, signaling that he is permanently committed to her. In bourgeois circles, this secondary household is known as the *casa chica* (little house), the implication being that the man accepts full financial responsibility for the woman (*la mantiene*). Of a working-class man, it would be said, *tiene una querida*, meaning that he has another woman to whom he makes regular financial contributions. The man has no intention of abandoning his legal wife. He divides his time between the two women and recognizes children born of both relationships by registering them in his name. (As of the 1980s, Mexican law made no distinction between children born in and out of wedlock, only between those whose father registered them and those whose father did not.) He may actually be a bigamist, having escaped detection by the authorities by marrying his two women in different states; more likely, he was only formally married to the first woman. Or he may never have married either.

As noted earlier, whereas male migrants tended to move back and forth between the rural and the urban areas, young single women, most of whom came to the city to work as domestics, rarely returned home. The numerical preponderance of women that resulted allowed both seasonal migrants and permanent urbanites like Jesús Sánchez to have two women, two households, and two sets of children. Seasonal migrants, meanwhile, would have a woman in the village and another in town. With improvements in health care, childhood and female mortality rates declined, whereas mortality rates of adult males, more frequently the victims of criminal violence as well as liver and heart disease, remained somewhat higher, thereby contributing to the imbalance of women of childbearing age in relation to men. It is our observation that these days, informal polygynous arrangements appear to be most common among bus and truck drivers or commercial salesmen who have to travel long distances in their work. A married man who is transferred to a different town may set up housekeeping there with another women with whom he lives during the week, returning to his wife on weekends. Like Jesús Sánchez, polygynists appear to take their obligation to provide each of their women with her *gasto* very seriously. "One cannot neglect one's family responsibilities. Those of us who are from the Bajío [north central Mexico] place great emphasis on this," one says grandly, as his legal wife, standing behind him, smiles grimly. She has often pointed out to us (in his absence) that her husband's notion of "fulfilling family responsibilities" differs drastically from hers. She reports that in the early years of their marriage, he gave her most of his wages, but when he set up a second household, his contributions dropped sharply, forcing her to make up the shortfall by taking in washing. Her "co-wife," meanwhile, also had to work for a living, for though "their" husband gave her money regularly, it was never enough. In the main, then, wives of working-class polygynists have to support themselves.

In an earlier generation, polygyny was widespread in Mexico,[25] but with the rise in the cost of living and the growing acceptability of divorce among the working class,[26] young men seem more reluctant to take on secondary households, regardless of how limited the financial commitment involved. As a result, the number of unmarried mothers is increasing. The typical *madre soltera* is in her twenties. If a teenager becomes pregnant, her parents can usually arrange a marriage with the young father of her child, whereas in the case of a slightly older woman, her lover may well be a married man who, rather than taking her as his otra mujer, is more likely to desert her.

Lourdes's daughter, Rocío, is a case in point. Rocío carried on an affair for several years with Guillermo, who is married and has two children. The first time she became pregnant, Guillermo persuaded her to have an abortion, but the second time, despite his ambivalence and her own family's opposition, Rocío went ahead with the pregnancy, hoping that when the baby was born her lover would set up house with her or at least register her baby in his name and help with her expenses. But shortly after Pati's birth, he broke off the relationship and refused any further financial responsibility. "It was a shock when my baby's father turned his back on me," Rocío admits, "but I've always earned my own living, and I can earn it for two as well as one." As for Lourdes, angered and hurt though she was by Rocío, she forgave her once her granddaughter was born. "What else could I do? Certainly I was mad at Rocío for getting pregnant again—she was twenty-six and she knew all about birth control. She should have known better, that's what I thought. But she wanted a child more than anything, and once she got her, what was the sense in my being mad?"

Why are men unfaithful? Cheating costs a husband nothing, wives would assure us, least of all his reputation in the community. On the contrary, it arouses envy and admiration. It is his wife and lover who stand to lose—when their man moves on, leaving them to raise his children alone. But women themselves are largely to blame for male promiscuity, so we were told. As mothers, they raise their sons to demand (*exigir*) and their daughters to give in (*cumplir*). "Mothers are always telling daughters, 'Prepare food for your brother, wash his clothes, iron his shirts. He's tired and hungry, so let him eat first.' Daughters are tired and hungry, too, but do they get special attention? Of course not! Is it surprising that a boy gets spoiled (*consentido*) and that when he grows up he expects his wife to wait on him just as his sister did? Or that, if his wife's annoyed with him, he goes out and finds another woman to tell him how great he is?" This last point, men are quick to confirm. They admit they chase women for excitement and—just as important—because of a lack of understanding at home. "I go out looking for work and find none, and when I come home empty-handed, instead of sympathy all I get from my wife is bitterness," one young man complains. "So out I go again, and this time it's not work I'm looking for but a woman, and women are easy to find!" Men have to protect themselves against a world that constantly belittles them. Hard as a woman's life may be, a man's life is harder, these women readily conceded. A woman spends her days at home with her children who love her or in her immediate neighborhood, but a man has to go out into a hostile world where no one knows or cares about him. Getting drunk with his *cuates* (buddies) and picking up women makes him feel better, at least for a while. Beating up his wife when he gets home may make him feel better, too. Jorge Gissi's observation[27] that the family is the only domain in which a poor man retains authority is underscored by Sylvia Chant and Peter Ward, and Caroline Moser[28] who viewed domestic violence as a reflection of the polarization of gender roles in low-income families. The city has always been a hard and humiliating place for a man without skills or connections. As Selby pointed out,[29] the rural face-to-face community, in which everyone can be located in relation to everyone else by reference to kin and fictive kin ties, fosters self-assurance and maturity; whereas in town, where no one knows or respects you, the development of those "other" macho traits of hard work, reflectiveness, and sound judgment is less likely. In a time of economic crisis, furthermore, when male self-confidence is under continuous assault, a significant increase in domestic violence hardly comes as a surprise.

Adjustment to Reality

For women of an older generation, early training, economic dependency, and physical fear combined to make putting up with mistreatment and neglect a necessity. A wise wife tried not to provoke her husband's jealousy and anger. She dressed modestly, wore neither makeup nor jewelry unless she was going out with him, and if he came home late she did not ask him why. "You let sleeping dogs lie," says Lourdes, recalling how once she suspected her husband was having an affair with her *comadre* who lived a few doors away in the same vecindad. Instead of confronting her husband, she packed up their belongings while he was away from home and moved their six children down the street and into another vecindad. When he returned, all she said was, "See, this place is better. The kids have more room to play." And that, she adds with satisfaction, "was the end of their affair."

Julia, thirty years Lourdes's junior, declares that as all men are *canijos* (dogs and womanizers), and you are not going to find one who is not, you had better put up with the man you have. Of her taxi driver husband who has the run of the city twenty-four hours a day, she says, "Of course he has other women—don't all men? But as long as he supports me and the kids and doesn't catch VD and pass it on to me, I don't care."

In the 1940s, Lewis found that women in nearby Tepoztlán were willing to tolerate marital infidelity just so long as their husbands continued to support them economically. Forty years later, most Los Robles women, too, had either accepted or were in the process of accepting a modus vivendi.

This is not to say that households headed by women are a rarity in urban Mexico. Rather, García and her colleagues[30] reported that in the two decades from 1950 to 1970, female-headed households in urban areas constituted between 15 and 20 percent of the total. Though most were headed by widows or women who had been deserted by their spouses, a smaller proportion were headed by women who, once their children were old enough to help out financially, had preempted marital desertion by setting up on their own. Chant and Ward, and González de la Rocha report similar findings in their studies.[31] Though female-headed households have been seen as more socially and economically deprived than their male-headed counterparts,[32] Chant and Ward challenge this view. They argue that because working women are far likelier to devote their earnings to family needs than men are, children in female-headed households may fare better, both because the domestic atmosphere is less conflictful and because household income is being spent exclusively on them. Be that as it may, none of our older informants or any of their mothers had elected to go it alone.

In an older generation, divorce, though made legal in 1917, was almost unheard of in working-class Mexico. "A woman would be *abandonada*," says Estela. "There were plenty of those. But *divorciada?* Never!" By the 1980s, however, divorce was becoming more acceptable. One woman, deserted by her first husband, obtained a divorce, as did another whose husband drank heavily, used drugs, and was blatantly promiscuous. It must be said that she divorced him only after he had beaten her so badly that she ended up in the hospital and her parents had promised her financial help.

Matilde, whose philandering husband shows no sign of leaving her, fantasizes leaving him and returning to Guerrero. "I shan't go home," she says, "because mamá would only tell me to stick it out with Pedro, despite his faults, just like she's stuck it out with papá." Instead, she will go to her sisters who she believes will be willing to help her financially. Other women, too, make their escape plans, which, given their *falta de preparación* (lack of education), always involve appeals to relatives for financial support. But though nowadays there may be a good deal of talk about divorce, women who remain in seemingly untenable relationships still greatly outnumber those who get out. After toying with the idea of divorce, one young woman, whose husband frequently beats her and their children, rejects it on the grounds that if she remarried, her new husband might mistreat her children, too. "Their own father does," she points out, "so imagine how much worse a stepfather could be!" And if she stayed single, she would have to leave her four young children on their own all day and go out to work. "No," she concludes, *"es mejor aguantar"* (it's better to put up with things).

In a survey, we asked secondary school girls, "To whom, in adulthood, is a woman emotionally closest?" to which the large majority responded, "Her husband." When asked the same question, women ten and fifteen years older were likely to reply, "Her children." With their adolescent dreams shattered, they have experienced shock, humiliation, despair, and rage in roughly that order and have come to accept that alcoholism, intermittent violence, or infidelity—and in some cases, all three—is a permanent feature of married life. Practical realism is now the order of the day.

A woman who has not laid eyes on her traveling salesman husband in three weeks remarks, "It would be nice to have comprensión from your husband, but that hasn't been my luck. Still, despite all the troubles I've had with him, I can't complain. . . . He's never let the kids and me go without." Comprensión may be lacking in her marriage, but she has economic security, and she is not about to turn her back on that! She will suffer her husband's long absences and the pitying glances of her neighbors who know as well as she does that her husband has another woman, if not two or three. A stable home in which to raise and educate her children comes at a high price—and she is prepared to pay it.

Given the opportunity, women want to be close to both husband and children, but the opportunity doesn't often come their way. Romanucci-Ross observed that because a Mexican wife expects and even anticipates her husband's emotional desertion, she binds her children to her, forcing them to side with her against him.[33] Indeed, like Russell Coberley[34] in the Chiapas community of Socoltenango, we found that though the marital relationship may be the functional core of the family, the mother-child relationship is its emotional core. One woman says of her father, "He never supported us as he should have. He never looked out for us. He left everything to mamá. Now, when I meet him at home, I'm angry. I don't feel he belongs there." Another woman tells us, "My kids no longer welcome their father. They resent it when he comes in drunk and falls into bed." She adds with satisfaction that at least her sons are older and tall enough now to protect her from his fists. In Los Robles, as in any other place, the family is the center of human existence, but access to it is not automatic. Since, commonly, children respect but do not love their father, if he loses their respect, he has no habit of intimacy or mutual affection on which to fall back. Thus, should he insist on pursuing purely selfish interests, they are more than likely to reject him and henceforth regard him with sullen contempt.

With her husband an emotional if not a physical outcast, the wife becomes the stable nucleus of family life[35] and reigns supreme in her home. She becomes, as Romanucci-Ross observed, a *macha*, who, though she may continue to be overtly submissive in face-to-face relations with her husband, in all other situations becomes increasingly self-reliant and, in effect, her own boss. Typically, middle-aged and elderly women are treated by adult children, especially daughters, with loving respect verging on awe. Younger women, meanwhile, are doing their utmost to inculcate the same veneration and strength of attachment in their offspring.

The survivors of decades of marital mistreatment and neglect, many women have emerged in middle age with a sense of humorous well-being. Though they may have failed to keep their husbands sober or faithful, they are confident of having done their best as mothers under extremely difficult circumstances, and it is from this singular achievement that they derive their self-esteem. As Lourdes Arizpe has suggested,[36] Latin American women often gain a social centrality and an emotional power through motherhood that women in Western industrialized countries lack. If, meanwhile, some of the younger women suffer daily torment on account of their *machos méxicanos*, it is from a conscious identification with their mothers, whom they saw abused, neglected, and betrayed just as they are, that they derive strength.

Nevertheless, some are beginning to reject the role of the *sumisa* (the submissive one). Rosa, for one, tolerated her husband's affairs for years knowing that if she were to confront him he would beat her up. But one day she recalls, "I decided I was tired of being his *pendeja* [cuckold], and I told him so, and when he punched me, I punched him back." Then, with a razor in her purse, she went out looking for his girlfriend, and when she found her, grabbed her and threatened to slash her face. "That kid was so scared, she left town for good!" Rosa reports triumphantly. As for her husband, he has not given up chasing skirts, but since her attack on his girlfriend, he has kept his affairs to himself—and his fists as well. Furthermore, when she does not feel like having sexual relations, she refuses him. In the past, knowing that he would either have insisted on his rights or beaten her, or both, she would never have dared do this. Eloisa, too, used to "take it" when her husband, Marco, slapped her, until one night when he was drunk and she was sober, to his astonishment she slapped him back. Since realizing she could hurt him—badly—if she chose to, he has not laid a finger on her. They still quarrel a lot, but because Marco has stopped hitting her, making up after one of their spats is that much easier than it used to be.

Part 2: *Married Life*

Social Supports

To negotiate one's way through a world that is often hazardous and hostile, face-to-face relationships based on mutual trust are essential to men and women in urban Mexico,[37] as much as in London's East End,[38] Lagos,[39] and Guatemala City.[40] These relationships provide the structure for social life without which, as Carlos Vélez-Ibáñez noted,[41] the individual would find living an extremely lonely proposition. But while Los Robles men had opportunities to develop social networks in the workplace, their wives, few of whom had worked outside the home since marriage, were much more restricted. Apart from trips to the store and the market and in the case of young women, escorting small children to and from school, they spent most of their time in the house and patio, attending to household chores. Entertainment consisted of watching television, downtown window-shopping expeditions, occasional visits to the cinema, and family visits. For pleasure they read magazines, cartoon books (*caricaturas*), and their children's textbooks, and many admitted that they scarcely read at all. Some looked back nostalgically on adolescent friendships, which, even in the case of women who grew up in Los Robles, had atrophied. With marriage, motherhood, and in many cases, husbands who jealously monitored their movements, they had little chance to keep up with old friends or to make new ones. A wife who spent time gossiping would anger her husband and incur the disapproval of her mother-in-law, for in a crowded vecindad or alley, by getting involved with your neighbors' business, you were as likely to make enemies as friends. Like Peattie's informants in Cuidad Guayana, Venezuela, ours expressed reluctance to complain when their neighbors disturbed them. If teenagers across the street habitually played loud music after midnight, our informants would grumble and do nothing. Better to let the parents deal with those kids, they would say. And when the parents did not deal with them, our informants were still unlikely to complain, since "all you get from complaints is resentment."

Around election time, Margarita was seen wearing a T-shirt bearing the

PRI (the government party) logo, but she quickly denied any interest in politics. A PRI candidate, in the neighborhood to make a campaign speech, had been seen handing out the shirts and one of her grandchildren had got one for her, but when election day came, she wasn't going to vote. Once in ten years a politician might do you a small favor, but mostly they were creeps. Some women reported having participated in efforts to bring services to the community, but they explained that once these goals had been achieved, their motivation for involvement with their neighbors had largely evaporated.

In this respect, Estela, who with her husband, Julio, was one of the first settlers in Los Robles, is an exception. With a grin, she remarks, "Nobody could keep me from getting to know people!" As an adolescent in Los Angeles, parental prohibitions against socializing after school made the friendships she made in school all the more precious to her. Some of her classmates—not her parents—arranged her wedding in June 1929, and afterward her girlfriends would come daily to visit her in her new home. When her parents and brothers and sisters moved back to Mexico two years later, she became even more involved with her female friends. In 1939, her husband became depressed, and of the fifteen months during which he was confined in San Bernardino State Hospital, she recalls, "I don't know how I would have survived that time if it hadn't been for my friends. They helped me in every way possible." More often, however, in Los Robles as much as in London[42] and Taipei,[43] close relationships are exclusively with kin, for while kinship may not guarantee *confianza*, it provides a likelier basis for it than do extrafamilial relationships.

The most intense reciprocity occurs between members of the three-generational *gran familia*, which Larissa Lomnitz and Marisol Pérez-Lizaur[44] have identified as the basic unit of solidarity in all social classes in Mexico. Every marriage brings together two families, giving rise to a rivalry between them for the allegiance of the young wife and, as they appear, her children. In the country, where patrilocal residence is still normative, the closest *economic* interdependence between women is likely to be between a mother-in-law and her daughter-in-law who are living together or next door to one another. But given that Mexican villages are highly endogamous, the daughter-in-law's closest *emotional* ties continue to be with natal kin who are living nearby. When they migrate to the city, rural people may maintain contact for many years, if not a lifetime, with kin whom they have left behind. Nevertheless, there is a pressing need to create in the urban environment a new network *(red de seguridad)* of the kind they had in the countryside.[45] In the city, too, kinship is the most likely basis of *confianza.* A relationship that before migration may have been quite superficial may be intensified in the new situation, in which family members now need each other more.[46]

In Cerrada del Condor, a squatter community of rural immigrants in Mexico City, Lomnitz found high levels of reciprocity among the families she studied. Although each nuclear unit kept cooking arrangements and household expenses separate, they shared kitchen, bathroom, and laundry facilities and tools and utensils, as well as the care of small children, the sick, and the old; they also provided each other with job contacts and small loans.[47] As noted earlier, our young informants who continue to live with parents or in-laws long after marriage are rarely happy with the situation. Poor though some certainly are, they live in the inner city in permanent structures, rather than on the periphery in shacks, and are more sophisticated and city-wise, less tolerant of parental authority and interference than the *paracaidistas* (squatters) with whom Lomnitz worked. At the same time, even though the establishment of a living arrangement separate from kin is their first priority, they wish to stay physically close, especially to their own mothers. One young woman laments the fact that while she lives rent-free with her in-laws, she is a twenty-minute walk from her mother— quite a distance if one has to carry two small children. By contrast, her many siblings all live just around the corner. "I want to see mamá every day, like they do," she insists. She hopes to persuade her husband to move closer. "Though that will mean paying rent, I'll be so much happier!"

In their discussion of la gran familia, Lomnitz and Pérez-Lizaur point to the key role that women in general and senior women in particular play in terms of conflict resolution, ritual performance, and transmission of the ideology of cohesion and mutual support. It is to mamá's that one goes on Sundays; it is mamá who sits in the (only) folding chair at picnics and who presides at celebrations; on Mother's Day morning the streets are filled with women of all ages, their arms filled with flowers, on their way to pay homage to *la reina de mi corazón* (the queen of my heart). But if an adult daughter's respect for her mother is a given, her love is not. A mother is expected to be sensitive to her daughter's needs and responsive to them insofar as she is able, and, inevitably, her failure in this regard gives rise to bitter disappointment. Soledad reports that her mother, Amelia, who has both a husband and a son to support her, "never brings me food or anything else, though she sees how poor I am. Every day she comes here and I share with her whatever I have. But I was sick for years, yet she never brought anything to me." Eloisa, too, has problems with her mother who lives in the same vecindad. As her husband, Marco, is unemployed, she often has to ask her mother for food and small monetary loans, requests that her mother resents, as she makes abundantly clear. Occasionally, if Eloisa has nothing in her house for breakfast, she sends her eight-year-old son over to ask his grandmother for a roll. "In the end she'll give him one, but she'll always make him wait a long time. That makes both him *and* me feel terrible." But afraid of outright rejection, Eloisa keeps her disappointment and anger with her mother to herself.

Some women find their mothers-in-law more sympathetic than their own mothers. Unable to share her unhappiness over her husband's infidelities with her own straitlaced mother, Inés recalls that in her suegra she found a staunch support. "Though she couldn't stop Antonio from doing what he was doing, she had confidence in me, and that made all the difference, it made my troubles possible to bear." A much younger woman, finding herself in a similar situation, reports, "My suegra assures me that her son chose me for life and that if he leaves me, she won't let his new woman set foot in her house." But more frequently, we heard complaints. Matilde, who spent several unhappy years with her in-laws, reports, "My suegra treated me like a servant. It was always, 'Do this, do that!' And whatever I did wasn't good enough. . . . Even now, so long after I left there, she's still angry that I didn't do things right when I was living in her house!"

Sibling relationships, in particular those that in childhood were especially close, are likely to continue throughout life, although widening economic differences tend to cause divisions. Speaking of her brother, now a prosperous businessman, a woman confides, "His wife is *pretenciosa* [a bourgeois woman] who looks down on us poor people. Though as children my brother and I were friends, he hasn't invited me to his house in years." Other than on ritual occasions, our informants saw little of their cousins. In the village, people routinely meet in the course of their daily activities, but, in the city, scattered in different neighborhoods, unless reinforced by compadrazgo (fictive kinship ties), extended kin tend to lose contact. Some of the older women had close relatives—siblings, first cousins, nephews, and nieces—at many social levels, from peasant farmers to factory workers to well-to-do professionals. The Mexican miracle had certainly worked for some people, allowing them to make their way from inner-city tenements to elaborate houses in exclusive suburban developments on the fringes of Mexico City, Guadalajara, and Cuernavaca. And in most cases, they had cut their ties with poorer kin, for as it was explained to us by those who had been left behind, *los ricos* "are afraid we'll take advantage of them. If we don't back off voluntarily, they'll soon cold-shoulder us."

As has been noted, opportunities for making friends are limited, especially for women isolated in single-family houses, though those who live in tenements have a chance to socialize with their neighbors, should they wish to, in the course of performing routine household chores. But women readily admit to a lack of motivation when it comes to making friends. Catalina attributes a lifelong lack of friends to shyness. "As a girl, I never liked talking to people. . . . When Joaquín and I had the store, I was obliged to, but then I didn't feel uncomfortable because I had a reason for being there, I wasn't in the store just to talk. I enjoyed hearing neighborhood gossip and even giving advice if people asked for it. . . . These days when I run into people I know in the street, I greet them, but I've no time to stop when there's still dinner to prepare for eleven people." After a pause, she adds, "Anyway, here at home I have my daughters. They're my best friends." With a shrug of her shoulders, a younger woman explains that with seven brothers and sisters right there in the neighborhood, she does not have time for friends.

Poverty, as well as lack of time and motivation, is a major impediment to making friends. Like Susan Eckstein in her Mexico City study,[48] we found that the poorest women were the most socially isolated. Nevertheless, even the isolate finds it necessary to overcome her inhibitions to find the godparents that the sacramental rites of childhood require.

Compadrazgo

In childhood, the Catholic church requires padrinos for baptism and for confirmation before first communion. In adulthood, padrinos are again required at marriage and for the raising of the Cross after one's funeral. There has been a proliferation, too, of secular events that also call for godparents, although here, the relationship between godparent and godchild has no permanent significance.

The immediate and widespread existence of compadrazgo in the New World and in Mexico in particular was due to its similarity to native forms of ritual sponsorship that were weakened or destroyed by cataclysmic depopulation in the century following the Conquest.[49] In a seminal article, Sydney Mintz and Eric Wolf[50] showed that the institution enhanced social solidarity by operating horizontally, linking members of the same socioeconomic status, and vertically, linking members of different socioeconomic status in patron-client relationships. Meanwhile, George Foster[51] demonstrated that compadrazgo supplemented kin relationships by providing the individual with economic and spiritual support. Emphasizing the spiritual-natural dichotomy that compadrazgo incorporates, Stephen Gudeman[52] argued that a child born of natural parents is by definition sinful, but with the sponsorship of spiritual parents (padrinos), he undergoes baptism, signaling rebirth. Compadrazgo, then, "implants a perpetual sacred obligation between persons," that is, between godparent (padrino) and godchild *(ahijado)* and, more important, between natural and spiritual parents *(compadres)*.

In Los Robles, it is believed that the most significant personal tribute one can pay another person is to invite him or her to be the baptismal godparent of one's child, and acceptance indicates a willingness to enter into a reciprocal relationship of great importance. Although women of the older generation report that their husbands chose their children's padrinos without consulting them, today the choice is likely to be made by both husband and wife. Working-class parents emphasize that, above all, they look for personal qualities of respect and trustworthiness when selecting compadres, to whom henceforth they will look for help in time of trouble more readily than to kin. For their part, the godparents commit themselves to helping their godchildren *moralmente y materialmente* (emotionally and economically) and to rearing them in the event that the natural parents die or are otherwise unavailable. In practice, although a madrina may have a special relationship with her ahijada, it is unlikely that she will participate in her *educación* (upbringing) as such, for, as was pointed out to us, "you shouldn't try to correct another woman's child, even the child of your comadre, because if you do, you'll just get in a fight." Fewer still can afford to help their godchildren economically, though some give small gifts on birthdays and saints' days. Again, on the death of both parents, grandparents and other relatives are much likelier to assume guardianship than padrinos, unless the latter also happen to be kin. Nevertheless, the relationship, which is first and foremost between adults, that is, between the child's parents and his godparents, and only secondarily between padrino and ahijado, is expected to last for the lifetime of the compadres.

Conventions for the selection of compadres vary, depending on community and class, but in general, Los Robles parents prefer to choose from their own age group, for as one woman points out, "There's no sense in asking older people because they may not live long enough to carry out their responsibilities." Thereafter, the formal *usted* replaces the familiar *tú*, and Christian names are replaced with the terms "compadre" and "comadre," indicating the respect with which compadres regard each other and the commitment to honor and aid each other, and, should disagreements arise, to work to resolve them. For, as de la Peña noted in his study of nearby Tlayacapan,[53] a quarrel between compadres or between padrino and ahijado is regarded as a sin "worse than a quarrel with your parents." Sexual relations between compadres are also considered a grave sin.

Some Los Robles families choose only relatives as compadres, thereby making sure that the expenses of celebrations and gift-giving are kept within the kin group. Relatives whom you choose as compadres will eventually reciprocate by asking you and your husband to become padrinos to their child, thus enabling you to repay whatever they may have spent on your child. Another argument in favor of choosing relatives is that disagreements between compadres are more easily resolved if they are kin; with more at stake, both sides are more strongly motivated to settle differences if they are related. Other families, meanwhile, habitually choose compadres from among friends, for as one woman says, "How can you respect your relative? You're too close, you know too much about her!" Estela recalls that her husband, Julio, was always the one who chose their children's godparents. When she had her first child in Los Angeles, all her girlfriends clamored to be her comadre. "But in order not to hurt their feelings by choosing one and not the other, Julio chose my sister, Concha, and my brother, Enrique. In fact, all our compadres were relatives. This was to avoid unhappiness, you see." Nevertheless, Estela herself became the comadre of many of her friends. "By the time we left California, I had ten ahijadas," she says proudly. And she explains, "As a baptismal godparent one's responsibilities are very serious. One promises to love, advise, and correct the child and help her economically if necessary, and all these things I have done at times for my ahijadas."

Newcomers to a community, lacking relatives close by, may have no choice but to invite nonkin to be their compadres. Thus, we see Julia, a lively, forceful person quite recently arrived in Cuernavaca, busily constructing a red de seguridad among her new neighbors as, one after the other, her four young children need *padrinos de bautizo* or *de primera comu-*

nión. She invites first her neighbor across the street, then another around the corner, and they in turn reciprocate.

The practice of selecting compadres who are your economic superiors in the hope that in future they will act as patrons to you and your family is frowned on in Los Robles. In part, this is because people who are better off than you are, afraid you might exploit them in the future, may well refuse your invitation, causing you humiliation. Someone who is your economic inferior, meanwhile, is unlikely to accept because of the expenses involved, for the religious rite itself occasions an exchange that cements the relationship between the child's godparents and his parents, with the godparents providing the baptismal or first communion clothes and the parents a dinner following the mass. "Because people could see how poor I was and that I wouldn't be able to afford to buy the baptismal clothes for their children, I was only invited once," one woman explains. Other women note, however, that these ritual exchanges could be waived. Thus, though better-off parents may not ask their compadres to provide the clothes, they nonetheless entertain them at dinner; similarly, poor parents sometimes accept the clothes without providing the dinner. Soledad recalls having to tell her compadres that she would make *mole* for them at a later date, but right then she could not afford to. "They were buena gente, and they understood," she adds. Meanwhile, Eloisa reports that their young friends frequently ask her and her husband, Marco, to be padrinos, and though Marco is reluctant to spend the money, she insists that they accept. "Becoming compadres is a great honor," she explains. "How can one refuse?" Besides, she points out, the money they contribute to the festivities provides assurance that if in future she and Marco need a loan, they will be able to borrow from their new compadres. People like themselves who lead a hand-to-mouth existence need as many potential sources of aid as possible.

If, for reasons other than death or migration to a distant place, the relationship between compadres comes to an end, there are likely to be hard feelings on both sides. Recalling her compadres, Pablo and Susana, Catalina says, "To begin with, they were just like us. They'd come in from the country and were making their way in the city just as we were, but when Pablo began to do well in business, Susana stopped respecting me. The usted suddenly reverted to tú. If we see each other in the street these days, she barely speaks to me. *Me desprecia*" (She looks down on me). Another woman reports that after her comadre got divorced, she started going around with a lot of different men. "What she does is her own affair, but still, I don't want to expose my daughter Natali to that sort of behavior, so I won't allow her to visit anymore. I know my comadre knows something's up because she keeps asking, 'When is Natali coming to see me?' But you should respect your comadre, and I no longer can."

Religious Participation

All our informants were brought up in the Catholic church and are practicing Catholics today, with the exception of Margarita, now an Evangelical Protestant, Ofelia, a Jehovah's Witness, and Irene, who has become a Mormon. Regardless of denomination, they assert that their religious beliefs provide an important source of strength. "My faith is a comfort to me, I don't feel so lonely," one says. "When I have a problem, I pray to Him for help and help is always forthcoming," says another. "I want to live a good life, a morally correct life," says a third, "because if I don't, I'm afraid of going to hell later." The older women, who often attend mass several times a week, report that in their younger years they went regularly also. "I'd leave the little ones with my oldest child," Inés recalls," and run across the street to church. We were lucky. Not once while I was out was there an accident at home. . . . In those hard years, I looked forward to going to mass more than anything." Our younger informants, although insistent on the importance of their religious faith, got to church much less often, if at all. The mother of several small children says regretfully, "Yes, I am *creyente* [a believer], but till my kids are bigger, I'm stuck here in the house. All I have are my *santitos.*" Like many of our informants, she has a wall shrine consisting of a picture of Christ on the Cross hanging above a small shelf on which stand statuettes of the Virgin of Guadalupe, San Antón, and other saints. Every night she recites her rosary before her shrine and on religious holidays places vases of flowers and a lighted candle on the shelf between the saints. Matilde, the mother of two-year-old Chucho, explains, "I like to hear what the priest has to say, but I have no one with whom to leave my son, and people don't like it when he gets restless in church." Why doesn't she leave Chucho with her husband? He is not interested in baby-sitting. How about her neighbor? They are not on such good terms. How about Tere, her ten-year-old daughter? Yes, well, Matilde says that the truth is, with four children, she does not have time to go to church.

Although some of the older Catholic women participate in religious organizations such as La Legión de María and Los Franciscanos, the younger women rarely do so. Again, lack of child care is the excuse most often given, together with their husbands' schedules. How can you go to a six o'clock meeting if your husband works the day shift in a factory? When he gets home, he wants you in the house preparing his meal, not praying in someone else's house or in church, decorating the altar! Only widows or women whose husbands have already retired are free to participate, so the younger women say.

The fact that throughout their married lives, women of the older generation have somehow found time to go to church regularly and to take part in church-related activities, whereas by and large, the younger women have not, reflects the secular trend observed in Mexican society as a whole. Rural-urban migration on a massive scale has left large segments of the population, married women in particular, with few social supports, a lack that the Catholic church might have addressed with much greater vigor than has been the case. Into this vacuum have stepped many foreign-based Protestant denominations—several of which are now strongly represented in Cuernavaca—offering their converts social supports as well as religious instruction. Indeed, in comparison with the Catholics, our Protestant informants are much more active in their respective churches. They look to their "sisters" for moral and emotional support and as a result of regular attendance at bible classes, are rather better informed about their religion than the Catholics whose instruction in most instances began and ended with catechism classes prior to taking first communion at the age of eight. Catalina speaks for many when she admits, "I learned to recite the rosary, but I never learned what the prayers meant."

The ignorance and superstition of his parishioners are issues that the parish priest, Padre Augustín, an adherent of the Liberation Theology, has been attempting to address through Bible study groups, one of which Catalina used to attend. "It was my husband's idea that we go," she recalls, "and he threw himself into those classes. I didn't. I was too shy. I'd just sit there, not daring to open my mouth. But I always did my homework, and from that I not only learned a lot about the Bible but I learned to read much better, too." She continues, "Really, those classes had an important impact on my husband. Beforehand he had been cold and demanding with me and the children, but as a result of them he became less critical and more understanding . . . less macho, one might say. As for me, I became less dócil. At home I began to speak my mind without being afraid. I'll always be grateful for what those classes did for our family."

Padre Augustín requires parents whose children are being prepared for their first communion to receive instruction for a year, and if they are absent from class on more than a certain number of occasions, their children are not permitted to take communion. Classes focus on biblical texts as a means of learning how to deal with problems of family life, developing a sense of community and stimulating an awareness of issues relating to social justice. Catalina's daughter, Gloria, who teaches a catechism class for children, reports, "Padre Augustín says that if parents want their fiesta, then they should learn something about spiritual life as well. So they, too, have their homework. They have to read and discuss the text of the week with their child and make sure he understands it." Soledad enthusiastically recalls her experience in the parents' classes. "I loved learning about the Bible, and even though I didn't know how to read, Padre Augustín never made me feel ashamed." Few fathers attend preparation classes, however, for religious—just like secular—education is still regarded as the mother's responsibility. Thus, although Rosa's husband, Hugo, attends classes prior to his sons' first communion, he is forever complaining about being the only father in his group. In the belief that it is social competitiveness more than religious devotion that motivates parents to have their children prepared for first communion, Padre Augustín impresses on them that a child does not require elaborate clothes or a celebratory dinner. "But few listen," observes Gloria. "Though they can't afford it, they still insist on making the first communion into a huge event." And for all the effort that he has invested in religious education and developing a sense of community, Padre Augustín admits that less than 20 percent of adults in Los Robles come to mass on Sunday. "Most of them, once their children have made their first communion, we never see again."

Earning a Living

Traditional ideas regarding sex roles are slow to change. Writing in 1976, Gloria Gonzáles Sálazar noted that in large measure, Mexican women had achieved legal equality with men; furthermore, the law protected and assisted them in their dual roles as mothers and workers, and yet their "opportunities are very limited and very conditioned both by the socioeconomic and cultural framework and by their own internalization of the values of masculine domination, which lead them to accept what happens as natural facts of life."[54] Challenging the prevailing wisdom that economic development benefited both sexes equally, June Nash and Helen Safa[55] pointed out that in Mexico, as in most of Latin America, those few women— whether single or married—who had salaried positions, providing some job security and fringe benefits, were more than likely to be engaged in traditional supportive roles, such as teachers, nurses, and secretaries. The great majority of working women, meanwhile, were employed in the informal sector in unregulated conditions for subeconomic wages. When they worked alongside men, their wages were 20 to 50 percent below those of their male co-workers.[56]

Reporting on working-class Venezuelans in the early 1960s, Peattie noted that women were not required or expected to submerge their personalities in the role of mother and housewife.[57] Work was acknowledged to constitute a very significant aspect of their lives. In contrast, in a study of Mexican women's work and fertility, Elu de Leñero[58] found that the social status of the urban family was seen as depending solely on the husband's achievements. As a result, when a married woman worked outside the home, she did so to increase purchasing power rather than because she wished to pursue a personal interest or because the structure of the family had been liberalized. Indeed, 57 percent of the women interviewed believed that the decision as to whether the wife should work should be up to the husband alone. González de la Rocha[59] observed that a working-class wife was seen as "belonging" to the household—in contrast to her husband, who "belonged" to the world of work. Given that she was viewed— and viewed herself—as synonymous with the household, if she was employed, she was seen as helping *herself.* Furthermore, she did not feel that as a result of bringing in a wage, which she usually dedicated entirely to household consumption, she improved her status in the family hierarchy. Graciela Rodríguez de Arizmendi and her colleagues[60] reported that changes in the legal status of women were necessary but not sufficient to effect a permanent change in their role and status. For women to cease to think of themselves as inferior, dependent, and confined to a supportive role, major psychological changes must first occur.

As of 1980, nationwide only 24 percent of women over the age of fifteen were reported as employed, virtually all of them in urban areas.[61] Though this figure was up from 19 percent in 1970,[62] a large majority were young single or widowed, divorced, or separated women lacking a man's support. Most, as before, worked in petty trade, light industry, and domestic service, and whatever their work situation, sexual harassment by male employers and co-workers was par for the course.[63] Many married women (whose economic activity went unreported) also worked either without pay in small family businesses or as laundresses, seamstresses, and the like, at or close to home, which allowed them to watch out for small children at the same time.[64]

In her mid-1980s study of women's labor participation in Querétaro, León, and Puerto Vallarta, Chant[65] found that despite traditional beliefs confining women to the home, in response to recession and drastic economic restabilization measures, couples were being forced to change their views, reorganize their households, and reallocate domestic chores to enable the women to undertake income-producing activities. González de la Rocha noted that in Guadalajara too, women were going out to work, leaving adolescent girls, whether daughters or young relatives brought to live in the household, to take care of domestic chores, a shift noted in other Latin American countries, which, like Mexico, had been plunged into recession by fiscal mismanagement and foreign debt.[66] In the poor barrios of Lima, desperate economic conditions were forcing women who had nobody to help them with domestic chores to organize at the neighborhood level to survive.[67] One important innovation was the *comedor popular*, or cooperative kitchen, set up by groups of twelve to fifteen women who took turns buying, preparing, and serving meals to participating families. Released in rotation from time-consuming chores, housewives were able to earn money at home by doing piecework for large producers. Not only did these women realize that their time had an economic value but they had the opportunity to develop friendships on which they could rely in other aspects of their lives, notably, for protection against abusive spouses. Most important, having learned to organize themselves—democratically rather than hierarchically—they went on to work together to secure services for the larger community.

At the time of this fieldwork, however, despite a steadily deteriorating economic climate, working-class men in Los Robles still saw themselves as providers and their wives as homemakers. The women, meanwhile, like those among whom Verena Stolke worked on coffee plantations in southern Brazil,[68] did not relish the prospect of the doble jornada, the double load of paid and domestic work that often amounted to eighteen hours a day. Most believed that if her husband could possibly afford to keep her there, a woman's place was at home. They explained their position in terms of the belief that children—grade school and high school students as well as preschoolers—needed their mothers. If economic pressures forced a mother to work, her children were pitied for being left in the care of another woman, albeit an aunt or grandmother. Invariably, those few women who expressed a desire to go out to work to obtain personal satisfaction were made to feel selfish—and guilty—by husbands, female relatives, and friends, who insisted that financial necessity alone justified leaving one's children.

Though our Los Robles informants strove to provide their daughters and granddaughters with professional credentials, most of them still regarded schooling as an insurance policy rather than a means to self-fulfillment. The more education a young woman had, the better job she could get while still single and the likelier she was to make a good marriage. From that point on, unless disaster struck, she should be supported by her husband while she herself focused her attention on children and domestic life.

Making Ends Meet in Los Robles

Looking back four decades to her early years in Los Robles, Estela recalls that with the first stage of house construction completed, her husband, Julio, left to work on the New York Central Railroad, his objective being to earn the money to set up a mechanic's workshop on his return. "I didn't want to go," Estela says. "I wouldn't have liked the climate, and if the girls and I had been with him, he wouldn't have been able to save." With Julio away, Estela found herself with the freedom to do pretty much as she pleased; she also found that she needed to earn money to supplement his remittances. She decided to go out to work, something to which, had he been at home, Julio would never have agreed. In 1929, she had graduated from junior high school in Los Angeles. "In those days you got a better education than you do now. Really, junior high school was like high school is today," she asserts. She knew someone in the Ministry of Education who knew someone else who "arranged" her papers for her, and overnight she became a third grade teacher! She taught school for five years until Julio returned for good from New York and set up his workshop, at which point she resigned her position. Although subsequently, she embarked on a succession of small-scale commercial enterprises, none of them required her leaving the house.

"For as long as I can remember, I've had a taste for commerce," Margarita declares. "I think it comes from watching my mother selling things.

When we lived in the mountains during the Revolution, she sold tortillas and later, when we got back to our village, vegetables, and cheeses. . . . As a child I used to daydream about boarding a train and riding into town and opening a store!" She got her chance eventually. "We rode to town by bus not train, and my store was only a stall outside the vecindad where we lived, but it was a beginning." While her husband, Edmundo, worked as a master mason on building sites, Margarita sold candles, soap, children's clothes, oil lamps, matches, and plastic children's toys—merchandise that a dozen other women in her immediate neighborhood were selling, too, and at almost identical prices. Rather than undercutting her competitors, Margarita's strategy was to win clients by extending minute amounts of credit. Within a year, her stall burned down and she lost her entire stock, but with money borrowed from Edmundo's father, she started again, and this time she had a real store with a counter, shelves, and a scale for weighing sugar and rice.

Performing domestic chores for better-off neighbors has long been the paid work most readily available to poor women. "Whenever Antonio didn't give me money or he didn't give me enough," Inés recalls, "I'd go running from house to house asking my customers, 'Have you any washing for me today?' Wherever we lived, I'd have my regular customers, and in an emergency I'd try and find others." Lourdes, too, worked as a laundress—for a "house of assignation." She would go downtown to collect the bed linen and take it home to wash. Hard and poorly paid as the work was, she derived a good deal of amusement from running into men she knew escorting women who were not their wives in and out of the place in the middle of the day.

As the economic crisis of the 1980s deepened, more and more women were forced to start earning money. Chant noted that in Querétaro, an industrial city that was hard hit at the outset of the crisis in 1982, it was poverty rather than a demand for their labor that propelled women into the work force. Thus, throughout the period of stagnation that lasted in Querétaro into 1986, the majority of economically active women were self-employed at home or in the neighborhood. This was true, too, of women in Los Robles. The few openings that manufacturing, government, and tourism, Cuernavaca's main sources of formal employment, had at this time were reserved for better-educated women. Thus, for the most part, our informants were obliged to do domestic work. They took in washing that they laundered at tenement sinks; they mopped floors, cleaned out drains and gas stoves, disposed of other women's garbage, and took care of other women's children. In a word, provided they were paid to do it, they would do almost anything. Often a husband, *deshonorado* (humiliated) by the fact that his wife had to work, insisted that she do so literally *in* the house, "so no one would know." As González de la Rocha observed in Guadalajara, to some men, even that was an unacceptable compromise; thus their wives were obliged to keep their income-producing activities secret. Catharine Boyle pointed out that in times of economic hardship, to women, female employment may be the logical solution, but to men, it is a further afront to their battered dignity.[69] Knowing this was true of her husband, Matilde, who earned money by doing chores for her neighbors, was careful never to allow him to see her "at work."

For women approaching middle age whose husbands were less insistent that they stay in the house, food preparation was a popular way of making money. The investment was small: a table on which to knead masa dough and dice the vegetables, and a charcoal grill. The profits, too, were small, but they could make the difference between a family eating and going hungry. Even in the hardest times, there seemed to be a market for fried snacks, and at midday one could not walk a hundred yards in Los Robles without passing a woman frying *quesadillas* or *gorditas*. Selling candy, tamarind paste, bubble gum, and sherbet to children as they passed one's house on their way from school was another means of making money. As soon as the last child had gone by, one would pick up one's glass jars and table and go back inside. Women sold Tupperware out of their homes; cosmetics, too, and shoes and children's clothing. "Everyone's selling something these days," Inés commented, "trying to make ends meet."

If compelled to look for employment outside the home, the only option that most women with little education had was to work as a domestic servant. Day work was infinitely preferable to a live-in position. Since employers rarely accepted children, a live-in job required leaving one's children with relatives; thereafter, a woman would only see them on her day off.

As noted above, factories in Cuernavaca were hard hit by the recession, and work in them was hard to come by. When, from time to time, they advertised for assembly line workers, the competition was extremely fierce. An applicant needed a primary school, if not a junior high school, certificate, a *palanca* (handle or sponsor), and to pass a written test. In the case of a woman, she might also be pressured by the foreman for a *probadita* (a little taste, i.e., sexual favors), but if she surmounted these hurdles and was hired, she received the legal minimum wage, medical insurance coverage, and admission to the wider world beyond the neighborhood.

Luz María, tired of begging her husband for money he doesn't have and making up the difference by baby-sitting, is desperate to get a factory job. She wants to work both for her family's sake and to save her own sanity. No longer caring what her husband thinks about it, she fills out an application, goes home, waits, and hears nothing. Eloisa, who has been working as a seamstress, has better luck. When her unemployed husband, Marco, is away from home for a few days, she arranges for her sister to watch her two-year-old and gets herself a job painting pottery in a small ceramics factory. But discovering on his return that his wife is working, Marco flies into a rage. "How dare you neglect your son?" he yells at Eloisa. "Because he needs food to eat!" she yells back (implying that Marco is not providing it). As soon as the factory opens next morning, Marco races over to curse out and threaten the proprietor. "Every time I get work, Marco does this to me," Eloisa says later. "He's jealous that I'm working and he's not. And he's afraid I'll have sex with the patrón, too." Defeated, she returns to her sewing machine, at which she earns only a fraction of what she would have earned in the factory.

For a brief period, Luz María lived and worked in the United States. She recalls her stay in Santa Ana with nostalgia. She insists that even the border crossing with the *coyote* (paid guide) was fun. ("It was just like a Sunday walk through the mountains!") She and her husband, Octavio, cleaned the homes of affluent Arabs whose lavish life-style astounded them, and when they cleaned office buildings, they marveled at what they found in the trash: brand-new folders, notebooks, and typing paper, some of which they would keep for their own use and some of which they would sell. But most of all, Luz María was impressed by the cleanliness of California cities. "Why can't they pick up the garbage here, too?" She would like to have stayed longer, but whenever Octavio went out without her, his uncle, with whom they were living, would try to have sex with her. "Even if his small daughter was watching, that didn't stop him," Luz María recalls with disgust. In the end, instead of confronting him, thereby causing a rift within the family, Luz María and Octavio returned to Mexico. She talks about returning to the United States "one day"; it is the only place, she says, where women like herself, without training, can earn a decent wage. Most women, however, even those who have actually been to the United States, do not care for the idea of living there. It is too far away and too rough and the people are too obsessed with money. All they do is go to work to earn it and come home and sleep and get up and go out to earn some more. Husbands, especially, dislike the States. They insist that since women are as likely to work full-time as men there, children are neglected. "Giving a kid a key and telling him to let himself into an empty house is no way to bring him up," we are told by a man who has spent several months in Los Angeles. No, men and women agree, you would not want to raise your children in the United States, especially not daughters. The people there are too liberal. Those Chicano boys expect girls to sleep with them on the first date! If the man wants to go *al otro lado* (to the other side), then let him, and if the woman has to go, then let her, too, but leave the children behind with relatives. If you decide you are going to stay up there, you should wait until you are properly settled before sending for the kids. And in the case of teenage girls, better to let *them* stay in Mexico!

Saving for the Future

Few of these women have savings accounts. Inés is the only one who has ever obtained a mortgage, and that was through her son, Alfonso, who at the time was working in a bank. Margarita has twice used her vecindad as collateral for bank loans to buy taxis, but few working-class people are in a position to borrow from a bank. Relatives and compadres may be good for small loans, but when you borrow from intimates, you are under great pressure to repay as soon as you can. The only source of funds available for major investments—short of paying exorbitant interest rates exacted by hire-purchase agreements—is the *tanda*, the revolving credit association.

Tandas, which are to be found at all levels of Mexican society from the poor to the upper middle class, provide "a scheme of forced saving that circumvents the individual's desire to spend already committed funds," notes Vélez-Ibáñez.[70] "Such saving takes place within the context of other relations of confianza, and the threat of losing prestige if obligations are unmet reinforces the stability of the rotating credit association." A tanda is organized by an individual who is respected in his home community or place of work, where he approaches between ten and twenty people, all of whom he is confident will abide by the rules. To be accepted into an already existing tanda, an applicant must come highly recommended by someone whom the organizer knows and trusts. Having drawn a number, each member contributes a fixed sum at, for example, weekly intervals.

Family shopping expedition

Tenement neighbors

Husband and son

Mother and baby son

Comadres

Disbursement, too, occurs weekly. Thus, in a group of ten, the member who draws number four will receive the pool in the fourth week of a ten-week cycle. Peer pressure forces members to save while reducing the risk of being robbed, as might happen were they to keep large sums of money in their homes. Tandas may be episodic, that is, set up to provide for one-time purchases or investments, after which they terminate, or they may last until the organizer withdraws, whereupon, in the event that no one else is willing to accept the leadership position, the association comes to an end.

Most of the women have been involved in revolving credit associations, to which they make their contributions out of the housekeeping allowances they receive from their husbands. When their numbers come up, they use their savings for building materials, household appliances, trips to Acapulco, children's private school tuition, and, in Julia's case, to live on when her husband, Pancho, goes on a binge. Each year Pancho, who is an alcoholic, makes a vow to the Virgin Mary to stay off the bottle for the following ten months. During that time, he works long hours as a taxi driver and earns good money, some of which Julia salts away in the tanda she has organized in their neighborhood. But when the fiesta in his hometown comes around, Pancho foresakes his vow, and for two months straight, his taxi is parked in the street outside their vecindad and he earns nothing. Then, until Julia corrals him and hauls him off to make another vow of abstinence, the family subsists on her savings.

Women may find making their tanda contributions very difficult, but, as Soledad puts it, if one falls behind in payments, necessity pushes one to catch up. "If I'd failed to fulfill my obligation, the group would have thrown me out," she explains, and with her reputation for trustworthiness ruined, she would never have been accepted by another group. "And how else, except through a tanda, can a poor person save?"

La Vida Casada: Two Women's Experiences

INÉS lives with her husband, Antonio, and two adult children and their families in a commodious house on a quiet street in Los Robles. In the backyard there is a small swimming pool. "We put it in recently," Inés explains proudly, adding, "I learned to swim after my sixtieth birthday!" To her, comfortable circumstances are still quite a novelty; most of her married life, she has been poor.

"Antonio and I were both nineteen when we got married, and we had nothing," Inés recalls, "but Antonio didn't want to wait any longer. His parents lived in another town and he was lonely, living with his uncle. Four years we'd been courting, and that was long enough. As for myself, I didn't want to wait any longer either, because I was madly in love." She adds wistfully, "I used to tell my daughters, you should be madly in love when you get married, because you'll need that to help you endure the suffering that's bound to come your way."

In adolescence, Antonio had learned the tanning trade from his uncle, but when that process was mechanized, he found himself out of a job. When they got married, he was working for a lumber company where he earned two pesos and fifty centavos a week. "We got by because things were very cheap in those days," Inés recalls. When he lost that job, Antonio joined the Sinarquistas, a far Right political movement whose aim was to save the Republic from the radicalism of President Lázaro Cárdenas and his successor, Manuel Avila Camacho. In the late 1930s and early 1940s, it claimed more than one million members in the Bajío, Antonio and Inés's native region. "Antonio had the gift of the gab, and the Sinarquistas spotted it and trained him to use it." Soon he was organizing for the party throughout north and central Mexico.

After a miscarriage in the first year of marriage, Inés soon conceived again and in 1942 gave birth to a son in her sister Estela's house in Cuernavaca, where Antonio happened to be working at the time. She went on to have ten children. "In those days," she says with a slight smile, "we'd never heard of birth control. We had as many children as God sent."

Inés and her growing family lived a peripatetic life. "Sometimes we followed Antonio as he went from town to town," she recalls. "Other times I'd take the children to my suegra's or bring them down here to my sister's. Antonio would come here, too, and for a while we'd live together as a family. Then he'd be off again." In 1947, he left the Sinarquistas, after which he picked up jobs here and there, in a bakery, a shoe store, a market. "He had no skills except for tanning, and there was no work in that any more—and making speeches," his wife says. Finally, after fifteen years of living hand-to-mouth, he learned how to drive and in 1962 found a job with a long-distance bus company whose depot was in Cuernavaca. In due course, his political expertise won him election as a union official, and it is in this capacity that he still functions. He is now close to retirement. "Everyone likes Antonio for his open character," Inés says. "He's cheerful and even-tempered, and he doesn't drink much. As you know, even now he's very handsome. *Ya me acabé* [I'm old already], but he's not. . . . There's only one thing wrong with him: he loves women."

Inés had been married for seven years the first time she discovered Antonio was unfaithful. "At that time he was traveling about all over the country, working for the Sinarquistas, while I and the children—I had three then—were living with my suegra in Acámbaro. The day I learned that he'd been expelled from the party for having an affair with his secretary, I thought I would die."

Inés goes on, "This girl, her name was Marisela. Years before, her father had been killed by the police while participating in a political demonstration, and she'd become a ward of the party [*hija del Sinarquismo*]. She was still very young, about fifteen, when my husband took a fancy to her and requested that she become his secretary. After that he brought her home to live with us. . . . As for me, I suspected nothing. I thought of her as a younger sister. . . . They'd go out on the road together; they were a team. He would talk to the men, and she would talk to the women. But the Sinarquistas were very strict about morals, and once the romance was discovered, they threw out both of them.

"When I heard, I wanted to kill myself. Then I thought, if I did, who would take care of the children? I decided to run away to another city where I didn't know anyone and I could hide my pain and humiliation. I didn't do that, either. I realized that if I ran away, mamá would guess about Antonio, and that would shock her very much. Of course, because Antonio earned so little, she was aware that I suffered economically, but that other way, because of a woman . . . no. As far as I know, she and papá never had problems of that sort.

"So what did I do? Having found out that Antonio was living with Marisela in Puebla, I told mamá I was going to join my husband, and even though he hadn't sent for me, I went there and rented a room. After that, he lived with her sometimes and sometimes with me. In the end he left her, but not before she'd had three kids.

"There were probably others before Marisela. There have certainly been many since. Antonio has never spoken to me about any of his women, and I have never asked," Inés says, "but I've seen their photos in his wallet, and photos of their children, too, and letters. . . . Once I found a letter from one of his kids. *Papá te mando muchos besitos* [Daddy, I send you lots of kisses], it said, and it was signed, 'Violeta.'"

When Antonio was hired by the bus company in Cuernavaca, Inés and her children followed him there. It was not long before she discovered she was not the only woman who had joined him. "He had another one living right here in the neighborhood! One day I found myself sitting next to her in the health clinic! Our eyes didn't meet. We didn't speak. We both looked straight ahead. But it happened that my daughter Susi and that woman's daughter were in the very same class at school. Susi used to talk a lot about her friend Celia. . . . I didn't tell her, and she didn't find out till much later that she and Celia had the same papá. Antonio stayed with Celia's mother for a long time, but eventually he got tired of her just as he had of Marisela, but she managed all right. Celia went to the university, and now she's a lawyer. One can do that much for a child if one only has the one."

Antonio has a different woman now, and that is not the only one, Inés adds with a chuckle. "He has to have his girlfriends on the side. Perhaps he still goes out chasing women because he's trying to stay young. I tell you, when he finally doesn't feel young any more, I hope one of the others takes on the job of looking after him. I don't want him sitting in my house all day, expecting me to wait on him!" At sixty-four, with trousers pressed, mustache clipped, and thick gray hair carefully brushed, Antonio still looks smart and far from old. He travels daily to his union's headquarters in Mexico City. Out of his office there he runs a small shoe business; he also publishes a union newspaper, writing all the articles himself. As Inés says, "He's always had a fountain of words, and now it's flowing onto paper!"

Antonio spends Monday, Tuesday, Thursday, and Friday nights with Inés; Wednesday, Saturday, and Sunday nights he is elsewhere. "He tells me he's working," Inés says, with a wry smile. "Anyway, it means my time is my own. As I don't have to stay home to get his breakfast, I can go to early mass." When Antonio returns to the house on Thursday and Monday evenings, he is wearing a different shirt from the one he had on when he left home. "He keeps another set of clothes in the house of la otra," says Inés. She doesn't know where this particular woman lives. In forty-five years of marriage, he has had so many otras. "Eight that I know about, and three other sets of children. He's a great one for falling in love, though it's never forever."

But for Inés herself, Antonio is the only man with whom she has been in love. "I stayed in love with him too long, that was my problem. I used to hope that he'd change—though mind you, he never promised to change. He knew better! You may be wondering why I had ten children with a man like that, and I wonder too now. Of course, in those days women didn't know how *not* to. We accepted as many as God gave us. But apart from that, Antonio loved babies and he wanted as many as possible. Each time I got pregnant I'd tell myself, this time he'll stay home with me, and for a while after each child was born he *did* stay home. But after two or three months, off he'd go again. The last baby was premature and died while I was giving birth to him, and the doctor said I mustn't have any more. Otherwise, in the hope of catching Antonio and keeping him, I'd have continued."

Of her husband's infidelities she says, "If he has to behave that way, it's his business." As for herself, she has remained entirely "loyal." This is not to say she necessarily disapproves of women who, out of economic need or loneliness, have love affairs. She recalls her neighbor, Luisa, whose husband had deserted her. "She wasn't pretty, she looked older than her age because she'd suffered a lot, but she was good-natured and everyone liked her. In the daytime she was in the vecindad, taking care of the house, but at night, as soon as the children were sleeping, she'd go out. She made her living by taking lovers, she'd have several at a time. But she was always home before daybreak to get her three kids ready for school. They were her pride and joy, she'd have killed for them. This was thirty years ago, before we had contraceptives, and soon she had another child, and then another, each one by a different father. On the Feast of the Kings her children got so many presents—one from each of their 'fathers'—that mine would be jealous. The old ones would say, 'Mamá, wouldn't it be better to have five fathers, instead of just one who hardly ever comes to see us?'" She smiles. "I could see their point of view, but I wasn't that sort."

During the great deal of time that she has spent alone over the years, Inés has received propositions from men. "But I'd be cold with them," she remembers. "I'd tell myself, 'You married Antonio for love, and despite what he has done to you, you still love him.'"

Indeed, it is only quite recently that she stopped loving him. "It happened like this," she says. "Antonio had been gone for a week, and though he didn't tell me where, I knew he was with a woman. The night he came home, we were in bed and I reached over to him. 'What are you asking?' he said. 'How can you expect a man who works as hard as I do to do that? Don't you know how tired I am!' On other occasions I'd felt rejected, but this time I felt angry, too. Not long after, my son Salvador told me that he'd been downtown at the movies with his children on a Sunday and they'd run into Antonio with a young girl. We have eight sets of grandchildren, and any Sunday at least five of them go downtown with their parents. Why did Antonio insist on taking his girlfriend to a place where he was bound to run into our kids? If he wanted to see that movie, well, he has a car and he could have taken his girlfriend to Cuautla—they show the same movie in all the towns round about. But he has no respect! He doesn't care how badly the grandchildren would be affected by seeing him and that young girl. . . . Till then I'd put up with everything, but suddenly I decided I'd had enough."

Inés continues, "We'd been sleeping in two beds pushed together, but now I pulled them apart. When the children saw, they asked me why I'd done it, so I told them, 'We're old now.' Antonio didn't say anything, but he's never once asked me [to make love] again. As for me, I wouldn't want to make love with him unless he left la otra, and he's not about to do that because her children are still young. So now I cook his meals and wash his clothes. If he has something to say to me, well and good, I answer, but I never start up a conversation. We never go out together, either. He doesn't invite me, and anyway, I wouldn't want to go in case we ran into one of his women. If I do go out, it's always with my kids. These days Antonio and I live like brother and sister. . . . Sometimes, I look at him and ask myself, did I really love him? Yes, of course I did! I know I did. I adored him, but that's difficult to remember now."

Having an *enamorado* for a husband is bad enough, Inés says, but one who does not support you and your children is even worse. Whatever Antonio earned—and he never earned much—they had to share with the "other" family. "There were many times when we didn't even get our share," Inés recalls. "You wonder, why did I stay with him? Because a little money occasionally is better than nothing at all, ever. I lost a lot of dignity by staying with him, but the alternative would have been even worse for the children. If it hadn't been for my faith in God, there were many times when I wouldn't have been able to endure the suffering. It's always been my belief that God sends you tribulations as a test, so that by overcoming them, you may grow strong." Once Antonio disappeared for six months, and that was the most difficult time she ever had. "You should have seen me then, running from house to house, begging for work." Inés shakes her head. "Then, my brother, Enrique, died in California and I asked his spirit to ask God on my behalf to send my husband back to me. And lo and behold, Antonio came walking through my door!"

But Inés did not ask him where he had been, or with whom, or anything. "I was afraid that if I did, he'd walk right out again and never give me a single centavo again. All nine of my children needed new shoes."

As a result of her own experience, Inés was determined that her children, daughters as well as sons, get an education. "If I'd had a way of earning a decent living," she explains, "I wouldn't have put up with Antonio the way I did." Certainly she would have been glad of their wages had her children quit school and gone to work, but she worked at her sewing machine fourteen hours a day to keep them in primary school. "At least I managed that," she says. "After primaria, they had to help each other. One would work while the other went to school, that's how they got their training. I know that these days everybody's suffering, but my daughters don't suffer the daily humiliations I did."

Inés goes on, "Young women today are much more independent than we were because they're used to earning their own money. If they don't like their husband's behavior, they tell him, 'I'm leaving!'" Her daughter, Nina, the administrator of a large Catholic school in downtown Cuernavaca, did just that. She married a nice young man with a good job, and they had a son. But when the boy was three, she got a divorce. "She saw right away that her husband was too attached to his mother, and it turned out that he was homosexual. After leaving him, she became friends with Raul and they started living together. Now they have a daughter, but Nina doesn't want to marry him," says Inés, with lingering incredulity. "She has her job and she wants to keep her independence." Although poor Mexican women may actually prefer to live in consensual union with a man, on the grounds that in the absence of any formal tie, they retain more freedom, it is something new for a lower-middle-class woman, typically the quintessence of respectability, to choose such an arrangement.

"Of course there are good and bad sides to this new independence," Inés adds reflectively. "Some young women are so determined to have their own way that they have no tolerance at all. They'll leave a man the first time he disappoints them. As for myself, I never had that option. Even if Antonio had been homosexual, I wouldn't have left him. How would I have fed my kids?"

Since she accepted him for what he is, Antonio has been easy enough to live with, Inés says. He has never beaten her; in fact, in forty-five years of married life, they have never had a serious quarrel. "He's unwilling to discuss anything really important. . . . So at least the children have never had to listen to us fighting. He's always in a good mood, and he likes those around him to be in a good mood, too. If anything comes up to make him unhappy, he walks out of the house."

In recent years, her greatest sorrow has been over her son, Alfonso, "who looked just like his father and behaved just like him, too." Alfonso, a bigamist in his thirties with two sets of children, left his second wife for a young woman named Mercedes whom he had met at the bank where he worked. But Mercedes's spurned suitor, a man with powerful political connections, had the lovers murdered. Convinced that the police would do nothing for "ordinary people," Inés and her family did not try to seek justice. They were also afraid of inviting further retribution. One afternoon, as she sits on the living room couch gazing up at the photograph of her handsome son in swimming trunks on the beach at Acapulco, Inés says sadly, "Perhaps he's better dead. At least this way he can't cause himself or others any more unhappiness."

OFELIA, aged twenty-four, lives in one room in a vecindad with her common-law husband, Arturo, aged thirty-two, three sons, and a daughter. Ofelia and Arturo first got to know each other in their native Oaxaca village when she was twelve and he was twenty. Ofelia was much too young to think of getting married, and they went their separate ways. At fourteen, Ofelia became pregnant by a local boy whom she did not marry. After giving birth, she left her son, Roberto, with her parents and went to live with a sister in the capital, where she worked as a servant and a seamstress while being courted by several men. Meanwhile Arturo, too, had moved to the city, where he was living with a woman by whom he had a daughter. It was after that woman left him that he began to court Ofelia, and when he found work in Cuernavaca, he asked her to go with him. "He didn't mind about Roberto," Ofelia recalls. " 'I'm no saint either,' he told me. 'We should forgive each other our sins.' " They didn't get married. "What's the point of a piece of paper?" Ofelia says.

When we first meet her she is obsessed with Arturo's relationship of several months with Elvira, the mother of four children by four different men, who, so Ofelia imagines, is much more sexually experienced than she. She recounts how, a few weeks earlier, she ran into Elvira and Arturo in the street. She flew at her rival, scratching her face and beating her until Arturo pulled her off. Then leaving her children behind, she ran away to her sister's in Mexico City. The next day, Arturo showed up the with the kids and, promising to give up his girlfriend, begged her to return with him.

He was so upset, so filled with remorse, that she gave in and went back with him to Cuernavaca, but there, within days, he resumed his affair. Beside herself with anger, Ofelia next paid five thousand pesos (about forty dollars) to a curandera who claimed she could get Arturo to break off with Elvira. But though he has broken out in boils, he is seeing his *querida* as much as before.

Ofelia, who has thrown all her savings down the drain, is losing weight rapidly—and her temper twenty times a day. She regrets having allowed Roberto to visit his grandparents in the capital, for fear that without him at home to help her control herself, she may harm the smaller children.

"My suegra says it's my fault that Arturo's unfaithful," she laments. "When I ran away from him a few weeks ago, I should have stayed away. I'm too soft, my suegra says, and perhaps she's right." Since her return, Ofelia has threatened to leave again on several occasions, "but before I reach the door of our vecindad, Arturo's after me, promising he'll stop running around. But of course he doesn't! He needs to chase women because it's the only way he knows to make himself feel good. Either that, or what they tell me in church is true—it's the devil in him that makes him drink and fornicate."

Ofelia maintains that she stays with Arturo partly out of pity. "He didn't grow up with two parents who loved him like I did. He still has scars on his genitals where his father beat him! Even now, when he talks about his childhood, he starts weeping. His father made him and his mother and brothers and sisters suffer so much! He took Arturo out of school when he was seven and put him to work for a living. He had another woman, and he gave all his money to her and none to my mother-in-law. He even forced Arturo to give him his wages, and he spent that money on his other woman, too! But for all that," she adds, "Arturo has always listened much more closely to his father's advice than to his mother's—and followed his example, too. Aside from having other women, his father always drank a lot. And look at Arturo—he's been drinking since he was fifteen!"

Ofelia comments that because the first woman Arturo lived with left him, he is afraid she will leave him, too. "Sometimes I see him coming into the patio after work with a desperate expression on his face, and I know he's thinking, 'She's not here, she's left me.' Then, when he sees me, he brightens up and relaxes. . . . He suffers terribly from insomnia. It must be that his conscience doesn't permit him to sleep peacefully. . . . And already, at only thirty-two, he's getting to look old."

Will her sons inherit their father's unhappiness, she wonders? Will they suffer as he does? Will they make their wives suffer as she suffers now?

Arturo often stays away for several days and nights at a time, and Ofelia admits that by ignoring the basic rule—that a husband not shame his wife before her neighbors by staying out at night—he causes her great humiliation. Her father, too, had many affairs, "but at least, *nunca faltó* [he always came home at night], he had respect for mamá."

On one occasion, when Arturo finally comes home, she slashes his face with a knife. "The way we fought was terrifying," she admits the next day. "I was even more afraid of my own anger than of his. I couldn't keep quiet either, so the whole vecindad heard us fighting."

After yet another night when Arturo has not come home, Ofelia goes to the restaurant where he works to look for him but finds he has left. The chief cook, who comes out to speak with her, hints that Arturo is having an affair with one of his co-workers. They stay talking for a while (he was better-looking than Arturo, Ofelia recalls later), and as she turns to leave, the cook gives her his telephone number, telling her, "Next time your husband doesn't come home at night, give me a call. You should pay him in the same coin he pays you."

On her return home, Arturo, who has arrived ahead of her, flies into a rage. Grabbing her, he slaps her and tears her dress. At work the next day, he learns of her conversation with the cook and, returning to the house, finds the piece of paper on which the man wrote his telephone number. Again he slaps her, threatening that if he ever sees her talking with another man, she will "have to take the consequences."

"Why can you have affairs but I can't?" she yells at him.

"Because you and I are different. I'm a man and you're a woman," he yells back. "And I don't intend to share what's mine with anyone else!"

Later, Ofelia admits that his response, violent as it was, gratified her. "Doesn't his getting so angry show that he cares? He's always telling me that if he left me, no other man would want me, but that man did!"

A newcomer to Cuernavaca, Ofelia had no relatives there and few friends. Lately, in the hope of finding help, she has begun to attend the church of the Jehovah's Witnesses, where she shares her marital troubles with her "sisters," many of whom have experienced similar problems. With their encouragement, she starts being able to put a little distance between herself and Arturo. Reflecting back to the time before he took up with Elvira, she admits that she used to wait on him hand and foot. But now, she says, "I'm less *atenta*. When we have sex, he accuses me of not loving him any more. 'Where did you get that idea?' I say. 'Of course I love you!' But he knows I'm lying. I'm complying with his wishes out of duty, and I can't hide it.

"Mamá put up with my papá until he grew old and quiet," she continues, "but I'm not aguantadora like she is. I have a strong character and a very bad temper, like papá. So far I've put up with Arturo, but if I run out of patience, I'll leave." She does not plan to go to her parents'. Several other women have told her of their bad experiences when, on leaving their husbands, their parents would not accept the grandchildren. "Papá, with his temper, wouldn't take in my kids either," she says. What she would really like to do is live on her own with her children. Confident that if things get any worse with Arturo and she has to leave, her own family will help her financially, her plan is to go to her sister's and build a house on the same plot. Meanwhile, she refuses to continue putting up with things as they are.

She has heard that wives with husbands like hers—canijos—can request the DIF (Department of Family Services) to dock their wages so that the families get enough to live on. You have to be legally married for that, and though she has never wanted to get married, if, as Arturo's legal wife, she would acquire certain rights, it might be worthwhile after all. In the meantime, a neighbor advises her that a television can be very beneficial to the marital relationship. " 'If it gets your husband to stay in the house, well and good,' my neighbor told me." Their TV was broken months ago and has been sitting in the shop ever since because of a dispute with the technician over the cost of the repairs. Now Ofelia pays the bill regardless and brings the TV home. Two days later, she reports that Arturo stayed home to watch it both evenings. Progress! The next step, she tells us, is to stock the refrigerator with beer.

Arturo establishes a new routine: he comes home from work, takes a beer, and sits down in front of the television. From that point on, their relationship improves steadily. Arturo spends Christmas Day with his family and helps Ofelia prepare pozole. This is a far cry from Father's Day the previous June or Roberto's birthday in August, when Arturo did not show up at all. Soon Ofelia confides that she is cleaning his shoes, ironing his uniform, and heating his bath water—in other words, waiting on him hand and foot. A month or two later, she reports, "Things are better than they've ever been between us. Arturo's coming home every night!" She adds with a laugh, "It must be because I've stopped picking fights with him."

By Easter, Arturo is substantially heavier. "He's eating properly now," Ofelia remarks. "It isn't like the old days when he never ate at home." She continues, "Now when he's annoyed it's over small things, like the kids fighting or Roberto being in trouble at school, not because I'm nagging him about Elvira." Is he happier? "Maybe." As for herself, she is happier than she has been in a long time. Her conversation with her husband is peppered with endearments and, in contrast to a year ago when she was talking about having her tubes tied ("How could I have more kids with *him*?"), she is thinking of "another daughter for Arturo."

Arturo has become a devoted family man. The children throw themselves on him the instant he comes through the patio door in the evening. How did this transformation occur? Ofelia grins, "I couldn't have waited thirty years till Arturo stopped drinking and running around of his own accord, like mamá did with papá. I don't have mamá's patience. I had to take steps."

La Vida de Soltera: Unmarried Motherhood

INOCENCIA, a tiny, fragile, white-haired woman, lives with her daughter, Carlota, two grandchildren, and her sister, Judith, in what was originally her parents' weekend house on the edge of the ravine that runs through Los Robles. She has had two heart attacks and a coronary bypass; she has a cataract in one eye, diabetes, and emphysema. "With all the *angustias* [troubles] I've had, I should have been dead long ago!" she says with a chuckle. What keeps her alive, she insists, are her responsibilities.

Judith towers over Inocencia, her junior by two years. A stout and forceful woman, she has practiced law for four decades in a country in which, in her generation, a professional woman was a rarity. In contrast, in her youth, Inocencia—whose formal education ended at the sixth grade—earned her living as a seamstress. While today Judith travels widely, Inocencia seldom leaves the neighborhood except to go downtown to pay the light and telephone bills. Judith lives primarily in a man's world, Inocencia wholly in the world of women. But different as their lives have been, in one most important respect they are alike: both are single mothers. Within four days of each other in 1960, Judith, at thirty-eight, gave birth to Ricardo and Inocencia, at thirty-six, to Carlota. Thenceforth, they joined forces. Inocencia stayed home and nursed both children, "as if they were twins." She adds, "I'd always wanted a son and there, I had one, as well as a daughter!" When the babies learned to talk, they both called her 'mamá' and her sister Judith, 'Chata,' a nickname derived from her slightly squashed-in nose.

Judith, meanwhile, went out to earn the "family" living—a necessary, if tempestuous, partnership.

"Judith has never been an easy person to get along with," Inocencia confides. "Even as a young girl she was proud and bad-tempered, and over the years she's got worse. When she was young she was so talented and ambitious, so self-assured. She always looked down on me because I wasn't as pretty or as smart as she was, and I wasn't at all self-assured."

At nine, Inocencia remembers waking up in the middle of the night and seeing that an electric cord in the room she and Judith shared was on fire. "I saw the flames leaping across the wall so I screamed and woke everyone up. The others put out the fire, but even so, I couldn't stop shaking and I stammered very badly, too. In fact, I was in such a bad state that I couldn't go to school. My parents took me to doctors, none of whom asked *me* how I felt. They just listened to my parents' account of what had happened. They said I was suffering from *mal de San Vito* and prescribed medicinal teas and baths of scalding water."

After several months of incapacitating anxiety, Inocencia recovered sufficiently to be able to return to school, but she could not concentrate properly on her studies. At twelve, when she finished primaria, her parents removed her from school and had her take a dressmaking course. Soon she was doing piecework for a Mexico City department store. "I'd go and pick up dresses that had already been cut out, and then I'd bring them home and sew them. If I made the smallest mistake, I'd have to pay the cost of the materials out of my wages." Her parents insisted that she contribute most of her earnings to the educational expenses of her siblings. One brother was in medical school, another was training to become an architect, and Judith was in preparatoria. A third brother, Felipe, the youngest member of the family, was the only one apart from Inocencia who did not become professional. "As children," Inocencia recalls, "Felipe and I were very close, and we are still. We're the shy ones. My parents wanted Felipe to become an engineer, but he worried so much about how much his education was costing that when he was thirteen he dropped out of school and went to work on the railways. We were both disappointments to our parents, although they were even more disappointed in me than in him. Mamá was especially. She was *muy recta* [very strict], and as far as I was concerned, very hard. It was impossible for me to please her." The best Inocencia was able to do was avoid *displeasing* her. Thus, as a teenager and young adult, she did her utmost to be placid, unproblematic, and above all, useful.

"When my sister turned fifteen, my parents gave her a quinceaños party," Inocencia recalls, "but when *I* turned fifteen, they didn't offer to have a party for *me*. I wasn't sociable like Judith." In her late teens, Inocencia begged to be allowed to take a course in practical nursing. "By then my oldest brother was a doctor, and I loved to read his medical books. Papá agreed to the course, but when the time came for me to work the night shift in the hospital, he made me withdraw. He wasn't willing to let me be in the streets at night without a chaperone." After that, she sometimes did office work for her parents' friends, or if someone in the extended family needed an extra pair of hands, she would be dispatched to Nuevo Laredo, Villa Hermosa, or Guadalajara, to take care of children, cook, do the shopping, or make curtains for the new dining room. Most of her youth, however, she spent at home working at her sewing machine.

Meanwhile, having qualified, Judith was practicing law and having love affairs. "Papá wanted her to marry a widower friend of his, but Judith didn't care for him at all. Instead she fell in love with that man's son! His name was Rogelio, and he was younger than she was and Papá didn't like that. . . . I don't know why Judith didn't marry someone else. She had many opportunities."

In contrast, Inocencia had few boyfriends. "Really, there were only two. The first my parents didn't like because he was several years younger than I was; and they objected to the second because, although he had plenty of money, he was a Zapotec Indian from Oaxaca. The fact was, I didn't want to marry either of them. I never thought very much about getting married, though I used to daydream about having a little boy."

Despite not having finished nurse's training, Inocencia knew enough to be able to help her brother in his consulting room, and there one day she bandaged up an engineer who had been badly hurt in an industrial accident. His name was Arnaldo, and after he recovered, he began courting her. "He came from a very poor family. I met his mother once, and she was a quiet, simple person. He was making his own way up in the world. Mamá didn't like him, but then, she didn't like anyone who came courting me. As for papá, by then he'd been dead for several years."

Inocencia had never made love with anyone before Arnaldo. "He hurt me a lot," she remembers. "It was difficult [*fue muy laborioso*], but that didn't matter because I was in love with him." A couple of months later, when she told him she was pregnant, he admitted he had a wife and three young daughters. " 'Don't worry,' he told me, 'I'll get a divorce and then we'll get married.'" With a shake of the head, Inocencia continues, "Although in my heart I knew that wasn't going to happen, I wanted to believe him. . . . We would go out together, like any married couple, and buy things for the baby which I'd hide in a trunk I had at home. I didn't tell a soul that I was expecting. In those days I was quite stout, anyway, and I wore loose dresses, so my family didn't suspect. Every day I was waiting to hear Arnaldo tell me, 'Now I'm divorced and we can get married,' but he never did. Finally, it dawned on me that I was going to have to handle everything alone."

When she was almost eight months pregnant, Inocencia found work through a friend as a housekeeper in the coastal city of Veracruz. One day, when her mother was out of town and she was getting ready to go to the station to catch the train, Judith rushed into the house in a distraught condition. "She begged me to help her because she was eight months pregnant, too! Her old lover, Rogelio, had married another woman about two years before, and Judith had gone abroad to recover, but when she came back, she'd taken up with him again, and this was the result. So of course I told her I was in the same state she was, and I was going to Veracruz to have my baby there. Straightaway she asked if she could come with me. I said I was going out now to see our parish priest, to get his blessing. While I was gone she should get her things together and we'd go away together. But when I told the priest what we were about to do, he said, 'Stay here, don't you move!' He went into another room and telephoned my brothers, who had all been married a long while by then and were living with their families on their own and told them to come immediately. He told them about Judith and me, and that we were their responsibility. They couldn't let us go to live among strangers. It was their obligation to take care of us. So we didn't catch that train to Veracruz after all."

Inocencia continues, "When mamá came back to the city and my brothers told her about our situation, she was very angry and bitter, but only with me, not with Judith. Rogelio, Judith's lover, was the son of her comadre, so of course she liked him even though he was married and had got my sister pregnant! But she'd never liked Arnaldo, and as for me, I'd always disappointed her, and now I was a source of shame as well. She decided that Judith and I should leave the city immediately. That way, our friends and acquaintances in the capital wouldn't find out. That was her main concern—that nobody find out. Judith and I were to go to Cuernavaca, to our weekend house. We'd give birth there and then we'd live there permanently, passing ourselves off as divorcées. So that's what we did. We moved down to Cuernavaca with mamá."

During the last weeks of their pregnancies, the sisters, both in their late thirties, were forbidden by their mother to leave the house and garden, which was surrounded by a high wall. "Mamá didn't want the neighbors to see we were pregnant. She kept the front gate locked all the time." She also forbade Inocencia to have contact with Arnaldo. "From the moment she learned about my pregnancy, mamá set about putting an end to my relationship with him," Inocencia recalls. "She insisted she was acting in my interests because Arnaldo was no good. As it turned out, she was right; but even so, she shouldn't have interfered."

Meanwhile, Arnaldo would sit in his car outside the gate, waiting in vain for Inocencia to emerge. Not until after she had given birth to Carlota ("I paid all the maternity clinic expenses myself," she says proudly) was she permitted to see her child's father again. "Then mamá let me out to go with Arnaldo to register my baby, but that was the only time. Eventually he got tired of not being allowed to see me and he went away."

Three years passed before he returned, and then it was to tell Inocencia that he had got a divorce—and was already married to a "wonderful" woman. "So you see," says Inocencia with a faint smile, "it hadn't taken him long to forget me. . . . He was a great enamorado. He'd be in love with one woman one minute and with another the next, and each love was the love of his life! He married his first wife in church and his second in church also, which of course is against religious law. The second marriage was up on the United States border, so he got away with it. But he left his second wife, the 'wonderful' woman, too. He said he wanted children, and she couldn't have them. The four he had already weren't enough for him, so he took up with his wife's maid! They're living in the capital now." Inocencia chuckles. "At least he didn't marry that one in church. In fact they aren't married at all, but they have a child, about the same age as Carlota's daughter, Yael. Every year Yael is invited to her birthday party."

As Carlota was registered in both parents' names—and Judith's son, Ricardo, was as well—their Los Robles neighbors have always assumed that both sisters were married, if briefly, to their children's fathers. (We knew Inocencia for six months before one day she said, "I have something to tell you. . . .") In this way, just as their mother intended, they have been able to pass themselves off as divorcées. For her part, however, Inocencia has never pretended to Carlota that she and Arnaldo were married. "Why tell her a lie? I said that her father and I loved each other at one time but that later on, we stopped."

Inocencia has always welcomed Arnaldo's interest in Carlota, intermittent though it has been. "It was important that she know her father. Whatever he's like, she knows now." He would arrive without warning and wait outside the gate until Inocencia came out. "He didn't knock because he was scared of mamá," Inocencia recalls. "Till her dying day, mamá never forgave him—or me either—nor did she allow him to set foot on this place." Once he had succeeded in making contact with Inocencia, she would bring Carlota out to him, and he would take the little girl off for an hour or two. Sometimes, too, Inocencia would take Carlota up to the capital for a visit with her father, expeditions that she kept secret from her mother. During the years that Arnaldo lived on the U.S. border, he saw very little of his daughter, but after he moved back to Mexico City, he began seeing her quite regularly again.

Inocencia has never received any financial help from him. Indeed, the only time he offered it, she refused. While Carlota was growing up, Judith paid the day-to-day expenses, and their brothers helped when they could. In emergencies, Inocencia drew on savings she had put away when she had been working. Numerous illnesses, both her daughter's and her own, were an acute financial stress. "But somehow we got by. I always felt that God was looking out for us." She and Carlota continued to live in the Los Robles house, which since the death of her mother has been owned jointly by her and her four siblings. There has never been much money for maintenance, and today it is in a very poor state of repair. The swimming pool has been empty for a decade; the garden looks like a jungle; the living room ceiling has a huge hole in it. "But at least we've still got a roof over our heads," observes Inocencia with a smile.

Once, when Carlota was little, Inocencia had the chance to marry. In her album there are several photographs of her, a radiant new mother with Carlota in her arms, and her novio, Mario, beside her. They even set a date for the civil ceremony, but at the last moment Mario's mother fell ill and Inocencia's mother insisted on postponement. "She told us that when parents aren't present at their children's wedding, it's bad luck, so we should wait till she recovered. But that took a long while, and by the time she was better, Mario and I had broken our engagement. Mamá said that in any event it was just as well I didn't marry him as he was ten years younger than I was, and when Carlota was fifteen, he'd only be forty-two, and I'd be fifty-two. That situation would invite trouble, she said, so I should forget about getting married and concentrate on bringing up my daughter. And that's precisely what I did."

Following the death of her mother, Inocencia suffered a severe heart attack after which she had a coronary bypass. Since then her health has steadily deteriorated. Carlota's out-of-wedlock pregnancy at eighteen was a heavy blow to Inocencia. She was briefly encouraged two years later by her daughter's marriage; but within the year, it had proved a failure, leaving Carlota, at twenty-one, divorced with two children.

The cruelest blow of all comes in 1984 with Ricardo's death during his last year of medical school. As Inocencia says, "Though I didn't give birth to him, I was his mother, and he was my son." A few months later, she suffers a second heart attack, which leaves her much weaker. From then on, the sisters have to hire a maid to do the housework.

Determination to see Carlota settled is all that keeps Inocencia alive. At last, at age twenty-five, Carlota marries a man who loves her dearly, and she and her children move with him to Mexico City. "She begged me to go live with them. She didn't want to leave me here with my sister," says Inocencia softly just after the wedding, "but I told her, 'I'm not coming. Married people need their privacy. I'll be all right here with Judith. After all, I'm used to her; I've lived with her all my life.'"

"*Ya se terminó mi trabajo* [my job's done]," she concludes contentedly one summer morning. "Now that Carlota's settled, I can die in peace."

Summary

Typically, these Los Robles women reported that during courtship they had looked forward to a loving and harmonious marital relationship in which husband and wife would work together for the good of the family. Although a few claimed that their original expectations had been fulfilled, others, confronted by alcoholism, physical abuse, and infidelity, had revised if not abandoned their hopes of finding companionship and mutual understanding in their marriages. Just as many had seen their mothers do in their own childhoods, they had shifted the focus of their affections from husband to children. For all that, the older women, their child-rearing days over, were likely to report a high level of personal contentment. This bears out a finding from a study of family life that Elu de Leñero conducted in the mid-1960s, in which men and women who identified raising a family rather than conjugal happiness as their most important concern reported greater satisfaction with their marriages.[71] Some of the younger women, however, continued to look to the marital relationship for their primary emotional satisfaction and were deeply hurt and angered when their husbands acted out their insecurities and frustrations in conventional machista ways. As we walked through the door, these young wives, desperate for support in the struggle with the world outside that enthralled their husbands, would begin to pour out stories of violence, betrayal, and threats of desertion. The humiliation they felt on account of their husbands' extramarital affairs did not appear to inhibit them from talking to us about them or about the "other women" on whom some admitted having spied and/or even phys-ically attacked. In contrast, the older women could only bring themselves to talk about their husbands' infidelities with great reluctance, and when they did, they had little to say. Soledad's husband, Jorge, had been living for years with another woman, but though Soledad knew who she was and where she lived, she claimed that she had never been to check on her. Catalina admitted that there were "rumors" about her husband and a cer-tain woman, adding, "But that was his business, not mine." Husbands' accounts of their philanderings concurred entirely with Catalina's view. Their affairs were *their* business. If any woman were capable of making a man feel guilty, she was much likelier to be his mother than his wife.

By and large, the younger women were not as submissive or long-suffer-ing as women of the older generation described themselves as having been in their youth. City-raised for the most part and schooled, if only through the sixth grade, they were more self-confident in relation to men. Instead of accepting as many children as God sent them—and their husbands wanted— they could plan their pregnancies, and most did, and rather than being burdened with the care of young children from marriage to menopause, they had time for and greater need of emotional intimacy with their husbands.

La Liberación de la Mujer (Women's Liberation) meant little to them. With the exception of Luz María, who had lived in the United States, they read very little and then, apart from the Bible, only cartoon books or women's magazines that undertook to make their readers better wives and housekeepers, not rebels against the domestic routine. They were in favor of equal pay for equal work, the provision of child care facilities, and mater-nity leave, but to them, these were largely abstractions. Most were in such dire straits financially that any wage was acceptable; and none worked alongside men or was employed in a setting that provided social welfare benefits. Feminism was all very well for rich women (*ellas que tienen dinero)*: if they defied their men, they had the financial resources to dispense with them. Just a few blocks away from Los Robles was a women's center that provided support to mothers raising families alone. But the women with whom we worked were unaware of its existence. Had they been, they would probably have regarded it as personally irrelevant. They were far more interested in staying in their marriages than getting out of them.

Nevertheless, in certain important respects, these young women were different from their mothers. But how different were their husbands from *their* fathers? In a study of parent-youth relations, Glen Elder[72] reported that in contrast with the United States, Italy, Germany, and Britain, where he found major value differences between oldest and youngest men, in Mexico, young men were almost as "authoritarian" and "undemocratic" as their fathers. Though Elder's data are a quarter of century old now, as one young woman told us, "Our *machos mexicanos* aren't going to change of their own accord. It's up to us to make them." Instead of keeping quiet, she and others like her challenged their domineering husbands on a whole range of issues, including overnight absences; some refused to have sexual relations at their husbands' behest and if struck, were likely to strike back. Their mothers had put up with things until, deserted, they were forced to make it on their own; but these young women set limits to the physical and emotional suffering they would tolerate. Thus, while Inés admitted that she "lost a lot of dignity" by staying with Antonio, Ofelia, forty years her junior, declared that "a lot" was "too much." Being "only" a mother to her children was not enough. She wanted a relationship of trust and understanding with her husband and convinced, despite all evidence to the contrary, that this was a possibility, continued to fight for it.

Within the household, a woman's life might have changed, but outside, it had changed much less. Like their elders, the younger women's intimates were mainly close kin. Though as a schoolgirl and later in the workplace, a woman might have had friends, after marriage her domestic work load, combined with her husband's disapproval of gossip, made the maintenance of old friendships and the development of new ones difficult. Women who were newcomers to the city, lacking relatives on whom they could depend, were likelier to flout the restrictions their husbands imposed on them. These new friendships often assumed a permanent character after conversion to relationships of fictive kinship, on which they hoped to rely in future for economic as well as emotional support.

Despite the hardship that la crisis imposed on the poor, traditional no-tions with regard to sex roles still largely prevailed in Los Robles: a husband should provide for his family while his wife took care of their home. A working-class man was still likely to view an employed wife as a threat to his manhood; for her part, a woman saw herself as entitled to her husband's support while she stayed home. Though of necessity many working-class men allowed their wives to earn money, a married woman who had to "help out," excluded by lack of training from professional occupations such as teaching or nursing which carried some status, looked for work that could be done at home, enabling her to combine an income-producing activity with domestic responsibilities—and at the same time save her husband's face. Those few younger women who managed to secure outside employ-ment ran up against intractable opposition from their husbands. In short order, they found themselves back home and as before, earning a pittance doing chores for marginally better-off neighbors. Though meanwhile, some might be able to delegate some of their own chores to adolescent daughters and sisters, rarely was a husband willing to help. Most working women had no alternative but to shoulder the doble jornada alone.

The only way out of drudgery appeared to be more training, leading eventually to an office job. Some of the younger women were eager to take adult education courses, but others, seeing women who, during the reces-sion, were unemployed despite their credentials, were skeptical about the benefits of further education. Again, given their husbands' attitudes, they doubted whether even if they were qualified and a job were forthcoming, they would be permitted to work outside the home. Thus, they focused their energies on educating their daughters, in the hope that when they married and had children, they would have the freedom to use their skills when and as *they*—rather than just their husbands—pleased.

· 4 ·

Con Todos Estos Chamacos: Child Rearing in the City

As children, these women assumed that one day they would be mothers, and for most, that day was not far off. Ofelia gave birth to Roberto at fourteen; Irene and Soledad were mothers at sixteen, Luz María and Eloisa at seventeen. By twenty-one, all but two had given birth. The younger women, as much as those of the older generation, view raising a family as their essential purpose. Those few who admit to wanting something for themselves—the opportunity to study for a professional credential in order to become "more than just a housewife," for example—emphasize how much their children stand to benefit from their increased earning power. Despite far-reaching changes in the society as a whole and in the conditions in which child rearing occurs in particular, their goal—to raise children who as adults, though economically independent, remain emotionally close—is hardly different from that of their mothers.

Pregnancy and Childbirth

A three-tiered medical system is in place in Mexico. As of 1980, 45 percent of the population had health insurance—government workers and their families through the Instituto de Seguridad y Servicios Sociales de los

Trabajadores del Estado (ISSSTE) and salaried workers in the private sector through the Instituto Mexicano de Seguro Social (IMSS).[1] Subscribers to these programs, which are financed by contributions from both employer and employee, have access to health services and medication free of charge. The self-employed and workers in the informal sector who do not receive coverage through their place of work may purchase membership in the IMSS program, but few do so. Rather, the wealthy obtain health care in the private sector, and the poor from Secretaría de Salubridad y Asistencia (public health) hospitals and clinics that provide services at nominal cost. Although due to cutbacks and budget restrictions its quality had been declining, nevertheless in 1984–85, Mexico could still boast of one of the most comprehensive health care systems in the developing world.

Until a generation ago, however, few medical facilities were available to poor Mexicans. The only attention that the great majority of women received during pregnancy was from traditional midwives (*parteras*). A partera would make her first home visit when her patient was about four months pregnant and thereafter would visit every month to determine whether the fetus was growing well and to give massages (*sobadas*) and advice, for the most part about morning sickness, backache, and diet. Since it was believed that pregnancy made the woman "hot," certain foods would be recommended to "cool" her. But because it was considered shameful to discuss such delicate matters with young women, especially first-time mothers, the partera would speak with an older female relative rather than with the patient herself. Meanwhile, women too poor to afford a partera's services during pregnancy went without. Though some were aware that they should be eating more and different foods—for their own well-being as well as for that of the unborn child—most lacked the resources to do so.

The delivery (*parto*) took place at home with the mother-in-law in attendance or if the woman was very young, in her natal home. A first-time mother would be told nothing in advance about what to expect in childbirth. "Why frighten them? If you worried them ahead of time, when it came the labor would be worse," says one elderly partera. "Most young ones made a racket anyway. Only with experience did they suffer childbirth uncomplainingly." She adds that though some of her colleagues used to chastise their patients for screaming—"They'd even slap their bottoms!"— she herself would do her best to console them, "because losing your temper never helps."

After delivery, the cutting of the umbilical cord, and removal of the afterbirth, the partera would concentrate on the baby, leaving the care of the mother to her relatives. Having bathed him in oil, she would put him to the breast right away, in the belief that colostrum cleaned the stomach and got his digestive system going. Each day—until the umbilical cord dropped off, a period of about a week—she would return to bathe the baby.

Estela, who gave birth to her first child in Los Angeles in 1931 with a Mexican partera in attendance, recalls being "scared to death." Although the partera had starting checking her months beforehand, she had not told her anything about the parto itself, and neither had her mother and grandmother. Catalina, too, remembers how frightened she was the first time she gave birth. "My mother and mother-in-law were living in the country, and only the partera and my cousin were with me. I tried telling myself, 'Everyone was born this way, this pain is normal. Be *valiente*, don't scream!' But I screamed anyway," she admits shamefacedly. In later childbirths she would arrange to have her children cared for by a neighbor. "Only people who are *muy ranchera* [real hayseeds] allow their children to see them giving birth," she explains. Nor should an adolescent girl witness childbirth in case she be put off motherhood for ever! Thus, one woman, whose younger unmarried sister was with her when she went into labor, immediately sent the girl away. "Just seeing me in pain terrified her. If she'd seen the parto, she might have died of fright!" Even Luz María, who routinely helped her mother during labor and escorted her to the maternity clinic, never stayed for the delivery itself.

Husbands were rarely present during childbirth. "That's women's work. It isn't a time for men," we were told. Matilde recalls, however, that on the one occasion her husband stayed with her, he proved very helpful. "He kept the fire going for heating water and changed the bloody cloths, just as the partera told him. And when it was time for the baby to come out, he supported me from behind while the partera held my legs open." But another woman tells how her husband came home in the middle of her labor and got "drunk because he couldn't stand to see me in pain. I lay in the bedroom and he lay in the kitchen, dead to the world!"

Until the expansion of health services in the 1960s and 1970s, poor women very rarely gave birth in hospitals. Lourdes, however, went into labor three months early with her son Angel and was taken to the Hospital Civil. "When my baby was born, he weighed so little that they put him in the incubator. The governor's wife had recently donated it, and he was the very first baby to use it. He had his picture in the newspaper, too," she proudly recalls. Her six subsequent deliveries all took place at home.

Today, prenatal care, consisting of a physical examination, blood test, tetanus injection, and iron and vitamin supplements, is routine in Cuernavaca. Better-educated women tend to go for a checkup in the first trimester of pregnancy, the less educated, in the second or even third trimester. The great majority of women also give birth in a medical facility. Those lacking insurance or the money for a private maternity clinic go to the Hospital Civil. "The overcrowding there is terrible," one woman reports. "You often have two women to a bed, moaning and crying, and those doctors and nurses have neither patience nor respect. They refuse to answer your questions or treat you like a human being." Staff in the ISSSTE and IMSS hospitals are reported to treat patients better, while women who give birth in private clinics have fewest complaints. But these clinics are very expensive, and women often delay being admitted until they are about to deliver and leave as soon as physically possible after the birth. Julia, for example, in labor with her fifth child, waited as long as she could at home before entering a nearby clinic and was already hooked up to an IV when the doctor informed her that, due to "complications," she would need a Caesarian section. Astounded by the price he quoted for delivery and aftercare, she told him she would stay only if he could guarantee the survival of her child. When he replied that he could not, she checked out and her husband rushed her to the Hospital Civil, where she was obliged to wait twelve hours for a Caesarian. Two hours after delivery, her newborn son died.

Some women in Los Robles—mainly young unmarried mothers who are ashamed to go to the hospital without a husband and rural immigrants who are shy of male physicians—still prefer to use parteras, who these days are traditional midwives who have taken Ministry of Health training courses and received certification. In the mid-1980s, only two remained in Los Robles. Though, at about forty dollars, their charge was expensive by local standards, they appeared to have plenty of work. In the neighborhood people joked about one who, before she became a midwife, had sold handmade tortillas door-to-door. Back in her village, Matilde had given birth to three children with a partera in attendance and, pregnant with her fourth child in Cuernavaca, considered a hospital delivery. But as she had no health insurance, this would have meant going to the Hospital Civil, which, given all the bad things she had heard about it, she was reluctant to do. Thus, when she went into labor, she sent up the street for the Tortilla Lady.

In an older generation, it was customary for a new mother to be relieved of all domestic responsibilities for the *cuarentena*, the forty days following childbirth, so that she could concentrate on caring for her infant and regaining her strength. At the end of the seclusion period, the first place she would go was to church to give thanks for her safe delivery. Ideally, during the cuarentena, a woman would be cared for by her own mother, which was often possible in the endogamous village, since in all probability she would be living close to her natal family. In the city, however, we found much variation. Catalina, whose mother had remained in the country, had her teenage sister come to Cuernavaca to help her. Margarita, meanwhile, who gave birth to eight children in town where she had no relatives, could only count on her husband. She recalls, "During the cuarentena, I'd just walk up and down, up and down with the baby while Edmundo did everything, even the cooking. Later when our family became so numerous that he couldn't manage alone, he would hire a girl to help."

A few days after Estela gave birth to her first child in her parents' house in Los Angeles, her mother, too, gave birth—to her tenth child. So it was her grandmother who cared for her while her younger sisters, including Inés, took care of their mother. After her parents moved back to Mexico, leaving her without close female kin in California, Estela would travel south to stay with her parents for the last few months of each pregnancy. After delivery, her grandmother would take care of her, just as she had the first time in Los Angeles. "She'd tell me, 'This is the one occasion in a mother's life that she can rest.' She'd cook and clean and wash and iron and watch my other children. I'd spend the first week in bed, only getting up to bathe, and the next five resting. All I did was nurse and change the baby and go out for walks in the evening, well wrapped up against *el aire* [cold drafts that are thought to do a new mother damage]."

Some women who observed the cuarentena with their older children later saw their support system collapse as their mother died, an aunt moved away, or a sister married. "With my younger kids I was lucky to get four days' rest," Inés recalls. Meanwhile, four days' rest was quite enough for Lourdes. "Mamá used to tell me to stay in," she remembers with a grin, "but I paid no attention. I couldn't wait to get up and go out!"

These days, the convention that a woman newly delivered of a baby should rest for forty days is all but forgotten. At most, one's mother comes to help for a week or two, or a younger sister is sent over in her stead. As a child, Luz María would take care of her mother postpartum, but when she herself gave birth to her son, her mother, who had also recently given birth, was in no position to return the favor. When Luz María arrived home from the hospital, her mother-in-law suggested she move in with her for a while, "But I knew what sort of person she was," Luz says. "After five days she'd have had *me* doing all the housework while *she* sat down to watch TV! Another bad thing about her is that she likes to play the radio as loud as possible, and when you've just given birth you don't feel like hearing that kind of music. And so," Luz María concludes, "I came back to my own place right away, and my husband was the only one who helped me."

Again, new mothers may still go to church to give thanks for a safe delivery, but they are in no particular hurry. Their babies may be several months old before they go.

Whereas the older women sewed all their babies' clothes by hand, today's mothers buy virtually everything in stores. In this tropical town, wooly sweaters, booties, hats, and leggings are favored, and at all times the infant is tightly wrapped in a *rebozo* (shawl) to ward against el aire, which brings bronchial infections. Disposable diapers are available in local stores but are too costly to use except on special occasions. Instead, Los Robles mothers continue to use machine-finished cloth diapers secured with a strip of fabric around the waist, while the poorest use any piece of absorbent cloth that comes to hand.

Infant and Child Care

After good health, docility is the characteristic that Los Robles mothers value most highly in their infants and young children, a preference that was also frequently expressed by mothers of babies studied by Lucille Atkins and her colleagues in Mexico City.[2] The "ideal" infant makes few demands for interaction; rather, he spends his day sleeping, or if awake, lying quietly in his bed. Though a certain amount of active exploration may be tolerated in an older child in the home setting, elsewhere, or in the presence of visitors, he should remain still and silent.

Traditional patterns of infant care were designed to contend with hazardous health conditions that until a generation ago resulted in infant mortality rates of close to 100 per 1,000. That an infant also needed social stimulation was hardly a consideration. A baby was breast-fed on demand, had a great deal of physical contact with his mother or caretaker in the daytime, and slept with his mother at night. More recently, public health measures such as mass immunization campaigns and the introduction of piped water, combined with rising levels of education and increased availability of modern medical care, have contributed to a rapid decline in infant mortality.

As conditions have become less hazardous and life expectancies have increased, infant care practices, too, have changed. Until thirty years ago, virtually all peasant and working-class babies were breast-fed. If the mother died in childbirth or was unable to feed her infant, a wet nurse—often a relative—was found as a substitute. A nursing bottle was used only to give a baby water in hot weather. The exception was the case of a child who had to be weaned before he could drink from a cup, who would be given cow's milk by bottle if his family could afford it and if not, gruel (*atole*) made of maize or rice. The convention was to breast-feed a baby for at least a year; beyond that, duration of breast-feeding reflected personal preference and economic resources. Margarita explains that she weaned her children at twelve months because her milk was no longer rich enough. "Cow's milk was better for them." But Inés, who could not afford to buy cow's milk, would wait until her children were about eighteen months. "If you didn't wean a child by the time he learned to talk, he'd become *muy chillón* [whiny], and I didn't like to be nursing a child who could walk around asking for the breast." Poor mothers who had many other mouths to feed often delayed weaning until well into the third year, with minimum supplementation.

Traditionally, a mother weaned her child as soon as she became aware of being pregnant. Some women claimed that the nursing child would harm the fetus, others that the breast milk, made thin and watery by the new pregnancy, would make the nursing child sick, a belief that Richard Currier, too, found in his study of folk medicine in Erongaricuaro, Michoacán.[3] But despite the prejudice against nursing during pregnancy, a very poor mother often delayed weaning until the arrival of the new baby.

By the 1950s, working-class mothers were starting to use powdered infant formula in emergencies. Lourdes, who had nursed six babies before her daughter, Rocío, was born with a cleft palate in 1958, recalls, "Because she couldn't suck on my nipple, she was pitiful to see. The bottle was easier for her, so that's what I gave her." Another woman who had nursed four older children remembers the difficulties she had with her fifth child. "From the start he refused the breast. When I tried to nurse him, all he did was cry. Breast milk would have been better for him, but what could I do except use a bottle? At that time [1960], I knew no other woman who gave bottles to her child."

According to a finding in the World Fertility Survey of 1975, only 77.6 percent of Mexican mothers reported breast-feeding their last child, however briefly; the proportion still nursing at three months had declined to 64.4 percent and to 55.5 percent at six months.[4] The newly delivered mother today receives conflicting messages from the medical profession. Whereas at the outset, she is strongly encouraged to nurse so that her baby receives some immunity from disease (no emphasis is placed on the emotional benefits of breast-feeding), should he get sick, the message abruptly changes. One woman recalls, "I nursed my son for a week and then he got diarrhea and the doctor told me to wean him. Formula was better for him, that's what the doctor said." By the age of two months, even if her child is in good health, a mother is likely to be told that breast milk no longer provides enough nutrition. Thus, even women who press on with nursing are more than likely to supplement with powdered milk, which results in a rapid decline in the output of breast milk. "My son liked his bottle better than his mamá, and soon my milk dried up," says one woman sadly. Again, with family planning a top government priority, medical professionals urge mothers to begin taking oral contraceptives as soon as possible after childbirth; but since oral contraceptives contain estrogen, which contaminates breast milk, mothers are told to wean their infants before starting on the pill. Meanwhile, the belief that breast-feeding spoils the figure is spreading. Young women are weaning their infants within a few days of birth, with the excuse that they do not have enough breast milk or their infants do not like it. "But vanity's the real reason," one grandmother says in disgust. "In our day, if your baby didn't like your milk, he soon learned to like it!"

In sum, though *la leche materna es mejor* (breast milk is better), as billboards and radio spots insist, since the 1960s, breast-feeding has been in retreat in Mexico. Though women who nurse for a very short period or not at all may invite criticism from older female relatives, their contemporaries see bottle-feeding in an entirely favorable light. Infant formula is available in every neighborhood store as well as, at a somewhat reduced rate, in government-owned CONASUPO grocery stores and free at Social Security clinics and hospitals. Pasteurized milk, though more expensive, is generally available, and farmers still ride into the neighborhood from the countryside bringing fresh milk in cans strapped to their saddles. However, most

Los Robles mothers buy powdered milk from the store, which the poorer mothers often overdilute to make it go farther.

In addition to a substantial financial outlay, bottle-feeding requires sterilization of the water with which the powdered milk is mixed. Though mothers are almost universally aware of this, those with little or no schooling are likely to turn off the heat immediately after bringing the water to a boil, thus failing to kill the bacteria. They are also likely to refill nursing bottles without sterilizing them.

Until the 1960s, when breast-feeding for at least a year was still almost universal, mothers employed a variety of weaning techniques, from putting coffee grounds, bitter herbs, or the juice of chili peppers on the nipple to having the child sleep with a grandmother or an older sibling for a while to get him to forget the breast. Though some mothers continue to use these methods, most report that since their babies are already accustomed to the bottle, the transition to full bottle-feeding is accomplished without trouble. Henceforth a child may continue to use a bottle (in addition to drinking from a cup) before naps and at bedtime until he enters kindergarten or even later. Though mothers are certainly aware that a young child needs milk to grow well (*crecer bien*), poorer women report that, unable to afford milk, they routinely substitute gruel or carbonated drinks, which have little nutritional value.

In an older generation, except for the very poor, who, as noted above, often waited much longer, mothers generally introduced solid foods at six months. Today, following current pediatric wisdom, Mexican health professionals are recommending the introduction of solids as early as two months, advice that better-educated Los Robles mothers readily accept. They begin with maize or rice gruel, mashed bananas, and store-bought infant cereal and go on to beans puréed in the blender (an appliance found even in very poor homes) and, as soon as he can grasp them, pieces of tortilla. More affluent mothers may also give their babies apple sauce and puréed beef and chicken livers. Just as the baby had no schedule for nursing or bottle feeding, he has none for meals either. If he fusses, his mother or caretaker will offer him something to eat regardless of the hour. In addition to home-prepared foods, a wide variety of snacks is sold on the streets and in the stores, and small children are constantly asking for—and being given—candy, packaged cakes, tacos, and *raspados* (cones of ice chips soaked in syrup), not to mention sodas. A fussy baby, too, will be given a taste, for mothers are much less interested in the nutritional value—or lack of it—of a snack than in placating their infants.

Because crawling on a dirty floor littered with potentially dangerous objects is hazardous, the sooner a child is upright, the better. As soon as he can sit up, he will be set in a baby walker, which elevates him from the ground. It is believed that if one takes the time to teach him, a baby will learn to walk more quickly. Apart from leading him by the hand, one technique is for the mother to put her "crawler" down in the sun-baked patio and move away, whereupon the heat on his hands and knees forces him to his feet and across the patio to her. Another trick is for the mother to walk backward, offering her child a crust of bread, "to encourage him, just as you would a chicken." Time invested in teaching your first child to walk is thought to be well spent, as he in turn will teach his follower, and so on. One woman recalls regretfully, "I was too busy doing chores to walk around with my daughter. All I had time for was to tell her, 'Come!' She didn't walk till she was fourteen months. If I'd helped her, she'd have learned faster."

In the countryside, mothers tend to be quite casual about toilet training, but in town, where toddlers spend so much time indoors, or if outside, share play space with many others, it is taken more seriously, especially because a child needs to be "dry" by age three to enter kindergarten. Toilet training should not begin until he has started to talk and can understand what the mother is telling him. "Then you put him on the *bacinica* [potty-chair] several times a day," a mother explains, "and teach him baby words for urination and defecation. During the day you take off his diaper and have him run about in underpants, encouraging him to tell you when he wants to 'go.'" Older mothers recall bathing a child who had an "accident" in cold water, but the younger women, remembering the cold baths of their own childhoods as humiliating, refuse to subject their children to them. Though some mothers reported that they slapped their toddlers for wetting themselves, we did not observe this, any more than we heard mothers praise their children for giving them advance warning. Girls, we were told, are easier to train than boys because they soon start to feel ashamed when they wet themselves, whereas boys do not seem bothered. By age eighteen months, children are usually dry in the daytime, but most are not dry at night before age two. In a vecindad where the communal toilets are usually dirty, mothers have small children use the bacinica until they reach school age, if not older.

Mothers sling hammocks from the rafters for their infants, and the more affluent provide cradles and cribs, but these are for daytime naps only. Very few of our informants reported that they slept alone with their husbands while their children were still young. It is believed that a mother's first responsibility is to her baby, and therefore she should sleep with him. Meanwhile, her husband may share a bed with the two of them, but if there are older children, he is much more likely to sleep with them in a separate bed than with his wife and infant. When a couple has inter-course, they place the baby in the hammock or crib and older children in a different bed or on the floor so that for a few moments they can be alone together. "That's how we poor people do it," says Lourdes. "As a kid, did I know what mamá and papá were up to? Of course I did. Did *my* kids know what Luis and I were up to?" She shrugs. "Well, what do you think?" After finishing sexual relations, the couple separates and rearranges the children.

Although a toddler is not moved out of his mother's bed immediately on the arrival of a new sibling, in time a small boy will start sleeping with his father and a small girl with an older sister, aunt, or grandmother who may be living in the household, too. Our older informants often reported never having slept alone in their lives. As children, they shared a bed with parents or siblings and for a short time after marriage, with their husbands; and once their children started coming, with them. As widows, many women choose to sleep with grandchildren, for as one elderly lady who shares her bed with a three-year-old grandson sheepishly admits, "I'd feel lonely sleeping by myself." This is not to say that Los Robles people are unaware of the middle-class practice of putting each child in his own bed in his own room. When building their homes, they, too, provide separate rooms for their children, but in the large majority of families, children continue to sleep with one or other of their parents until they are well into grade school. Meanwhile, as an indication that this reflects a strong cultural preference and not just scarcity of space, the extra bedroom is used as a store.

You should not expect small children to be easy, our informants told us. They are going to have *berrinches* [temper tantrums] and wet their beds; they are going fight with their brothers and sisters and refuse to share their toys. But given maternal firmness and the passage of time, they will learn better. In addition to the conventional run-of-the-mill problems, children nowadays are having others that a generation ago were unknown. Refusing to fall asleep at night is one that mothers often complain about. Inés recalls that when her children were small, they had no bedtime schedule. When they were tired, they simply fell asleep on a lap or in someone's arms, or they stayed up and went to bed with the adults. But whereas thirty years ago, before electricity and television, everyone was in bed by eight-thirty, these days, parents and older children are staying up later, and mothers report that their toddlers are often so alert and active that even after their parents are in bed, they are still roaring around the house. Again, Lourdes recalls, "When we were young we always felt hungry at mealtimes because we were poor and we didn't get much to eat. But people are better off now, and they buy their kids all sorts of snacks, so that when they sit down to dinner, they have no appetite. They're *melindrosos* [finicky]. They're always saying they don't like this or that."

"Kids are so *caprichoso* these days," another grandmother complains, and she points to a newspaper photograph of starving Ethiopians. "Next time my grandchildren refuse to eat the bananas I've bought them and say they want pears, I'll show them that picture!"

Birth Control

Women of the older generation, some of whom had ten or twelve children apiece, regard birth control as nothing short of miraculous. Lactation and abstinence were the only methods of birth control they knew. Traditionally, a husband was supposed to "care for" his wife, that is, abstain from sexual relations not only during the cuarentena but for several months thereafter. This would allow his wife to recover from childbirth and her child to get a good start in life before a new pregnancy deprived him of the breast. Ingham notes, however, that by the 1960s in Tlayacapan, this custom had largely been abandoned by younger couples, and it is our impression that in larger urban centers it had been abandoned even earlier. Thus, while our oldest informants report birth intervals of at least two years, women who were bearing children in the 1950s and 1960s commonly report intervals as short as a year.

Those who were medically advised against having more children long before menopause, lived anxious lives. Catalina was only twenty-seven when, after bearing six children in nine years, she was told that another pregnancy might kill her. As a very religious person, she did not regard sterilization as an option, and in the mid-1950s, contraceptives were unavailable in Mexico except to the sophisticated upper middle class. Thus, for the next twenty years, she had a cousin who lived in Laredo, Texas, send her vaginal suppositories. She did become pregnant once and, in contravention of her religious beliefs, had an abortion, an experience that was traumatic and that she feels guilty about to this day.

Since 1976, a vigorous government-sponsored family planning campaign has been underway in Mexico. The proportion of women of childbearing age using contraceptives rose from 30.2 percent in that year to 44.7 percent in 1982.[5] Due initially to soaring increases in the cost of child rearing and, since 1982, to the economic crisis, most young couples in urban areas today want a much smaller family than the one in which they themselves grew up, and wives want even fewer children than their husbands. When it comes to deciding whether or not to have "one more" child, however, husbands, for many of whom children, costly as they are to raise and educate, are still necessary proof of masculinity, tend to get their way.

In the survey that we carried out in Los Robles in 1983–84, 90 percent of our respondents reported having used a modern form of birth control at some time. The pill (*píldora*), IUD (*dispositivo*), and Dopa Prevera injections are available at nominal or no cost in Social Security and Ministry of Health facilities to any woman who requests them; oral contraceptives are also available in pharmacies, as are condoms, foams, and jellies. At the same time there appears to be a good deal of ignorance about how to use them correctly. Believing that the pill provides protection only on the days she takes them, Matilde reports that on those days that she does not, she avoids intercourse. Irene, convinced that she cannot get pregnant because she has only one ovary, does not use birth control and becomes pregnant with César. Ofelia, meanwhile, who has had three pregnancies in three years, reports that she has tried several contraceptive methods and because of their side effects, has abandoned all of them.

Sterilization by tubal ligation (*salpingo*), the preferred contraceptive method in Mexico,[6] is available to women who are over the age of twenty-five or who have already borne three children. "Two sons are enough," declares Eloisa, just twenty-five, as she waits impatiently to have the procedure. She wants "no more crying children." Matilde, too, is planning to have the salpingo. She insists that four children are all she and her husband, Pedro, can afford. Just as important, once finished with childbearing, she intends to slim down and smarten herself up so that Pedro will again find her attractive, leave his current girlfriend, and return to the conjugal bed. She admits she has not yet discussed the subject of tubal ligation with Pedro. Whether or not they can afford another baby, Pedro, the machista, may still want one.

Abortion, though illegal, is a very common practice, especially among married women. (Because *aborto* refers both to medical termination of pregnancy and miscarriage, it was not always clear to which women were referring.) If her period is delayed and she suspects she is pregnant, a woman may get an injection to regulate her menstrual cycle. Commonly known as *tirando el niño* (throwing out the child), this procedure, which is not defined by the medical authorities or by the woman herself as an abortion, is only effective within two weeks of conception. Thereafter, a pregnant woman may try one of a number of herbal teas, widely used as abortifacents, that she either prepares herself or obtains in the neighborhood. If they fail, she will probably go to a partera. In 1985, the Tortilla Lady was charging seventy dollars (thirty dollars more than for a delivery) to induce an abortion by inserting a screwdriver or a length of rubber tubing into the uterus. Once the abortion was underway, the woman would have herself admitted to a hospital where the process could be medically concluded. Those who could afford double or triple the partera's fee went to one of several neighborhood doctors who were known to perform abortions in their consulting rooms or private clinics.

Health Care

Studies of Mexican folk beliefs and practices have shown that although there is some overlap, by and large, people make clear distinctions between illnesses for which they seek modern medical treatment and those requiring the attention of traditional practitioners.[7] We, too, found that mothers differentiated between *las enfermedades de los doctores* and *las de los curanderos*. Those in the first category, which included diarrhea, vomiting, bronchitis, and high fevers, were thought to require "scientific" attention. The second category included folk illnesses such as *nervios, embrujamiento* (witchcraft), *coraje* (rage), and others, more specific to children, such as *mal de ojo* (evil eye), *empacho* (indigestion), and *susto* or *espanto* (soul loss).

Las enfermedades de los doctores are believed to stem from natural causes, namely (depending on the mother's level of education), from *microbios* (germs) or extremes of heat and cold; treatment should be in a clinic. By contrast, las enfermedades de los curanderos, believed to be "personally" transmitted, should be treated by a folk specialist.

Through the 1960s, smallpox, typhoid, measles, whooping cough, diphtheria, scarlet fever, tetanus, and polio were common killers in Mexico. All of these, as a result of more recent door-to-door immunization campaigns, have either been eradicated or their incidence markedly reduced. Even so, Los Robles mothers unanimously identify childhood illnesses—gastrointestinal and upper respiratory infections, in particular—as their gravest concern, although promptness of response to symptoms varies considerably with level of education. We found that mothers who had completed primary school monitored their children's physical condition more closely and sought medical attention faster than did mothers with less education, a finding that Jiménez Ornelas corroborated in a study of the determinants of under-five mortality in two low-income communities in central Mexico. Thus Luz María, who studied to the eighth grade, worries a great deal about her two-year-old being underweight and spends long hours waiting for him to be seen at the (free) Ministry of Health clinic. When they get to the head of the line, she bombards the medical staff with questions and later berates herself because she cannot afford to buy the special foods the doctor recommended. By contrast, Julia, who dropped out of second grade, is much better off than Luz María and talks incessantly about the toys she plans to buy her children for the feast of the Three Kings. Meanwhile, she seems quite unconcerned by the chest infections from which her toddler suffers one after another. At last she gets worried enough to take him to an expensive private doctor but afterward, repeatedly forgets to give him the medication the doctor prescribed.

Alternatives to Modern Medicine

In the countryside, Soledad recalls, virtually every woman knew how to prepare teas, poultices, and enemas for the treatment of common childhood illnesses. "Mamá was very clever with medicine. She knew which bark was good for indigestion and which leaves were good for bronchitis. She even had an antidote to a scorpion's sting. All this she learned from her mother, who was a curandera, too." In town today, there are still some women who give massages and know how to prepare *remedios caseros* (home remedies), which they provide—usually free of charge—to their neighbors. Their ingredients include herbs and the leaves and bark of trees growing in their patios, animal fats, and oils. Some curanderas still trek out to the edge of town to gather plants in the open countryside; others purchase their materials from *yerberos* (herbalists) in the local market. Some have medicines for several childhood ailments, while others specialize in the treatment of earache, fainting fits, or bleeding anus.

At the Conquest, the Spaniards brought to the New World a set of beliefs, based on a simplified form of Greek humoral pathology, according to which the body required a proper balance between the four bodily fluids or humors, namely, blood, yellow bile, phlegm, and black bile, the first two of which were deemed "hot," and the second "cold."[8] As the onset of disease was thought to indicate a humoral imbalance, medical practice focused on the restoration of harmony by the addition or subtraction of heat and cold through purging, vomiting, bleeding, cupping, and diet as well as medicine.[9] In contemporary Mexico, illnesses such as chest cramps, earaches, headaches, rheumatism, and tuberculosis are still commonly believed to be caused by el aire (a cold draft), while too much heat is thought to cause digestive illnesses, kidney ailments, rashes, and sore eyes and throat. With the exception of diet, however, other aspects of humoral medical practice have been abandoned, and although virtually everyone continues to believe that "cold" illnesses require "hot" foods, and vice versa, we found little agreement as to which foods were which. As one woman explained, "In the country, people used to be very careful about foods—which one should eat when one was ill with such and such and what one shouldn't—but as for myself, I've been living in the city for so long that I've forgotten a lot about those things."

As noted above, some illnesses are believed to be caused by supernatural or magical power transmitted by individuals; for their treatment, one goes to a folk healer. Several mothers reported that their children had suffered from the effects of the evil eye (mal de ojo). The evil eye is transmitted by inheritance or chance contact to unfortunate people who, as a result, have the power to cause malaise in young children. This power is involuntary (those who have it cannot control it and may not even be aware when it is active); thus they are to be pitied as much as their victims. Mothers also reported embrujamiento and, most frequently, susto. One mother recalled that all five of her children had suffered from it, several more than once. An emotional condition that follows a shock or trauma, susto, is very common throughout Latin America and Hispanic communities in the United States. In their study of Indian and mestizo adults in the Valley of Oaxaca, Arthur Rubel and his colleagues[10] found that the onset of susto was closely correlated with inadequate performance of adult social role and a heavier

than ordinary disease load, but just as in Tlayacapan, where Ingham found
that two-thirds of reported cases involved children, in Los Robles, susto
appears to be mainly an affliction of early childhood.

If a child cries for more than an hour and refuses to be comforted, his
mother will conclude that soul loss has occurred and that a *limpia* (cleans-
ing, purification) is necessary. She asks a friend with a forceful character
and strong religious faith to be her *comadre de limpia* and accompany her
and her child to the curandero. At the time of our fieldwork, Father Manuel, a Catholic priest in his eighties, was the best-known curandero de susto
in Cuernavaca. He told us that as an adolescent he had received the Holy
Spirit in his native Guerrero and since that time had been a curandero,
specializing in "family problems" as well as the treatment of susto. Although healing *(curación)* was a priestly function as much as baptism or the
giving of the Eucharist, of late, few priests were willing to undertake it,
which explained why he had gained such a following in recent years. Alleviation of the child's condition was impossible without first pinpointing the
event that had precipitated it. Though the mother herself was often unable
to do this, empowered by the Holy Spirit, the curandero could recall the
exact circumstances in which the child received a shock. Indeed, mothers
would express astonishment over the accuracy with which Father Manuel
described events of which he could have had no prior knowledge. Having
determined the cause of her child's fear to the mother's satisfaction, in a
ritual that he performed on three successive days, the curandero would call
on the Holy Spirit to pass through both him and the comadre into the
afflicted child. The efficacy of the ritual, Father Manuel hastened to point
out to us, depended more on the faith of mother and godmother than on
his own power or prayers.

The Spiritualist temple, which stands on an unpaved street behind the
cemetery, is another source of healing for children as well as adults.
According to Kaja Finkler, the Spiritualist church, which originated early
in this century and has grown steadily throughout Mexico and in the U.S.
border states, "is both a vehemently anti-Catholic religious movement and
a non-biomedical health care system."[11] In their role as healers, the Spiritualists provide treatment for chronic illnesses that modern medicine has
failed to cure, through "emotionally charged symbols, derived from the
sufferers' collective experience, which, even if they fail to eliminate pain,
help make it tolerable." Most congregations are founded by women who
at one point were sick and put themselves at the command of one of four

divinidades (spirit beings) who appeared to them during their illness.[12] On recovery, they became spirit mediums and established temples in which they offer *catedras* (sermons) on Sundays and healing sessions during the week. As Finkler noted, the Spiritualist theory of disease incorporates natural and supernatural phenomena: symptom alleviation is effected by a limpia, a salient cultural practice that ritually terminates the sick role.

Since it was founded in the 1950s, the Spiritualist temple in Los Robles has grown from a shack into a spacious two-story building. Healing sessions—for which there is no charge—are held there on Tuesday and Friday afternoons in a large room over the temple itself. Usually three curanderos (male and female) are on duty under the supervision of Doña Gloria, the temple's founder and director. Though a sprinkling of better-off people may be present, most of those seeking treatment are women and children from the poorest class. Given the anti-Catholic position of the Spiritualists, our informants tended to express considerable reservation about them. Nevertheless, many admitted taking their children to their healing sessions. Some went out of desperation, after trying medical treatment without success; others, because they lacked health insurance and were too poor to go to a doctor or even to pay the nominal fee charged by the Ministry of Health clinic. But just as the efficacy of the susto healing ritual depends on the faith of the child's mother and her comadre, so, too, Doña Gloria told us, "without faith our limpia has no effect."

Religious pilgrimage, too, is viewed as a way to health. People from Los Robles regularly make pilgrimages to sacred places throughout Mexico to request all manner of boons (*hacer pedidos*) and to give thanks (*dar gracias*) in the event they are granted. Frequently the health of their children is the issue. The two sacred places most often visited are the shrines of the Virgin of Guadalupe at La Villa in Mexico City and of El Señor de Chalma in the state of Mexico. Both places of pilgrimage in pre-Columbian times, they received Christian rationales soon after the Conquest and have remained the most important centers of popular religion ever since.[13] Though pilgrimages may be made throughout the year, December 12, the anniversary of the apparition of the Virgin before the Indian, Juan Diego, at the Aztec shrine on the same site, is the preferred day for going to La Villa; Holy Week and May 3, the fiesta of Santa Cruz, for visiting Chalma.

Eloisa recalls going to Chalma several times by bus. On one occasion, however, when her son, Abram, was very ill, she promised El Señor that if he recovered, she would take him across the mountains to Chalma on foot.

He did recover, and the following Holy Week, feeling extremely fearful, since she had heard many stories about pilgrims losing their way and falling to their deaths in the ravines on either side of the mountain path, she set off with her husband, Abram, and Abram's padrino de bautizo. As it turned out, tiring though it was, she thoroughly enjoyed the journey. The cooperation and sense of solidarity among the pilgrims made a deep impression on her. "It was an experience that drew us all together," she says. Looking back, she marvels that she walked so far, "but if something's very important, somehow you find the strength."

Parent-Child Relations

The formality that once characterized parent-child relations is less evident today. Whereas in an earlier generation children addressed their parents as *usted* (the formal "you"), nowadays in Los Robles one hears *tú*. Catalina notes with envy that her daughter and nine-year-old granddaughter embrace when they take leave of one another in the morning and again when they are reunited in the afternoon. "I wasn't brought up like that at all," she says. "My mother was my *jefa* [boss]. When I had children of my own, even though I wanted to be affectionate and quite different from the way mamá had been with me, I was shy. Something was always holding me back." Inés, too, enviously watches the exchange of affection between her daughters and their children. "When my kids were young, I was always so busy," she remarks. "I didn't have time to appreciate them or teach them anything that wasn't essential." When they were small, she taught them how to greet people properly and how to say good-bye. "Even little ones have to know that," she says. But she did not have the time to tell them stories or to read to them. "I had to save that for my grandchildren." She does not deny that her daughters lead stressful lives. Besides working just as hard as she did and coping with difficult husbands, they worry about how to attain and maintain a standard of living of which she never conceived. But for all that, she says, with family planning, they have only two or three children—instead of the tribe she had—and thus more time to be friends with them. Indeed, watching mothers and children, we often observed an ease and pleasure in each other's company such as our informants regretfully reported had been lacking in their own early lives.

As it is generally believed that naughtiness and disobedience should be dealt with on the spot, mothers, who are at home all day, are usually the disciplinarians. Most regard physical punishment as a natural and essential component of child rearing. By sparing the rod, you spoil the child, and once spoiled, a child will give you nothing but trouble. Older women report beginning in the first year of life with light spankings (*nalgadas*) on the hands and buttocks; by the time a child was two or three, they would be using a switch and by four, a belt. Now, with their children long grown, they say that if they erred, it was on the side of not being firm enough, especially with their sons. "I ought to have been harder on Andrés," says Inés of her oldest son, "but most of the time he was growing up, my husband wasn't around, so I had to handle him by myself." She goes on, "The trouble began when he was ten and I caught him stealing from my purse. He said he wanted money to go to a fair, and so to teach him a lesson, I made him take a job after school as a delivery boy. I let him keep what he earned—it was never more than a few centavos—in the hope that if he had his own spending money, he wouldn't steal from me again, but he kept on doing it." She couldn't beat him—he was taller than she was by that time—so, at her wits end, she sent him to seminary. "But the monks said he had no vocation and sent him back!"

Most of the younger mothers, too, regard physical punishment as right and necessary. "I've already given my daughter [aged four] two thrashings today," one announces. "She does what she wants, and she had to understand that in life you can't keep on doing that." "I don't want any *chillones* [whiny kids] here," another declares as she swats at her three-year-old son. But some mothers express guilt about physical punishment. Luz María admits to threatening two-year-old Héctor with a slipper but adds hastily, "I only do it to make him listen. I rarely carry out my threat. I don't want him to be afraid of me like I was of my parents. I want him to be *más como mi amigo que como mi hijo* [more like my friend than my son]." Of her handling of eight-year-old Abram, Eloísa says shamefacedly, "It's always *gritos, insultos, nalgadas; gritos, insultos, nalgadas* [screams, insults, slaps], and afterward I feel terrible." As adolescence draws nearer and children grow as tall and strong as their mothers, beatings taper off. Instead, mothers try talking to their children, and punishment consists of forbidding them to go out with their friends. But as one woman admits, "There's not much you can do to influence teenagers, especially boys. They already have their way of being [*forma de ser*]." As a last resort, you can send them to live with relatives in another neighborhood or even another town, in the hope that after cooling their heels, they will listen.

Even though from babyhood, you have tried to handle sons and daughters identically, they turn out differently, mothers insist. Boys are more *inquietos y tercos* (restless and stubborn); girls, *dulces y más cumplidas* (sweeter and more tractable). And though there certainly are girls who are restless and stubborn as well as boys who are sweet and tractable (qualities that mothers appreciate), on the whole, girls are easier to raise than boys. Mothers also insist that from an early age, children manifest certain character traits *(rasgos)*, and there is little one can do to change them. Lourdes says of her son, Fernando, "From when he was little he was headstrong. I beat him, I pleaded with him, I locked him in the house, but nothing made any difference." He grew up to be a drunkard and a womanizer, and though she grieves about him and for the harm he does himself and others, she does not blame *herself* for how he has turned out. You do your best to point your children in the right direction. More than that, you cannot do.

The mother-child relationship may be warmer and more egalitarian than it was in the past, but most working-class fathers still keep their distance. Though they may enjoy playing with infants and going on outings with older children, day-to-day involvement seems to have little appeal. Apart from el gasto, women of the older generation report that they expected no help from their husbands with the care and upbringing of children—and received none. But younger women see things differently. One speaks for many when she says, "I'm the only one who watches out for the children. Carlos just drops off my housekeeping money, then he's gone again. But the children need their father's attention as well as mine!" Indeed, a desire for husbands to play a more important role in domestic life is often expressed. Instead of being out with their cuates, or—worse yet—with la otra, these young mothers want them at home. They want help with child care and discipline and, later on, with decisions about schooling, occupational choice, and employment. As Matilde says with a sigh of frustration, "My husband shouldn't leave everything to me." This new model of parenting comes in part from the media. Television, which almost everyone watches several hours a day, presents an image of the middle-class family in which the father is on intimate and affectionate terms with offspring of all ages. It also comes from the slow but steady erosion of the wall between domestic and working worlds, the world of men and the world of women, and from necessity. Raising children is becoming an increasingly complex and challenging enterprise. To do it takes two parents, the younger women insist.

Child Rearing in the City

Help with Child Care and Domestic Tasks

Our informants, most of whom have lived for long periods with or next door to kin, report that help with small children is rarely offered. "It isn't like in the countryside," one woman explains. "There you'll find more cooperation than you do in town." When help is offered, it comes at a price, says Luz María, who lives in the same vecindad as her mother-in-law and two sisters-in-law. She prefers to take care of her son on her own, with occasional help from her husband, rather than listen to their criticism. Most mothers insist that one can only depend on help from one's own older children, and, as primary school draws to an end, only from daughters; the streets, they say, will claim the boys. Ofelia reports that whereas until recently, her son Roberto performed his chores willingly, now that he has turned ten she has to bargain with him to get them done. Girls Roberto's age, meanwhile, often see their work loads increase exponentially, to a point that by the end of primaria, they are spending four or five hours on household chores each day. When we asked sixth-grade girls (twelve-year-olds) what they wanted most, many replied, "time to play."

Rites of Passage

Everyone celebrates birthdays and saints' days, albeit very simply. Recalling her own birthdays as a child, Catalina says that her parents and siblings would sing Las Mañanitas (Happy Birthday to You), and the family would eat mole or pozole and maquasote, a sweet bread that her mother baked in a can in the ashes of the cooking fire. "I always received a little present, too." Flipping through an album of photographs of her own children standing beside many-candled cakes, dressed in their best, Lourdes says, "In my family we used to make something special out of birthdays, and when I had kids, I did, too." This tradition continues to flourish in the new generation. Sixty guests attended the party Lourdes's daughter, Rocío, gave to celebrate her daughter Pati's first birthday. Following a photographic session in the patio, decorated with balloons and paper streamers, for which Pati wore three different outfits, dancing to a stereo began and continued past midnight, by which time the birthday girl had been asleep for several hours. A trestle table ran down the center of the patio, at which guests—ten were Rocío's compañeros from the textile factory where she worked, the rest, relatives—sat in shifts to eat two enormous cakes (one chocolate, one vanilla), followed by pozole that Lourdes had been preparing for three days and jello molds. Coca-Cola, beer, and brandy were also served. To Rocío, a single mother, it was of the utmost importance to demonstrate to her family— who had condemned her for having a child out of wedlock—that a year later she and her daughter were doing well.

Each child requires padrinos for the sacramental rites of childhood (baptism, confirmation, and first communion), the observance of which, as far as working-class people were concerned, used to be confined to the church itself. But as living standards have risen, it has become mandatory, even in poor families, for the child's parents to honor their compadres with an elaborate meal. Long in advance of her daughter's first communion, Julia decides to serve roast pork and brandy (as well as beer) at the party to follow; and several dozen guests will dance to live music (rather than a stereo). But by the time she has saved enough money, instead of eight or nine (the usual age at first communion), the girl is almost twelve years old.

In recent years, another religious rite of passage, the *presentación*, has been added to the list. At age three, dressed in a tiny tuxedo or a white crinoline, a child is presented to God at a special mass, followed by a party. "I never heard of such a thing when I was raising my kids," one grandmother declares, "but now all the parents want them. One of my granddaughters was very young for her age, so I said, 'Wait till she's five when she'll be able to manage an occasion like that.' But my son and daughter-in-law wouldn't listen; they went ahead, and the child had a tantrum right there at the church door!" By contrast, Catalina's grandson, Israel, behaved like a perfect little gentleman at his presentación, which was attended by fifty-five guests.

These days, the completion of each stage of the educational process also requires a madrina (but not a padrino) and a festive meal. When a child graduates from kindergarten at age six, his mother selects a godmother for him, and another when he graduates from elementary school. On each occasion, the madrina presents the graduate with an arrangement of paper flowers, and in return, his parents entertain her at dinner. Although these are much smaller affairs than the party following a baptism or first communion, the same expensive food is served. "When this custom with the paper flowers came in, I told my kids, 'Look, if that's what you want, I'll buy you them myself and save the money for the comida,'" Inés recalls. "But nowadays, when the time comes for their children to graduate, parents feel pressured to do things the right way."

Schooling

Without exception, these mothers believe that the acquisition of a trade or profession is a young person's most important goal. Inés, raising nine children in the 1950s and 1960s with sporadic support from her husband, vividly recalls the sacrifices she made so that her oldest son could get an education. "These days, kids study either in the mornings or in the afternoons, so they can get a little half-time job and bring some money in. But when my children were young, the school day was much longer. They went to school from eight till three, with a break for lunch, and after they came home they had a lot of homework. A child either went to school or he went to work," she explains. "There wasn't time in the day to do both. Often I'd say to myself, 'If Andrés were bringing home a wage, life would be easier for all of us.'" Although a lot of other women she knew let their sons drop out, Inés believed that his only hope of getting ahead—and the rest of her children's, too—was through education. She managed to keep him in school long enough to get his primary certificate. "Then he went to work and helped educate the others," she says. "That's how we did it. As soon as one child finished, he went to work to help his follower."

Today, almost all children in Cuernavaca complete six years of primary school. Of those who go further (86% in 1982),[14] a large majority complete three years of secundaria, and many go still further. To accommodate such high enrollments, state schools have two daily sessions of five hours each—as opposed to only one of seven hours when Inés's children were going to school. Although by law, children under the age of fifteen are forbidden to work, one-third of the sixth and ninth graders whom we surveyed in 1983 held part-time jobs. The girls worked as maids, sales clerks, and machine operators in tortillerías, the boys as supermarket baggers, mechanics' assistants, gardeners, and dishwashers. Some reported giving half their earnings to their mothers, but most kept their money to pay for clothes, school uniforms, books, and transportation.

Though some mothers talk in terms of wanting their sons to learn an oficio (trade) and their daughters to complete a carrera corta (short training) in practical nursing or kindergarten teaching, for example, others are more

Mother and children

ambitious. Rosa dreams of her son becoming a pilot, Verónica of her daughter becoming a doctor; Irene wants her oldest son to be an engineer and Luz María talks about moving to the United States so that her son, Héctor, will grow up bilingual. As Frances Rothstein, who worked in the neighboring state of Mexico, noted, the myth of mobility through education is extremely powerful, and even though, in a deeply depressed economy, almost every professional field is flooded, parents are not about to discard it.[15]

In most families, it is up to the mother to supervise homework. One barely literate young mother fusses over her daughter as she struggles to make sense of her science assignment, confusing the child even further. Another, who dropped out of school in the third grade, tells her son who is failing arithmetic, "You have to keep trying. I wish I had!" If a poorly educated mother can rely on her oldest child to help his younger siblings, all may be well, but too often, a child who at six and seven years of age could not wait to go to school in the morning is beginning to get lazy at eight and nine, a tendency that intensifies in adolescence when girls get distracted by boys and boys by life in the streets. It is usually up to mothers, too, to deal with the school authorities. They register their children at the beginning of each academic year, attend fund raisers, and meet with teach-

Family vecindad

ers about their children's progress. For their part, teachers tend to look down on parents as ignorant and irresponsible, a view that some do not bother to conceal. Not surprisingly, then, mothers are reluctant to go to talk to them, and when weeks if not months go by before they respond to a summons, they confirm the teacher's prejudices. "These people just don't care about their children's education," they complained to us, an assertion that in most cases could not be further from the truth.

Street life: dancing to a cassette recorder

Two Women's Experiences of Motherhood

SOLEDAD, a slight woman of forty-nine, has borne twelve children, nine of whom survive. Her black hair falls well below her waist. "Despite all the grief I've had, I have no *canas* [gray hair]," she observes, sounding slightly bemused. Her face, though lined, is still beautiful. Ashamed of her few remaining discolored teeth, she has a habit of holding her hand in front of her mouth as she speaks. A reserved but gracious hostess, she retains the shy formality of the countryside from which she came to Cuernavaca at age thirteen.

Her household consists of herself, three teenage children, four out-of-wedlock grandchildren, and four married children and their families—twenty-one people on a property ten meters by five, sitting astride a public footpath that runs beside a stream into which everyone in the neighborhood dumps their garbage. From dawn until late at night, people are continually walking through the narrow patio that lies between Soledad's house and her corrugated iron kitchen. A few passersby greet her, but most walk through in silence.

Soledad's first child, Laura, was born in 1951 and her twelfth, Manuel, in 1970. All but the two youngest children were born at home with the help of a partera. After delivery, her maternal grandmother who lived close by would help her for a few days, but her mother, who also lived in the neighborhood and for some years in the same house, never offered to help. "She's not that sort of person," Soledad remarks with a shrug. Her third child died in infancy, her fourth and fifth children in early childhood. As she did not have the money to take them to the doctor, she is not sure why they died. "Let's say, it was lack of medical attention."

Soledad had her children close together—eleven in sixteen years—and because she was too poor to buy milk, she would continue nursing until she was about to give birth again, when she would rub a bitter herb on her nipple. "That way the baby would learn that the breast wasn't good for him any more. . . . And then suddenly, there was another baby, and he'd be so sad."

She says she would have been happy to have had only five children. "Five one can afford to feed." But she went on having babies, because "in those days women didn't know how not to." Josefina, her eleventh child, was a breach birth, and after a very difficult labor, she went to the Hospital Civil to give birth. She bled for many months afterward, and the doctor warned that she might die if she had another child. The only way she knew to avoid getting pregnant was by abstinence, which led to constant fighting with her husband, Jorge. Soon she was pregnant again, and after Manuel was born she was sicker than ever and so weak for so long that her older children despaired for her life. It was during that period that Jorge started spending almost all his time in Santa María, a village on the outskirts of Cuernavaca, two hours' walk above Los Robles, where he had borrowed some land. "He also had another woman there," says Soledad. "He'd call out her name in his sleep: 'Alejandra, Alejandra!'" But as Soledad never went up to the village, she never saw her.

After a few years, Alejandra left Jorge, who soon replaced her with a widow whose children are all grown up and gone. But despite having another woman, Jorge continues to come down to Los Robles every couple of weeks with his donkey, Tobaco, loaded with corn and charcoal and Soledad's housekeeping money in his pocket. Usually he leaves after eating, but if he is sick or drunk, he spends the night. Now that some of their sons are grown up and can protect her, he does not beat Soledad any more. But from time to time, he still demands his conjugal rights, and for fear that if she refuses him he will deprive her of the little money he gives her, she complies with his wishes. "I used to lie there with him thinking, 'If I get pregnant I'll die and then who'll take care of these kids?'" she says. Only since reaching menopause a couple of years ago does she no longer dread sexual relations.

Soledad first met Jorge, an illiterate boy who worked with his father making charcoal, when she lived in the mountains above Cuernavaca. When she moved into town, they started courting in secret. He loved her very much, she remembers, while for her part she pitied him, knowing that his mother was dead and his father was a drunkard. At seventeen, he, too, was already a heavy drinker, but she told herself, "It's because he misses his mamá so much and he's sad. Once we're married, he won't need to drink any more." Unhappy at home with her mother and stepfather, Trinidad, who, as she approached puberty, had started sexually molesting her, she thought that marriage offered a way out. And so at fifteen she eloped with Jorge to Los Robles, to a one-room shack divided by sheets of cardboard into four small cubicles that he shared with his father and seven younger siblings. "When I went with Jorge, I'd had my period once," Soledad recalls. Five months later, already pregnant with Laura, she and Jorge were married by the parish priest. Only after they had twelve children together did they have a civil ceremony. "The law used to require a birth certificate," Soledad explains, "and coming from the country, we had none." It was only after the law was changed that they married.

Far from giving up drinking at marriage as Soledad had anticipated, Jorge drank harder. When he got drunk he would beat his wife, and instead of going out and earning a living, he would stay at home with a hangover.

Soledad's first five children were born in her father-in-law's shack. "There were so many of us living there," she recalls, "and yet I had nobody to help me. As my suegra was dead and Jorge's brothers weren't married, there was no woman in that place with whom I could leave my kids, so whenever I went to the river to do the washing, I had to take them all with me. It was a nightmare," she recalls.

She joined a tanda in her neighborhood, into which each month she invested the small amounts of money that she earned as a laundress, planning to buy a plot of land when her number came up. But before it did, she and her family were out in the street. "My suegro said he wanted to enjoy his last days, so he sold his place, spent every cent of the money on alcohol, and within a few months was dead." For almost a year, Soledad and her children moved around from one relative to another, waiting for her number to come up, and when it did she took her three thousand pesos and an additional sum borrowed from a cousin and bought the plot on which she and her family live today. Lying along a polluted stream, in a ravine that little sunlight enters, it is one of the least desirable house sites in the neighborhood, but it was the best she could afford. Though Jorge had not contributed to its purchase, as head of household, he put his thumbprint to the sale agreement, and so by law he, not Soledad, is sole owner. Some years ago, at Laura's urging, Soledad engaged a lawyer to press her rights to the property, but, she reports, "That man did nothing for me except take my money."

When the family moved onto the plot it was December, the coldest time of the year. To begin with, they lived in a hut hastily constructed of cardboard and wooden crates. Soledad took Laura, then aged nine, out of school and put her to work in a tortillería. The girl gave three-quarters of her wages to her mother, who put the money into the tanda, and whenever her number came up, she would buy materials—lumber, nails, corrugated iron sheets—for a permanent house. At that time there was no electricity in Los Robles, and they had to carry water from a spigot half a mile away (piped water and electricity were installed in the 1970s). Primitive though these conditions were, they were an improvement over where they had lived before. Three of her children had died there, but once she was in her own place, she lost no more.

As her husband has lived apart from her most of their married life, Soledad has had to bring up their children virtually on her own. "Even when he comes, he pays no attention to the children," she says. "He just eats and sleeps here. That's all he's ever done, apart from quarrel with me." Whether or not their children got to school did not matter to him, she says. But nothing matters more to her, and she has done everything in her power to see that her children get an education. "That's the only way poor people have to get ahead." With the exception of Laura and Victoria, a year younger, who was so inquieta that after three months she had to be taken out of primary school, all her children have studied up to secundaria, and two beyond. "And yet none of them is ambitious," she says with a deep sigh. "Other people's children salen adelante [get ahead] and help their parents, but none of mine has. . . . Things are very bad economically right now, and yet, instead of going out and looking for work, my sons stay home. They say it isn't worth their while to look for work because there is none."

In effect, when Laura left the tortillería to get married four years ago, Soledad lost her only reliable wage earner. Now her hopes are pinned on her two youngest children, Josefina, sixteen, and Manuel, thirteen, who both go to school in the morning and work in the afternoon. At present, after paying their expenses, they have nothing left to give their mother, but one day in the not too distant future . . .

Soledad's own children are almost all grown up, but she still has four out-of-wedlock grandchildren to raise. Of their mother, Victoria, she says, "While the others were learning, she was here at home with me until, at fourteen, she went to work with her sister in the tortillería." With a shake of the head, Soledad continues, "After that, she was callejera, always in the streets, first with this one, then with that one, and all of them were married men. . . . When Jorge discovered she was pregnant, he flew into a terrible rage—with me as much as with her. . . . The next time she got pregnant, he broke three of *my* ribs. After she delivered, I thought, 'Whatever happens, she mustn't get pregnant again because if she does, Jorge will kill us both!' I was so scared that I tethered her to a post in the patio, as one would a goat, but she escaped, and sure enough, before long she was pregnant. . . . When Martita was born, what could I do but accept her, just as I'd accepted the others . . . and after Martita came Carlos."

Soledad pauses. "As she doesn't love them, it was better for them to stay with me than go with her when she got married. These *chamacos* understand that she's their mother, but it's me they call Mamá." Meanwhile, Victoria, who lives in a neighboring colonia with her husband, a much older man, and their two children, comes to her mother's house almost every day. To an observer, she looks unkempt and seems distracted, and her speech is sometimes garbled. Her children appear markedly less well cared for than the four who are living with Soledad. "She comes because she's restless, not because she wants to see the kids she left with me," her mother confides. "When she's here, she ignores them." Nor does she help support them, even though her husband, alone among Soledad's four sons-in-law, earns a fairly decent living.

Soledad has watched many TV programs about health and nutrition, and she knows that her grandchildren's small stature is due to poverty and poor diet. "Martita's nearly eight, but she looks like a five-year-old, and Carlos, who's six, looks four," she remarks. "When they were little, to make it go further, I'd mix their Nido [powdered milk] with too much water, and so they didn't grow well. I should be giving them fruit and eggs, but I can't afford to." Small as it is, she cannot afford the Ministry of Health clinic fee either, and so when the children are sick, she asks Laura to take them to the parish clinic where medicines—which have been donated and are sometimes out of date—are given to patients without charge, sometimes to the Spiritualist temple.

Meanwhile, she struggles to educate them, just as she did her own children, a task that she admits may be beyond her. After Rosalía, the oldest of Victoria's fracasos, had repeated third grade three times, the school put her out. "Since then I've tried to get her to go to evening classes," says Soledad, "but she refuses. The law says she has to keep studying till her fifteenth birthday, but she knows no one's going to run after her. . . . So there she is, out of school before she's even learned to read properly!" Miguel, ten, and Martita, seven, are in primaria. Carlos ought to be in kindergarten, but as his grandmother cannot afford to buy him a uniform, he has never been enrolled. His older siblings also "skipped" kindergarten, for the same reason: no money for uniforms.

Soledad managed to find padrinos for each of her children, all of whom have been baptized and confirmed. "To begin with, when we were all poor together, our compadres respected us," she says. "But after a while, when they went ahead and we stayed back, they started to look down on us. . . . They were afraid we'd ask them for favors, which, as our compadres, they'd be obliged to grant, and so when my kids went knocking at their doors— and padrinos are supposed to answer to their ahijados—they wouldn't respond, as if they weren't at home. When they moved out of Los Robles without telling us where they were going, it was clear they weren't interested in knowing us any more." Of her grandchildren, only the older two have been baptized. "For Rosalía and Miguel I found a woman to be their madrina who didn't know our family all that well so she was unaware of what Victoria's really like. But for the other two, I couldn't think of anyone. . . . Comadres have to respect each other, and no one can respect Victoria."

Ashamed of being looked down on for her poverty, she has virtually nothing to do with people other than immediate kin. "Mamá comes most days because she doesn't have anything better to do. She never helps me, though, she just passes through." Of her five siblings living nearby, none comes to visit and she does not visit them. "I had a good friend once," she says wistfully. "It was she who invited me into the tanda. She was such a good woman, so *comprensiva* [understanding], but now she's dead."

Apart from her daughters Laura, who lives in the room she and her husband built overhead, and Carolina, who lives across the patio, Soledad's closest companions are her grandchildren. "When they're small, children are so nice," she says. "But later they change, they become rebellious and they don't want to stay with you any more. If you wait long enough, a daughter may become your friend again, but a son never does. When boys go to the street, they're gone for good. . . . I used to shout at my kids but *coraje* (anger) makes my blood pressure go up. I can't breathe and I feel as if I'm going to die. It's better not to get upset like that. . . .

"I look at these little ones (as she speaks, Carlos and Martita are cuddled up, one on either side of her) and I know they'll turn away from me one day. . . . I've seen it happen so often that I should be used to it by now. I should be tired of kids and their problems. I should be happy when the youngest ones get big and off my hands, but no, I tell you, I'll feel very sad."

VERÓNICA, a lively, gregarious woman of thirty, lives in a vecindad with her four daughters and two sons. For the past several years, her common-law husband, Rubén, has been stationed in Chilpancingo, the capital city of Guerrero, five hours away from Cuernavaca, where he works as a driver for the federal government. An affectionate husband and father, he usually visits his family on weekends. Verónica has never seen the place where he lives in Chilpancingo—she does not even know his street address—but believes he has another woman there. "I don't know if I'm the first wife or the second," she says. When a neighbor is shocked to discover that her own husband is having an affair, Verónica tells her, "I went through that, too. I suffered a lot, but I stuck with it and now I'm happy again." So long as Rubén provides for her and her family, she claims she will not worry about *la otra*.

She likes to talk about Rubén's generosity to her and the children and to boast about the toys he brings at the feast of Los Reyes. She derives great satisfaction, too, from her bank account in which she keeps the "cushion" that she has built up over the years by exaggerating her expenses to her husband and getting him to give her more money than she needs. She is proud that Rubén has bought two pieces of property, one near her parents in Cuautla and the other in his hometown, Jonacatepec. On the second he has built a shop, and he wants Verónica to move there to manage it, but she adamantly refuses. She will not go to her parents' either, she declares. She wants him to buy a (much more expensive) plot in Cuernavaca. Confident that by and by, he will comply with her wishes, she daydreams about the house she will build with three bedrooms, a *sala*, a *comedor*. . . . In the meantime, she and her six children are living in one room in a vecindad, but she hastens to point out how much larger it is than their neighbors' rooms and that, instead of having to share with dozens of others, they have their own toilet and shower.

Rubén is Verónica's second husband. When she was seventeen, she eloped with a boy from her hometown and married him *por lo civil*. Within a month, her new husband had left her for another girl, and so, already pregnant, Verónica returned to her mother and stepfather. After she gave birth to her daughter, she discovered that her parents had made arrangements to have the baby adopted by a North American couple, but in the face of her suicide threat, they abandoned their plans because as she says, "They knew I was capable of doing it."

Leaving her baby with her mother by day, she went to work in a factory in Cuautla and there met her present husband, Rubén. "It was love at first sight," she recalls. Later, pregnant with his child, she joined him in Cuernavaca and gave birth to a son. She and Rubén have never been formally married. In the first place, as she was never divorced from her first husband, she is not free to marry, and second, though he has never come out and said so (and she has never asked), Rubén may not be free to marry either.

Verónica's desire to have a large family is unusual for a woman of her generation and level of education. It seems to stem from a wish to compete with her mother who, though she gave birth six times, lost all but two children; perhaps, too, it comes from her lonely childhood. In any event, her attempts to use birth control have been at best halfhearted. She gave up the pill because it made her gain weight and made her skin blotchy and the IUD, because it hurt her. At one point, she considered tubal ligation but decided against it after she heard that when women over thirty—her own age—get their tubes tied, they have trouble. What kind of trouble? She can't say exactly. . . . Perhaps she will get (Dopa Prevera) injections instead. Rubén, meanwhile, welcomes each addition to the family. "I'll just have to work harder so that all the children get ahead," he says cheerfully.

Verónica is fastidious about hygiene. "My neighbor teases me because I change my baby's diaper three times during the night, but unlike her baby, mine can't stand being wet!" She adds proudly, "Whenever I take her to school, the teachers always ask to hold her because she smells so sweet." Indeed, arriving before eight in the morning, a visitor finds all her children bathed and dressed. She apologizes for not taking more pains with her own

appearance, hastening to add that when she does, "I'm often proposi-
tioned. Because Don Rubén is away so much, men think I'll go with them,
but I always send them packing. I'm not the kind of mother who waits till
her kids are asleep so she can do those disgusting things!" Her energies, she
insists, are focused on the welfare of her children.

Their health especially concerns her. Through Rubén, who is a government employee, she and the children have access to the ISSSTE program,
and she is forever taking one child or another to the clinic. Once there, she
knows how to "work the system" to receive attention promptly instead of
waiting for hours in line.

As neither she nor her husband has close relatives in the city, the only
help she can count on is from her children. She wants her sons as much as
her daughters to learn how to run a house, for, as she says, "I'm not going to
be with them their whole lives." Though all but the smallest have their
chores, the main burden falls on Beatriz, her twelve-year-old daughter from
her first marriage. She delegates much of the washing, cooking, and infant
care to her, and since the other children are still too young to go out in the
street alone, it is Beatriz who runs all the errands. The minute Verónica
leaves, Beatriz, who is usually very quiet, starts ordering her siblings about
in imitation of her mother. And, just as with her mother, her orders often
fall on deaf ears.

In her frustration, Verónica is continually taking swipes at her children.
"I like to hit them with the slipper because it only leaves a mark for a
moment," she explains. But if they continue to defy her, she uses a belt,
which leaves a welt. "I can't stand it when they don't listen, and I can't
stand it when they yell either. Whining I can tolerate, but I lose my temper
when they yell. I get so mad, I'll beat them on the back of the legs, the face,
anywhere! If they try to run away, I beat them on the soles of their feet."
She hopes that when her children are older, she will be able to reason with
them, but so far, she cannot; and so with physical punishment her only
tactic for dealing with misbehavior, she hits her kids if they keep on asking
for something that she cannot buy right away, if they are slow to catch onto
what she has been trying to teach them, or if they wet the bed. Or if they
get poor grades.

To Verónica, nothing is more important than education. "It's good to be
something in life—unlike me, who's nobody," she says, and her eyes fill
with tears as she recalls her own school days. She was a good student, and
when she finished secundaria, she was offered an athletic scholarship to a

teacher's college in the northern part of the country; but her mother insisted that she refuse it on the grounds that she would be going too far away. And why would a girl want so much education anyway? "If I'd taken that scholarship, I wouldn't be a housewife and your servant," she tells her children bitterly. "Or at least, if I were a housewife, I'd be a housewife with a degree after my name."

In her own case, she says, she received no encouragement, but she is going to see to it that her children receive all the encouragement they need to go as far as they are capable of going! Children, she declares, are not naturally smart. "You have to pull intelligence out of them. That's why I scold mine so much." She closely supervises their homework, berating them loudly when they are distracted or make mistakes. "You're lucky, having me to help you," she tells them. "As your grandmother couldn't even read, I had to do my homework all on my own."

So eager is she that her children get ahead, that she falsifies one child's birth certificate so he can enter school a year early. Meanwhile, long in advance, she worries about Beatriz's examinations. "The girl works so slowly," she complains. "She won't be able to answer all the questions in the time allowed. Maybe, to help her stay calm, I should give her a tranquilizer on the morning of the exam."

Verónica is intelligent, energetic, meticulous. A curandera, her remedies for indigestion and the evil eye are much in demand in the neighborhood. Her advice to distraught wives is listened to and heeded. She is clever with money: she plans, she budgets, she achieves long-range goals. Her talents may be better suited to running a business than raising a family, however. She wants things done her way every time. Her vivacity has a brittle edge, and beneath her determined manner there seems to lurk a hurt and lonely little girl. Nevertheless, her marriage appears to accommodate both her longing for love and her desire for independence. She only sees her husband for a few days each month, and as she does not live with him, she is able to keep her ambivalence about him almost out of consciousness. But she does live with her children, and problems do arise from her relationship with them. She enjoys being pregnant; her steadfastness during childbirth is a source of pride, and she insists she finds babies enchanting. But when they get older and—inevitably—start to thwart her, she has great difficulty controlling her anger. She claims she wants to be friends with her children, but by insisting on being their jefa, she squelches their affection. Surrounded by them, she tends to feel isolated and trapped. "If only I weren't just a mother," she laments. "If only I'd taken up that scholarship and made something of myself!"

Summary

Raising children in the 1980s was a rather different undertaking from what it had been a generation ago. With contraception, childbearing had become an option rather than an inevitability, and the medicalization of health care had made childbirth itself and the rearing of children less harzardous. As living standards rose and modern medical care became available to most city dwellers, infant and child mortality rates had plunged, reducing maternal preoccupation with survival. Many mothers now chose to forgo breastfeeding, almost universal in the working class only twenty-five years ago, in favor of easily available infant formula. Traditional sleeping arrangements, by which the mother shared a bed with her young child in order to monitor him as closely as possible, remained largely unchanged, however. A mother was still more likely to sleep with her baby or toddler than with her husband. It may well be that this prolonged experience of physical intimacy in infancy and early childhood instilled a conviction that contact with others was pleasurable and so contributed much to the warmth and sociability characteristic of Mexicans generally and of working class Mexicans in particular.

But if the survival of children was now considerably more assured than it had been a generation ago, child rearing presented other challenges. Preparing children for adult roles in an urban industrial society required greater investments of parental time, thought, and economic resources than ever before. Traditional approaches to parenting were no longer adequate to a task which, as in the past, mothers tackled largely alone. Of necessity, the younger mothers in this study appeared to be more self-reliant than, by their own account, the older women were at their age and lifestage. Shouldering almost total responsibility for the household, these young mothers received less practical support than women of the older generation claimed they had had when they were raising small children. If in the past, female kin helped each other in the postpartum period and with routine child care later on, by the 1980s, this was much less common.

Looking back on parent-child relations in their own childhood and remembering them as formal and reserved, our informants often expressed a desire to be emotionally closer to their children than their parents had been to them, and in this many appeared to be successful. By contrast, even if fathers were involved with smaller children, as they got older and more demanding, paternal contact decreased, a situation about which mothers bitterly complained. For though a young husband might see no good reason to alter traditional sex roles whereby he provided and his wife cared for their children, his wife was eager for change. She wanted both a more attentive and communicative husband and companion, and a more responsive partner with whom to share the concerns that raising a family entailed.

· 5 ·

Se Acaba la Lucha: Widowhood and Old Age

In 1960, life expectancy at birth in Mexico was 57. In 1990, it was 69.[1] Not only are people living longer than they were a generation ago but, as in most of the world outside South Asia, on average women are living significantly longer than men: whereas in 1990, male life expectancy at birth was 66, female life expectancy was 73.

In the countryside, the burden of support for elderly parents usually falls on sons, most often on the last born, who, on condition that he take care of them in old age, the father designates heir to his property.[2] If his older brothers leave for the city, the youngest son is expected to remain at home and in the event that he also migrates, to take his parents with him or to send home money for their support. Although a daughter's emotional ties to her parents may remain strong, at marriage she passes financial responsibility for them to her brothers; in future, only if they default will she be expected to support their parents economically. In the move to the city, however, a father loses the control he once had through property and inheritance rights and, as Lomnitz noted,[3] tensions in the father-son relationship tend to surface. The likelihood is that as he has been only marginally involved in their daily life, his children, who often grown up fearing rather than feeling affection for him, will resent having to contribute to his support once he ceases to be economically productive. As the mother-daughter relationship appears better able to weather the rural-urban transition, young couples often find themselves living nearer the wife's parents than the husband's, thus putting themselves in line to accept financial responsibility for them later on.

Without social security benefits or pension plans, most elderly Mexican parents continue to look to adult children for economic support but often with less confidence than parents did in the past. As we have seen, in recent decades, many factors have combined to reverse the intergenerational flow of wealth. In the countryside, children were expected to provide a rapid financial return on parental investments of time and resources. In town today, however, the investment required is much greater and repayment is slower and less reliable, and to their dismay, parents are beginning to realize that resources invested in the rearing of children do not guarantee an economic return to themselves.

Adult children, encumbered by the heavy demands of their own families, may well find the economic support of aging mothers a severe if not intolerable strain. "In the past there were always a few who turned their backs on their parents," Soledad remarks. "When help was needed, they vanished, leaving the burden to their brothers and sisters. These days, with everything costing so much, there are many more who do this. Some, as before, do so shamelessly, but most feel very bad about it [*se sienten bien feo*]. If they had something to give, they would give it, but they have nothing."

Support from Adult Children

Single adult children are expected to live with parents or close relatives and to give a portion of their earnings—usually half—to their parents, in equitable compensation for the expenses involved in their upbringing. They may also, through their place of work, secure health insurance for them. When they become formally engaged, however, they sharply reduce their financial contributions so as to save for a home of their own after marriage. As one elderly woman observes, "You can count yourself lucky if the novios pay for food. If you press them for more money, they'll only quarrel with you, marry *de repente* [just like that], and go off to live with anyone who'll give them house room." Once married, contributions to the parental household usually cease entirely, with no guarantee that they will be resumed at a later date, should parents become infirm or, in the case of mothers, widowed.

Thus, emotionally close though they usually are to their children, instead of feeling entitled to their economic support, elderly women are likely to express considerable guilt and anxiety about making demands.

Of our older informants, only Margarita, with eight (of eleven) living children, is financially independent. Though her sons and daughters are generous with presents, she continues to pay all routine expenses herself. Once a year she visits her older son in Chicago (where she goes to the dentist) and her younger son in Houston (where she sees her ophthalmologist and where she once received an award from a woman's organization for being an "outstanding mother, grandmother, and greatgrandmother"). Both sons keep urging her to move north permanently, but with a chuckle, she says, "Why would I want to live in Houston or Chicago when everyone knows Cuernavaca has the best climate in the world!" Most important, her property is in Cuernavaca, and she dislikes being away from it for any length of time. "I want to be sure that everything's as it should be," she says. She sees her six daughters, all of whom live close by, frequently. Indeed, her youngest daughter, Gaby, lives with her family across the patio in one of the rental units. "She's always been *muy apegada* [very clingy]," says her mother, somewhat disparagingly. Nevertheless, having her within earshot—but not under the same roof—has worked out very well for Margarita. Gaby is there to run her errands and to cook for her when she does not feel like cooking herself and to stay out of her way the rest of the time. "After raising so many children and baby-sitting so many grandchildren, I *prefer* my own company," she declares. "My daughters are always finding maids for me. They say that at my age, I oughtn't to live alone. But as fast as they bring me those maids, I send them away. So long as I pay my bills myself, no one tells *me* what to do!"

Other mothers who are entirely dependent on adult children spend a great deal of time and emotional energy devising strategies to ensure they get the funds they need. One is supported by a daughter and her husband, in return for taking care of their house while both of them work; another elderly widow cooks the main meal of the day for two married daughters, their husbands, and three single adult children as well as several grandchildren. In return, all the adults involved contribute to her support. A third woman spends long hours each day serving behind the counter in her son-in-law's grocery store.

According to the stereotype, the Mexican grandmother's concern is focused on her grandchildren for whom she is an ever-ready source of warmth.[4] While many do indeed take care of grandchildren, this is as often out of financial necessity as choice. Inocencia, with her triple bypass operation and many other health problems, has charge of two preschoolers from early in the morning until eight at night, while their mother—her daughter, Carlota—is at work. "I think I'm too old to be looking after little kids," she says. But since she as well as they depend on Carlota's salary, she adds, "I either do it, or none of us eats."

Meanwhile, Luz María's widowed grandmother is being supported by her youngest daughter, Isabel, whose training as a teacher she financed with profits from her stall in the central market. As her other children are all married and having a hard time making ends meet, they cannot help her. Thus, the realization that Isabel is becoming involved in a serious romance makes the elderly woman extremely anxious. If the girl gets married and stops supporting her, will she have to go back to selling vegetables in the market?

Catalina has run into legal problems over the rental property her husband left her, and for the three years since his death, instead of supporting herself, she has had to rely on two single children, Cristina and Rodrigo. "My husband never intended for me to live off our kids," she laments. Worse yet, Cristina is thinking about marriage, after which Rodrigo will be Catalina's sole source of support. "And what will become of me when *he* gets married? He and his wife should be free to get a place of their own. They shouldn't have to stay here with me, out of obligation." No one knows the trials of living with an elderly mother better than Catalina, whose own widowed mother lived with her, Joaquín, and the children for twenty years. In return for her keep, she did much of the housework while Catalina minded the family store. "Mama was a bad-tempered, critical woman, and living with her was very difficult. Yes, I paid dearly for the help she gave me. But at least she was *my* mother. I'd have found living with my suegra even worse!" With a sigh she adds, "Rodrigo's wife shouldn't have to put up with me."

For a woman whose husband has two families, widowhood is particularly problematic. "Savings? Antonio hasn't saved a cent," says Inés. "Someone in my position has to start planning for being old a long time in advance." Planned she has, and she now looks forward to a modestly comfortable old age. She lives with two married children who, when they were single, lent her money for the down payment on her house. The mortgage is all paid off now, and the house, much improved and extended over the years, is divided into four apartments, one each for the two children and their families, one for herself and Antonio; the fourth she rents out. Each month Antonio gives her the equivalent of eighty dollars with which to pay utilities and taxes and keep the house in repair as well as feed herself and him, too, on the four nights a week her spends with her. Fortunately, as she says, she is used to saving every leftover bean and stale tortilla and putting a little aside as well. This small sum, together with the rent she receives and the money she earns sewing uniforms for the local orphanage, she keeps in a savings account that was paying her up to 100 percent annual interest in the mid-1980s. She uses her savings to help her children with down payments and business ventures and in one case, with the cost of going up to Chicago to work. She regularly baby-sits two of her grand-children and makes shirts, shorts, and dresses for many of the others. Once a month she travels to Guanajuato to take her turn, along with her sisters, caring for their ninety-nine-year-old mother.

Given the support she is providing her daughters and daughters-in-law while she is still vigorous, she seems confident that when she becomes infirm, they will care for her with the same devotion that she and her sisters care for their mother. Furthermore, at Antonio's death, she will be entitled to a small widow's pension. "After all, I'm his only legal wife," she points out with a smile.

But Soledad, who at forty-nine already feels *acabada* (worn out), says that she cannot even count on having a roof over her head when she is old, for though her husband did not contribute to the purchase of her plot or the house construction, he is the titleholder. He could put her out at any time and has often threatened to do so. "I sent my sons to school hoping that they'd help me," she says ruefully, "but though they are men now, they do nothing for me." As her four married daughters are not in a position to help her, either, her hopes are pinned on her two youngest children, Josefina and Manuel, who are still in school. "They haven't turned away from me." She adds uncertainly, "At least not yet."

Looking back, these older women often express wonder at how far they have come. All of them were born elsewhere, and most grew up in poverty. They wanted to provide their children with a better start in life, and most have managed to do so. Margarita and Inés both have sons who attended the university, as did Inocencia's daughter; three of Catalina's children went to university also, and one, Rodrigo, graduated as an engineer. Now many grandchildren are university students or in academic high schools, preparing for professional careers. Only Soledad and Lourdes, both of whom married alcoholics trapped on the margins of the economy, describe themselves as *gente humilde*—not only poor but humbly so.

Our middle-aged and elderly informants appear to be less controlling of and emotionally closer to their adult children, to their daughters in particular, than they recall their mothers being to them and their siblings. With their grandchildren, too, they are warmer than their mothers were with their own children, reflecting a general decrease in formality between generations in urban Mexico. By the same token, the shyness and reticence that by their own account characterized them as young women, has, in most cases, been replaced by a forthrightness that sometimes surprises even them. Steeled by their struggles, they have emerged articulate spokeswomen for their own interests, as well as the interests of close kin.

Meanwhile, the younger women worry that they are not doing enough for their mothers who, after "suffering for the sake of us children," they feel are entitled to their unwavering attention and support—whether or not they want or need it. Matilde, for one, saves every cent she can from her earnings as a laundress so that when she goes home on her annual visit, she can present her mother with a "respectable" sum. She insists on doing this, even though her mother, aware of how poor her daughter is, has specifically released her from all financial obligation.

As Matilde and others scrimp to help elderly mothers, they look at their children and say they cannot imagine them grown up and supporting *them*. "It may not be a question of their not wanting to help," one says, "but of their not being able to. With so many responsibilities of their own, how will they manage to help *me?*"

Few young husbands have jobs that will one day provide retirement pensions. None has money in the bank. Their wives talk about buying plots and building vecindades, of becoming landlords and living off their rents. Then, with a shrug and a smile, they say, "Or maybe I'll have to go down to the zócalo and stand with my hand outstretched to passersby, saying, "Señor, Señora . . . give me, give me." They are only half joking, for they all know the story about the old woman whose children went to live in Los Angeles and "forgot" her; and the one about the daughter-in-law who gave her aged mother-in-law so little to eat, she literally starved to death. Similar fates could await them, too.

In the meantime, though it may take considerable energy on their own part to keep idiosyncratic support systems in place, the great majority of

"With age comes satisfaction"

Earning one's keep by taking care of grandchildren

Mother and daughter

elderly working-class Mexican women continue to be helped by their children and younger kin. As Henry Selby found, households headed by elderly widows, if smaller, are not worse off on average than households headed by younger women, or even than households headed by men. It appears, then, that filial piety, reinforced by affection, can still be counted on in urban Mexico.

Two Women's Experiences of Widowhood and Old Age

LOURDES has been widowed twice, once at twenty-three and again at fifty. She now lives with her only daughter, Rocío, and her granddaughter, Pati, in a single rented room.

"Every Saturday when I was a girl I'd go dancing," she recalls. "That's how I met my first husband, Javier. He was a guitarist in a group that played in the zócalo. I'd been around musicians all my life because papá was one. Before we moved into town, he'd earned his living playing the fiddle, and though he got another job in Cuernavaca, he still played his fiddle at fiestas."

Her father had grown up on a hacienda, the out-of-wedlock son of a

Negro cook and a Spanish bookkeeper. "Mamá had a different background altogether," Lourdes explains. "Her parents had come from Spain to Mexico, where they'd done well enough to send mamá to boarding school in Mexico City." There she learned to speak French and to do embroidery— and to dance the flamenco. "She was mad about dancing," her daughter recalls with a smile. "She met papá when he was playing in an orchestra and ran off with him soon after that. Her parents were horrified. They didn't want her marrying papá! Aside from being poor, he was *natural* and a *negrito*. They begged mamá to come home, but she refused. Poor and black as he was, she married papá and had thirteen children with him!"

Lourdes's mother had been fifteen when she eloped. Lourdes was just a year older when she ran away with Javier. "He left me in his village with his mother while he went to ask my father for my hand. Only after he'd received papá's permission to take me—which papá *had* to give, seeing that I'd gone already!—and we'd been married in church, did we sleep together."

In the daytime, Javier worked the land he had inherited from his father, and at night, he played his guitar in a bordello in the nearby town of Cuautla. "He drank a lot, and when he was drunk, he beat me," Lourdes remembers. "I was very unhappy, but because I'd run away with him, I knew I had to stay. We didn't have children and at the time I thought it was my problem, that I was infertile. Only later did I realize that he was the one with the problem, not I. He was diseased from all the prostitutes he'd been with."

When Javier was killed in a road accident, his young widow rejoined her parents in Cuernavaca. "Javier's uncle sent me money each month," she recalls, "and I imagined myself living happily in the vecindad where I'd grown up and helping mamá for the rest of my life." But one day a neighbor showed her a photograph of her handsome brother, Luis, a silversmith who made earrings and bracelets for sale to tourists in the zócalo. Lourdes continues with a smile, "He was three years younger than I and so good-looking! Right up till his death he never lost his looks. . . . So I agreed to go out with him and before I knew it, I was four months pregnant. He asked me to marry him because he loved me, but even if he hadn't, he'd have asked me because he was a good man and the baby was coming. I was twenty-six by then, which was considered old to have your first child. Mamá was very worried about me. She'd been only sixteen when she had her first, but my son, Mario, was born at home without any trouble."

Lourdes goes on. "Luis was *muy cariñoso*. I loved him then, and I still do." She adds with a shake of the head, "Only once did I hear gossip about him and another woman, but I never had any proof. No, his problem was alcohol, not women."

At first Luis drank in moderation, but as the years passed, his drinking increased and his productivity decreased accordingly. "Not that he drank in the house, mind you. I wouldn't allow that. He'd go out and sit on a bench with his friends. There were several men and an old woman, and they'd drink anything they could lay their hands on. When Rocío was born with a cleft palate and Luis saw how her top lip was attached to her nose, he couldn't accept her. He never did accept her, either, even after she'd had the operations and wasn't ugly any more. He was always bitterly ashamed of her." Lourdes adds sadly, "He was very cruel to her sometimes."

It was after Rocío's birth that Luis began drinking *en serio*. It was not long before he stopped working, and Lourdes, working as a domestic servant, became the sole provider for a family of eight. Some employers were good, she remembers, and others were very bad. "One said to me, 'Look how dirty you are!' So I told her, 'Señora, where I live, the patio isn't paved, and when it rains the earth turns to mud. If you lived where I live, you'd be dirty, too!" With a chuckle, Lourdes adds, "She fired me."

When Luis came home drunk, like her first husband, Javier, he would often beat her. They were living with her parents then, and so long as they were alive, she could take it. But one day after they were both dead and she did not have their love and support any more, she decided she had had enough. " 'Either you stop this,' I told my husband, 'or I'm leaving you.' Well, he did stop! He went back to making a living and I stayed at home with the kids. But suddenly, after eight years, he began drinking again, and five months later, at the feast of San Antón, he was dead. As we were on our way to the cemetery, I saw people celebrating their saint's day, and there I was with my grief."

By that time, three of Lourdes's six children were grown and two were married, with families of their own. Only Eduardo, at 23, was still a bachelor, and it was to him that Lourdes turned for help with supporting the younger three. "One day Eduardo said to me, '*Mamacita*, I want to study to become a teacher, and if you help *me* with my expenses, when I get my certificate, I'll help *you*.' So that's what we did. I worked for my sister, Herlinda. Her husband had a lot of property and a lot of money, and while Herlinda sat in her living room, I took care of the cooking, cleaning, shopping—everything. I did it for six years so that my son could study."

Because Lourdes worked long hours, she could not supervise her children as closely as she feels she should have. "The two youngest, Rocío and Arturo, weren't so bad," she recalls. "It was Fernando who gave me the headaches. He and his friends would go *de pinta* [play hooky] from school, come home, and finish off every crumb of food they could lay their hands on. And that was the least of it! At thirteen, Fernando got the clap from prostitutes in the cantinas next to the slaughterhouses. They're all shut now, but then they were still open. I knew what was up when I noticed he couldn't walk properly. . . . And right after he was cured, he took up with a woman with two kids already. She had two more by him, but when he was eighteen, he left her. I told him, 'Those kids are your responsibility. Your father stuck with me when he got me pregnant, and you should stick with her, too.' I begged him to go back to her, but he didn't listen. Maybe if his father'd still been alive, he'd have listened. . . . Who knows. Anyway, she took her kids to her parents in Guerrero, and the next thing I knew, he'd left for California with a new woman. . . . He hasn't laid eyes on those kids since."

By the time Eduardo graduated from the teachers college, Lourdes had developed diabetes and high blood pressure, and the Social Security doctors advised her to stop working. Eduardo, who at that point was still single, took a job in another state, and from there he sent money home every payday, making it possible for his mother to retire, just as he had promised. Rocío, with whom Lourdes was living, also helped her, as did her other sons. Two gave her money for her special diet, and one did house repairs and maintenance. With Fernando occasionally sending back money from California, Lourdes received a rather generous level of support, to which, after bringing up her children almost single-handedly, she felt fully entitled.

More recently, as economic conditions have worsened, she has become increasingly anxious about whether and at what level support will continue. Her conversation focuses on who among her children has been to see her lately and who has not, who has brought her money or meat or fruit and who has not. With the exception of Rocío, all her children are married, and, with families of their own, they find their resources stretched to the utmost. Instead of continuing to receive her "allowances" and living independently, her sons are suggesting that she move in with one of them. "But none of them's willing to take in Rocío," Lourdes reports. "And I'm not willing to move without her. They're still angry with her for having Pati. They were all ashamed when she gave birth without a husband, and they haven't gotten over it yet. They say she's *promiscua*—yes, that's what they say, even though they're far worse themselves. I know because they tell me all their secrets. 'Who are you to point a finger?' I say to them, and yet they do. . . . So I tell them, I can't leave Rocío till she marries, but what with the child and her cleft palate, that doesn't seem too likely," Lourdes finishes with a sigh.

Although she is gratified that her sons want to take her into their homes, she will not accept any of their offers. Aside from her unwillingness to leave Rocío, she is convinced that were she to move in with one couple, her other two daughters-in-law would try to persuade their husbands to cut their contributions. "They'd say, 'Now she has a roof over her head and food to eat, why should we go on helping your mamá?' No," she concludes, "it's better if I stay here with my daughter."

So far, Lourdes's children have done their best to meet her financial needs, in part because they genuinely love and admire her for past struggles on their behalf and in part because she expends a great deal of time and energy making herself indispensable to them. Her doctors may have told her she should not work outside the home, but that does not mean she cannot work *at* home. From time to time, she baby-sits her sons' children, cooks for fiestas, supervises first communion celebrations, and offers her sons a sympathetic ear at any hour of the day or night. Most important, six days a week she takes care of Pati so that Rocío can go out to work. "My sons say I shouldn't be doing it, that it's too much for me, and that at my age, with diabetes and all, I should be resting. But I tell them, 'I love that little girl, she's my best friend.' Besides, Rocío has no one to help her except me." Lourdes claims that before Pati was born, Rocío was moody and erratic. She would work for a while, and then she would quit, quarrel with her mother, and run off to a friend's house for a week or two. "And then I'd have no money for my light bill. But now Rocío has the child, she's had to settle down. These days she's serious and responsible. She knows very well she's got to earn a regular living." As a result, mother-daughter relations have greatly improved.

After Lourdes is knocked down by a municipal garbage truck and breaks her ankle, she is laid up for several months. But despite a good deal of pain and discomfort and four operations, followed by daily physical therapy, her spirits are excellent. There she sits in her oldest son Mario's house, surrounded by sons, daughters-in-law, and grandchildren, all of whom come to visit every day. With a broad smile, she remarks, "My kids keep telling me,

'Mamacita, when you die, you'll have to take us with you because we couldn't stand being left alone' "

ESTELA, aged seventy-one, lives with her husband, Julio, eighty, in a large house they built themselves on a quiet street well away from the commercial area. With the help of her daughter, María, Estela runs a boardinghouse in the main structure. She and Julio live in a small apartment in the rear.

Julio has a serious heart condition, and Estela, who has Parkinson's disease, talks slowly and with great care to compensate for an involuntary shaking of the head that interferes with her speech. Their declining health is far from their only concern. A son-in-law recently lost his fight with cancer, leaving his wife, Estela, and Julio's oldest daughter, Julieta, without any means of support. After trying and failing to get her husband's army pension continued, she has been forced to leave three teenagers at home and take a job as a live-in housekeeper. There is long-standing concern, too, about another daughter whose husband abandoned her; a retarded grandson is a constant source of worry, as is a granddaughter who, at fourteen, married a boy she did not love because he had made her pregnant and now, at twenty-one, is divorced with two children to support. Whatever worries her children worries Estela, too, and ways to solve problems are debated in her kitchen, to which most members of her family come each afternoon. One by one, they come through the flower-filled patio to kiss Don Julio as he sits in the doorway in his wicker chair; then they pass on to kiss Estela.

Although Estela is sometimes discouraged, it is never for long for, as she explains that she has received two blessings that go far to compensate for whatever difficulties beset her. "The first," she says, "is comprensión. In my family we have always been able to understand one another. The second is *amistad* [friendship]. I've spent a lifetime making and keeping friends, and now I have more than I can count!"

After living for many years in Los Angeles, Estela and Julio returned with their four daughters to Mexico in 1940, but instead of rejoining their parents in their native Bajío, they came to Cuernavaca, which was fast becoming a popular wintering spot for North Americans, attracted by the climate, the scenery, and—at that point, still—the rustic atmosphere. One of Julio's sisters had already settled in the town, and it was through her husband that Julio found a job as an interpreter in a resort hotel.

For the first year the family lived in a vecindad, after which Estela sold her sewing machine and a carpet that she had brought down from California in order to buy a plot in Los Robles. "In those days, there were just a few huts in this part of the colonia," she recalls. "There were no streets, only cattle paths. There was no light, no water. Nothing. But it was pretty and so quiet, too. I soon got to know my neighbors, the few that were already here, and I watched as new people bought plots, built houses, and raised families. Then I saw their children marry and have children themselves. Today I can't walk a block without some child running up and greeting me, 'Granny!' I've been his grandmother's friend for forty years and he's seen me in her house so often, he thinks I'm his grandmother, too!" Smiling, she adds, "It's just the same in Los Angeles. I've as many friends and honorary grandchildren there as I have here."

One day soon she is going to hand over the boardinghouse entirely to her daughter, and then she will be free to accept some of the invitations that her friends have been pressing on her for years. First, she will visit in Veracruz, Monterrey, and Guadalajara; then she will go up to California to her daughter, Sarita, who as a young woman went to visit her madrina in Los Angeles, married an American, and stayed. "Without the boardinghouse to pull me back here," says Estela, "I'll have time to visit with all my girlhood friends, my comadres, and ahjidas." As she has long-standing invitations from many former boarders also, she might go on to see some of them in Colorado and Oklahoma. Not that she is starved for company, mind you! On the contrary, the telephone rings constantly with friends calling to chat. "I should leave it off the hook," she says, "but I don't like to do that because I never know when someone might be looking for serious help, not just a gossip."

She knows what it is like to need serious help. She herself has needed it often. The worst period in her life was when they were living in California and Julio got sick and was in the mental hospital, refusing to eat. "He said he couldn't take food out of our daughters' mouths," she says gravely. "Nothing anyone said could persuade him otherwise. It was fifteen months before he was eating properly again." In the meantime, her friends rallied round her. Having helped her find a place to live near the hospital so that she could visit her husband easily and moved her in, they came to see her regularly. "They saw to it that I never got too low." Then her friend, Elsa, who ten years earlier had been her madrina de boda and arranged her wedding, suggested they go into business together. "The girls and I were on county relief," Estela recalls, "and as you can imagine, that didn't go far enough. Before Julio got sick, I'd asked my mother down in Acámbaro to send me a few embroidered blouses to give away as presents, but by the time they arrived, Julio was in hospital, and so Elsa said, 'Instead of giving those blouses away, you should sell them! I'll help you. Come on!' So together we sold them, and then mamá sent some more and we sold them, too. That way, I was able to supplement my checks."

After Estela and her family moved back to Mexico, she and Elsa continued their business. "I'd send blouses up to her and she'd sell them, and with the three hundred dollars I saved, Julio and his friends built the first two rooms of our house—the rooms we use now as the comidor and the sala. As our money ran out before we bought a door, at night we'd have to block up the doorway with the table!" Even now, when she walks through the original rooms, she sometimes finds herself thinking about those blouses and what a good friend Elsa was to her.

In the 1950s, Estela sent her two oldest daughters to Los Angeles to live with one of her comadres. They worked for a year in a factory and on their return, gave their mother most of the money they had earned so that she could add a second story to the house. As soon as it was finished, she began to take in boarders. "The older two paid for the construction, and between them, the younger two bought most of the furniture—sofas, chairs, carpets. . . . And that was just the beginning. Over the years, they've given me so many things! I've got four televisions, three blenders, two washing machines, and more electrical appliances than I could ever use, and all of them are presents from my daughters!"

The pensión has been a lot of hard work, she says, and quickly adds, "But it's all been worthwhile because I've met so many people I'd never otherwise have met." For although to begin with, her boarders were teenage girls from the neighboring state of Guerrero, in Cuernavaca to learn to become secretaries, later they were joined by foreign priests and nuns, en route to the new frontiers of Christendom in the slums of Lima, Managua, and San Salvador and in the meantime studying Spanish at a nearby language school. In her living room, Estela keeps a stack of albums filled with pictures sent by former boarders and a pile of shoe boxes, crammed with letters, many bearing foreign stamps. "Now I have friends everywhere," she says with immense satisfaction. "If you set me down in almost any country in Europe or Latin America, I'd have a place to stay."

She has had hard times but no unmitigated disasters, and now, surrounded by loyal family and friends, she refuses to let her husband's declining health, much less her own infirmities, daunt her. Although two of her daughters have financial difficulties, the other two are rather well-to-do, and she is confident that when the time comes for her to give up the boardinghouse, she will not lack support. "God has been very good to me. He's allowed me a quiet life," she says, "and for that one should be very grateful, no?"

Summary

On a warm evening in Los Robles almost every doorway frames an elderly lady perched on a straight-backed chair, gnarled hands folded in her lap, peacefully watching the street. Some elderly ladies may be a good deal less serene than they appear, however, for in a country in which the poor are without government pensions, support for the elderly falls on adult children who these days are finding it more and more difficult to meet their obligations. Most of our informants grew up with widowed grandmothers whom they recall doing their full share of domestic chores and, when they became infirm, dying in short order. But with better medical care, Mexicans are living longer, and today's elderly appear less confident of commanding their children's support than they once were. In some parts of the developing world, notably, China, filial piety still virtually guarantees the elderly the support of adult children. In Taiwan, Hill Gates reported[5] that increased educational and occupational opportunities have better equipped sons and adopted daughters to fulfill traditional obligations. But elsewhere, as Sally Falk Moore noted of the Chagga of Tanzania, old people "express keen disappointment that modernization has deprived them of the privileges and regard they expect."[6] Again, Marvin Goldstein's Nepalese informants in the city of Kathmandu voiced doubt that today's sons could be depended on any longer to take care of their parents.[7] Our informants, too, were keenly aware that they had to negotiate for support that in the quite recent past would have been considered by children, as much as by aging parents, theirs by right. While the "successful" elderly were able to live off rental income and thus conserve their independence so long as they had their health, poorer women were having to make themselves as useful as possible to adult children, thereby building up credit for the time when their health failed and they could no longer "earn their keep." Knowing that once they stop contributing their services, they lose their bargaining power, these elderly women, like Lewis's informants in Tepoztlán in the 1940s, feared physical dependency much more than death.

By being useful, they earned economic support but not necessarily respect. In the study of working-class families that he carried out in Ciudad Netzahualcoyotl Izcalli in the state of Mexico, Vélez-Ibáñez[8] identified two kinds of three-generational families. In the first, which he called "historic," the grandparent, valued for personal qualities such as stoicism, intelligence, and the ability to solve problems, was "listened to" by children and grandchildren. By contrast, in the second, "ahistoric," family, the grandparent who lacked such qualities failed to offer his descendants a viable role model or a sense of continuity with the past. This kind of individual was regarded as "just another mouth to feed," an impediment to the gratification of the rest of the household. Some elderly women in Los Robles were highly respected, in just the way Vélez-Ibáñez described, for the vigor and determination with which they had pursued their family's interests in the past and because, in the present, often despite ill-health, they continued to make a significant contribution. But others, lacking the personal charisma that, from the perspective of their children, transformed drudgery into a mythic struggle, were housed, fed, and clothed but otherwise ignored.

In the meantime, younger women would laugh at the notion that the infants they were nursing or the children they escorted through the streets to school in the morning could ever support them. "No," they would say, "when we're old, we'll live off our savings." But chances are that in old age they, like their own mothers, whom they were helping *como se pueda* (however one could), will look to a "best" son or a "best" daughter to support them and furthermore, that one or the other, or a combination, will come through.

· 6 ·

¿Cumplir o Exigir? Urban Women in the 1990s

Many researchers who worked in urban Mexico from the 1950s through the 1970s portrayed working-class family life as at once mutually supportive and hierarchical. Males were dominant, females subordinate and long-suffering of their menfolks' heavy drinking and philandering as well as of physical abuse. But in the decade of the 1970s, Mexican society experienced some very important changes, including massive expansions in the educational and health care systems and, following the launching of a nationwide family planning campaign, a rapid decline in fertility. The objective of our research in Los Robles, then, was to understand how these radical innovations had affected family life and relationships, especially women from childhood through old age.

In the early months of fieldwork in spring 1984, we heard much that seemed to confirm what we had read about Mexican family life in the anthropological literature. Women of all ages commonly described childhood homes in which conjugal roles and responsibilities were so clearly defined that it was possible for parents to get by with very little communication. So long as a wife did not try to interfere with her husband's "freedom," she and her children stood a fair chance of living in peace. But if, like Lourdes's mother, she confronted him with his infidelities, likely as not, there would be screaming children and a bruised and bleeding wife. Again, when a husband came home drunk and spoiling for a fight, violence was par for the course.

Today many working-class couples continue to live largely separate lives, and often, too, women have to deal with hard-drinking, philandering men. But rather than see this as the natural order of things, these city-bred women are less willing to be, as Rosa once put it, *el objeto y gata del marido*; in other words, they are not willing to let themselves be screwed by their husbands. Like Lillian Rubin's California subjects, they want companionship in marriage; they believe that husbands and wives should share concerns and responsibilities—and one another's confidence. Rejecting the role of aguantadora, they more readily admit their anger at neglectful spouses—and at intruding mothers-in-law and recalcitrant offspring as well. Instead of "keeping quiet and putting up with things," as Manuel Sánchez's wife, Paula, did about her husband's long affair with Gabriela, young wives are likely to demand explanations for overnight absences, and, rather than taking the beating this demand provokes, to defend themselves vigorously. Again, while some wives still resign themselves to their husbands' heavy drinking and its consequences, others, seeing alcoholism as a disease, cajole and browbeat their men into joining Alcoholics Anonymous. "You have to stand up to your husband," one young wife declares, "and be as *exigente* of him as he is of you. Or else, how will he change?" If, despite her determination, her husband does not change, provided she can marshal the support of parents and siblings, she may leave him; and if he leaves her, she is more confident of being able to provide for her family, on her own if need be, than her mother was.

Her confidence has many sources, not the least of which is education. By 1987, 62 percent of women aged 15 to 49 nationwide had completed primary school; furthermore, though rural-urban differentials were still substantial, the average level of education in urban areas was considerably higher. In the 1990s, then, the great majority of urban mothers of young children have some secondary schooling, if not more. Our research shows that though literacy skills poorly mastered in overcrowded schools may deteriorate through lack of practice, the social experience of schooling fosters a self-confidence that remains throughout life. In the classroom, where she is expected to apply herself *for her own benefit*, a girl who at home is being raised within a male-dominated structure to be compliant and to work for the good of the family, undergoes a process of resocialization. School is a new universe that operates according to different rules. Rather than giving orders that children are expected to obey without comment, as is typically the case with unschooled parents and their offspring, teachers engage in verbal *exchanges* with their students, using a formal language that is significantly different from the language used at home. They ask questions and expect answers, and that goes for their students, too. Again, school is a place where, judged on her own merits, a girl can—and frequently does—beat out the boys for first place. The longer she stays in school, the more likely she is to be convinced of her own efficacy—vis-à-vis males in particular—a conviction that stays with her into adulthood, marriage, and motherhood. She is likely to discuss family problems and make decisions jointly with her husband, rather than her husband keeping his own counsel and making decisions on his own. Paradoxically, despite her proven competence as a household manager, in an earlier less-schooled generation, a woman's authority was strictly delineated. Though she had complete responsibility for house and children, she had little to say, for example, about where the family lived.

Modern medical care, which scarcely existed for the urban poor a generation ago, is now widely available. Unlike her mother, who gave birth at home with a midwife, today's young woman receives prenatal care and gives birth in a clinic, thereby much enhancing both her own and her child's chances of survival. That she has the capacity to control her reproductive life is another very important source of self-confidence. Between 1970 and 1989, the average number of children a Mexican woman bore declined from 6.7 to 3.4.[1] Instead of having six or seven children as her mother did, today's young woman is likely to have if not the two or three she might prefer, then no more than the three or four her husband insists on. Again, though the father may still have the last word on family size, the health care of her children is largely the mother's responsibility. Closely observing them for signs of illness, if she notices any symptom she regards as serious, she will promptly take them to a medical practitioner rather than a curandera. Prepared by her education and familiarity with that other, extra-domestic universe, she gives a coherent account of what appears to be the problem, answers the physician's questions, asks questions of her own, and understands—and follows—the instructions she receives.

Under-five mortality (U5MR), that is, the number of children who die before the age of five for every thousand born, is the principal indicator used by UNICEF to measure the well-being of children. Figures for 1989 place Mexico in the middle category of countries and her two immediate neighbors, Guatemala and the United States, in the high and low category, respectively. While the decline in U5MR since 1960 has been steep in all three countries, Mexico's decline—from 140 to 51—has been steepest, a reflection not only of the extension of health care services and rapid urbanization, which tends to reduce mortality at all ages, but of the rising educational levels of the mothers using those services.

From her school experience, today's young mother has absorbed a new model of how to interact not only with authority figures like doctors and nurses but with her own children as well. In effect, from earliest infancy, she is readying them for school, responding to their signals visually and verbally, as teachers do with their students, and not so much physically, as her mother responded to her when she was a small child. When her baby cries, she does not simply pick him up and try to soothe him by nursing or rocking him. Rather, she looks down at him, meets his gaze, and, even though he is still many months short of being able to reply, greets him. When he smiles and coos, she smiles and talks to him, engaging him in a mock "conversation," the precursor of a real conversation. As a result, her baby soon becomes a loquacious toddler whose demands for her attention increase exponentially, making child care a labor-intensive task requiring much more energy than it did of an earlier unschooled generation of mothers who raised their children to be seen and not heard.

When women had as many children "as God sent," a baby might not even be walking when his mother became pregnant again and, in preparation for the arrival of her next child, weaned him. Before the recent precipitous decline in the birthrate, brothers and sisters more often than overburdened mothers were the primary socializers of small children. As we see in rural Mexico, where large families are still common, mothers rarely engage their children in play. "I haven't time for playing. That's what children do," we were told. But as mothers hold their infants in their arms or on their laps, their older children are crowding around, talking, laughing, and inviting their baby brother to join them, and as soon as he has the necessary motor skills, he does so. From his siblings, he learns to take turns and to share, to cooperate rather than to compete. In Mexican society, despite meritocratic innovations, kinship ties are still very important when it comes to making one's way in the world. Thus children learn to play games according to rules that encourage cooperation with siblings, on whom they will need to rely throughout life, over autonomy and individual achievement.

But the urban mother who plans her pregnancies so that her first child is in kindergarten by the time the second is born is much more socially involved with her children. As a result, rivalry between siblings—initially over their mother's attention and later, over everything about which competition is possible—is much more in evidence. A mother is likely to find two children who squabble constantly and compete for her attention far more taxing than six who play quietly together, leaving her free to attend to her chores.

At every age and stage of development, the mother-child relationship today is likely to be more intense and more egalitarian than was the case in the past. A daughter of an earlier generation would honor and respect but not necessarily love her mother. By contrast, in childhood and thereafter, today's daughters are less awed by and emotionally closer to their mothers. They feel freer to share confidences and express opinions, and when, in old age, roles are reversed and mothers look to adult daughters as well as to sons for support, it is on affection more than filial piety that they base their appeal.

Today's mother's childbearing days may soon be over, but the preparation of children for their adult roles demands greater investments of time and resources than ever before. Whereas her own mother may have wanted her and her siblings to be secretaries or technicians or, simply to be "empleada," she is more ambitious for her sons and daughters. She may well aspire to their entering professions that require university training—and great parental sacrifice. To many mothers, a girl's education is even more important that a boy's. "My daughter must be ready to make her own way both at home and on the outside," was a comment we frequently heard. "I don't want her to suffer as I have."

If mothers and children are more one anothers' friends than they once were, the change in the father-child relationship is less marked. Working-class men still tend to see their fathering role as limited to that of provider. Manuel Sánchez complained bitterly that his father did not attend his graduation from primary school and that in the ordinary course of events he was cold and distant. Many husbands and sons whom we knew in Los Robles said the same about their fathers, and now that they themselves are fathers, some do try to behave differently. But though they enjoy carrying their babies about the neighborhood on a Sunday and taking their older children to the park and on trips to visit relatives, for the most part, these outings occur only when and if it suits them. As in the past, few men spare much time for their offspring.

Once mothers, jealously protecting the primacy of their relationship with their children, would often deliberately encourage the exclusion of their husbands from the domestic circle. But today, as economic necessity compels many women to combine earning a living with household responsibilities, the old distinction between adentro and afuera—inside and outside the home—becomes less clear. Like women in the Western industrialized world, working Mexican women want help from their husbands with their "double load," help that as yet is rarely forthcoming. Unless there is an extra pair of adolescent or adult female hands in the house, most working wives continue to perform household chores virtually unaided.[2] Even more important, they want help with raising the children. By this, they do not only mean that husbands "distract" the younger ones while they prepare dinner but rather, that the children's upbringing become a *joint* venture. They want their husbands to help with homework and talk to teachers; they want them to advise, counsel, discipline, and plan for the future. But though some fathers participate more in the rearing of their children than their own fathers ever did, they remain a minority. Afuera still claims much more of most men's time than their wives believe it should.

In 1982–83, the first year of the economic crisis, Chant in Querétaro and González de la Rocha in Guadalajara were already seeing large numbers of women, previously full-time housewives, entering the work force. In Cuernavaca, however, women were somewhat slower to respond. Smaller and less industrialized than either Guadalajara or Querétaro, Cuernavaca is a southern city and, despite the Populist tradition of Emiliano Zapata, in certain respects a more conservative place as well. In 1984–85, a working wife was still a source of shame to many husbands, and a married woman, forced to generate an income to keep the family afloat, did so at home if she possibly could to save face for her husband. By contrast, in the 1990s, the two-wage family has become the norm. Though many women still work at home, others are leaving infants and toddlers in the care of mothers, mothers-in-law, and neighbors and going out to work in factories, offices, and stores, a development that a few years ago would scarcely have been countenanced by husbands and by few of the women themselves. Driven at the outset by necessity, they received an additional boost from the economic upturn of the late 1980s. At the local level, this resulted initially from the flight of government agencies, businesses, and private citizens from Mexico City following the 1985 earthquake. As pollution levels in the Federal District grew more visibly dangerous, the flight became a stampede. At the national level, meanwhile, President Salinas's policies encouraging foreign investment, the liberalization of international trade and the decentralization of industry, and providing for the privatization of state-owned companies served to usher in a period of renewed economic growth after almost a decade of stagnation.

This is not to say that the ambivalence husbands and wives once shared about the mothers of young children working has disappeared, but, given their difficulties in making ends meet, couples have been obliged to come to terms with it. Eloisa, whose husband once beat up her employer, forcing her to quit her job, now works full-time in a factory even though her younger son is only in third grade. Luz María, who has a child in kindergarten, also works in a factory. Though these young women find the doble jornada burdensome, their work provides major benefits in addition to a livelihood. Not only do they have a life afuera but they also, by bringing in a wage and paying half—if not more—of the family bills, secure a much greater role in family decision making.

It is now thirty years since, with the publication of *The Children of Sánchez*, Manuel, Roberto, Consuelo, Marta, and their father, Jesus, established themselves as the most celebrated informants in the annals of anthropology. Admiring of Lewis's work as we certainly were, we began this fieldwork with an awareness that the Sánchez children had lost their mother at ages two, four, six, and eight, respectively, and a devoted stepmother in adolescence. Thus, we were inclined to understand the personal disorganization, irresponsibility, and bursts of self-recrimination of the brothers and the impulsiveness and despair of their sisters as symptomatic of depression stemming from early losses rather than from poverty. Troubled as the young lives of many of the Los Robles women had been, none had lost her mother in childhood, and in adulthood, though their lives were far from easy, they communicated, even in very troubled times, a determination to contain their distress and to do right by their children. Their husbands, meanwhile, tended to appear more fragile.

After following these Los Robles families for several years, I became convinced that urbanization and rapid social change, such as Mexico has experienced over the last half century, has been harder on men than on women. In urban as in rural areas, raising a family is a woman's life's work, and in that regard, pressures and deprivations notwithstanding, the city offers many advantages. Access to modern medical care considerably enhances her children's chances of survival, just as educational facilities enhance their prospects for social mobility. Whereas there is virtually no paid employment for a woman in the countryside, in town, she has several options—low-paying but options nevertheless. A man, meanwhile, excluded from the mainstream of the industrialized economy that requires more and more formal training, struggles to provide for his family at the margins of urban life.

My experience in Tilzapotla, a town of 4,500 inhabitants one hour's drive south of Cuernavaca, served to strengthen my conviction that, by and large, working-class men pay a greater price than women for survival in the urban area. In Tilzapotla, too, there are plenty of young fathers with a minimum of marketable skills. There is irresponsibility and infidelity, heavy drinking and domestic violence—but less, it would appear, than in Los Robles. In Tilzapotla, it seems, lineage provides some protection against humiliation. As the son of X and the son-in-law of Y, both respected men, you, too, are respected. Husbands and fathers eat breakfast, dinner, and the evening meal with wives and children; sons know how fathers earn a living and soon start working alongside them in the fields and the corral. There is more *comprensión* between couples, a deeper conviction that they are working together for a common future. Admittedly, Tilzapotla is an unusually prosperous little place, and its prosperity is based less on agriculture and the local limestone quarries than on remittances from Chicago and Los Angeles. Most males over the age of eighteen have been to the "other side," where a long-established pattern of both seasonal and permanent migration supplies newcomers with the networks they need to find jobs, housing, and companionship. Los Robles men go to the "other side," too, but they are relatively few in number. Poor urban husbands and fathers, lacking the resources to make the journey north and the contacts to find employment on arrival, are likely to be trapped at home in the rut of underemployment with consequences for family life that have often been described.

It is not my intention to laud family life in the rural area, which, thirty and forty years ago, men and women left in droves and which many are still leaving. My point is that my experience in one particular rural community made clearer to me just how hard the city is on those men who, in good as much as in bad times, are near the bottom of the economic pyramid. Small wonder that when boys become men, so many respond to failure by the lights of the larger society in culturally conventional ways. Like the lower-class black men in Elliott Liebow's study, *Tally's Corner,* many young husbands we knew in Los Robles sought refuge and solace with their cuates in the street. There, "where the measure of man is considerably smaller, and where weaknesses are somehow turned upside down and almost magically transformed into strengths," a young man could be "instead of a poor provider and negligent husband and father, once again a man among men."[3] Intermittently, at least. If women are beaten by drunken husbands in their own kitchens, husbands are almost as often beaten by their drunken cuates and compadres on the street corner. Again, if we heard much about marital abuse, we also heard much about criminal violence—whose victims were almost always male. The only brother of one of our informants was murdered, as were the sons of two others. In none of these cases was the murderer—though he had been identified—apprehended. "For the poor there is no justice," we were repeatedly told.

Alcoholism, violence, sexual promiscuity, fragile marital relationships: these are common features of family life among the poor of North America as much as of Latin America. There appear to be important differences, however. Unlike poor Latin women who are depicted in study after study as single-mindedly devoted to the welfare of family, those described by (among others) Howell in Washington, D.C.,[4] and by Janet Fitchen in rural upstate New York[5] were almost as likely to drink heavily and engage in extramarital affairs as their partners. In Los Robles, many of the men we knew were alcoholics, but among the women, only Soledad appeared to have had a problem with alcohol, which, "for the children's sake," she managed to overcome. While husbands freely boasted of their sexual conquests, only one woman, Eloisa, admitted to an extramarital affair. That Mexican working-class men and woman conform to different standards of personal behavior reflects a difference in priorities. Men place the demands of the world afuera on a par with—if not above—those of adentro. As their wives matter-of-factly explained to us, self-indulgence affords men, albeit momentarily, compensation for disappointments and defeats incurred "out there." As for women, "With so many responsibilities, can one afford to indulge oneself?" they would say with a shrug.

In the 1990s, as much as in the past, motherhood and raising a family remains the chosen destiny of the overwhelming majority of Mexican women. Though some young women, embittered by soured romances, talk about avoiding marriage and raising children alone, only a few actually go that route. In Caribbean societies, with roots in slavery and the plantation economy, as in Central American countries, with a more recent history of war and displacement, the matrifocal family, consisting of a woman and her children without a resident senior male, is very common.[6] As Peattie observed in Venezuela, in high unemployment situations in which men cannot be relied on to bring in a wage and, when they are not working, are expensive to support, male-female relations tend to be fragile.[7] Having children in common is insufficient cause to stay together. Moreover, women are often better able to make a living—and to support themselves and their children—in the informal economy than are men. In Mexico, by contrast, despite a long recession in which many working-class men had great difficulty making a living, there does not appear to have been an appreciable increase in either matrifocal families or single motherhood. Less than 2 percent of the women of childbearing age whom Julieta Quilodrán[8] surveyed in a 1983 nationwide study of fertility were single mothers, that is, had never married or lived in consensual union with the father of their youngest child. Following Quilodrán, Selby and his colleagues found that of the households in a study conducted in ten cities during the 1980s, only 6.2 percent were headed by women and of them, only one quarter—again, less than 2 percent of the sample—by never-married women.[9] In sum, for all its shortcomings, the two-parent family appears to be flourishing in Mexico.

Today's young woman comes to adulthood with a different sense of her self than her mother did. At least publicly, her mother accorded her father—regardless of competence or the degree to which he accepted responsibility—the dominant role in the family while she pursued her primary objective, the welfare of her children, by hard work, self-denial, and manipulation of spouse. Her identification with her children was total. By caring for them, she cared for herself. If they throve, she throve. If they failed, she failed also. Today, her family's welfare is still a young mother's main—but not only—concern. Women of an older generation devoted their energies to the care of others. Undeniably, they suffered, though with confidence that they would reap the reward they sought: the loyalty of children and grandchildren. But their daughters have eaten of the fruit of the tree of knowledge, and though they, too, are committed to the care of others, they have begun to demand the right to care for themselves as well. The rewards they seek in future will be different from those women sought in the past, and the attendant risks may well be greater. For fulfillment of the domestic role virtually guaranteed self-worth, which, outside the home, may prove both harder to come by and harder to sustain.

Postscript 1991

Of the fifteen women on whom our study focused, INOCENCIA died in 1987, and I lost touch with VERÓNICA, IRENE, and OFELIA after they moved out of the neighborhood.

At age 81, MARGARITA was at last convinced by her daughters that she should not stay alone, and a granddaughter, a university student, came to live with her. "Anyway, she's out at her classes all day, so she doesn't bother me that much," commented her grandmother, who was still making regular trips to visit her sons in the United States. On her return, she would lament that her American grandchildren spoke ungrammatical Spanish and used slang words she did not understand. However, she was much more concerned about the dangers they encountered daily on the west side of Chicago and southwest Houston whose streets were "full of drugs and criminals." If only her sons would bring their families back to Cuernavaca! But in Chicago, Salomon had retired from working in a factory to take care of the apartment building he now owned; and in Houston, Lot's business was thriving. No, they would never come home.

Following her husband, Julio's, death, ESTELA began spending about half the year in California with her daughter. This enabled her to see a good deal of her junior high school friends, who, as she reported, "are all getting older, too."

Postscript 1991

As ever, INÉS's focus was her family: eight children, twenty-six grandchildren, three great-grandchildren, most of whom she saw every week, if not every day. At age 72, she radiated energy, determination, and satisfaction with the way in which, in the larger scheme of things, her life had turned out. After open-heart surgery, her husband, Antonio, was slimmer and as dapper as ever. Having always fancied himself a writer, in semiretirement, he was going daily to mass and writing a book about Catholic family life. Meanwhile, his schedule—Monday, Tuesday, Wednesday, and Friday nights with Inés and Thursday, Saturday, and Sunday nights with la otra— had not changed.

In 1987, LOURDES's only daughter, Rocío, got married in a big church wedding and moved away with her little girl and new husband, leaving Lourdes alone in Los Robles. But after three years of marriage and two babies, Rocío was deserted by her husband, whereupon Lourdes, at 70, moved in with her to baby-sit the children while Rocío went out to work. Long as her own days were and hard as life was for all of them, Lourdes reported that without question, she was a lot happier than she would have been had she been living by herself. "So long as my daughter needs me here," she said, "this is where I'll be."

When I first met CATALINA, she was a new widow, grieving and deeply unsure of herself. I saw her recover from the death of her husband, who had insisted on keeping full control of the family's business affairs, and for the first time in her adult life, truly find her feet. By age 60, she had become the confident head of her large and demanding family.

SOLEDAD's life, meanwhile, had become a little easier. Her four out-of-wedlock grandchildren were growing up. They continued to give her *mucha lata* (a lot of trouble), but with Rosalía married and Carlito, the youngest, in the fifth grade, the end was in sight. When I first knew Soledad, her hopes for the future had been pinned on her two youngest children, Josefina and Manuel, who were both in school. Though Josefina had since married, at 22, Manuel was still single. Cuernavaca was enjoying a construction boom that provided low-wage but steady employment for young men like him who had no particular skills. A gentle, industrious fellow, he was supporting his mother, just as she had planned he would. His older brothers and brothers-in-law, who, with their families, had once crowded into Soledad's house "to save rent," were also working. Three had moved out to places of their own, and the house and patio were much quieter. "Too quiet," Soledad said somewhat regretfully, though she conceded that it was a source of satisfaction to see her children getting ahead at last. She reported that she no longer suffered from nervios. As for her husband, Jorge, he still came regularly, and at least half the time, he came drunk. His donkey, Tabaco, had gray whiskers now.

In 1984–85, most of the younger mothers had been full-time housewives. Though several earned money as laundresses, seamstresses, and so forth, Rosa, whose younger son had already begun primary school, was the only one who was employed outside the home. By 1991, the outside employment of working-class women had become rather common. For though Cuernavaca was booming and unskilled men could again find work, their wages were not enough to support a family. Some women, like ELOISA and LUZ MARÍA, whose intelligence and self-confidence made up for a lack of junior high school certificates, were working in factories. Others were engaged in petty trade in the street where, in the mid-1980s, no self-respecting husband would have permitted his wife to spend any time at all.

ROSA's parents-in-law were dead, and her husband, Hugo, had inherited their vecindad, which Rosa managed. Hugo, who in the 1980s had been unemployed for long periods, again had regular work, but even so, Rosa had kept her job as an aerobics instructor. Their two sons were both in high school, the older one headed for university. Hugo's wages and their rental income together were still not enough to educate two boys, Rosa insisted. Of course, she had to work! She taught trainee teachers now instead of teenage girls and housewives—and loved it. The last thing she would ever want to do was quit!

Notes

Bibliography

Index

Notes

Introduction. Mexican Women in Historical Perspective

1. Oscar Lewis, *Five Families* (New York: Basic Books, 1959).

2. Oscar Lewis, *The Children of Sánchez: Autobiography of a Mexican Family* (New York: Random House, 1961); *La Vida: A Puerto Rican Family in the Culture of Poverty—San Juan and New York* (New York: Random House, 1966); "The Culture of Poverty," *Scientific American* 215:19–25; *A Study of Slum Culture: Backgrounds for La Vida* (New York: Random House, 1968).

3. Lewis, *The Children of Sánchez*, xxv.

4. For critiques, see Eleanor Burke Leacock, ed., *The Culture of Poverty: A Critique* (New York: Simon & Schuster, 1971), and Charles Valentine, *Culture and Poverty: Critique and Counter-Proposals* (Chicago: University of Chicago Press, 1968).

5. Anthony Leeds, "The Concept of the 'Culture of Poverty': Conceptual, Logical and Empirical Problems, with Perspectives from Brazil and Peru," in Leacock, *The Culture of Poverty*, 226–284. Lisa Redfield Peattie, "The Structural Parameters of Emerging Life Styles in Venezuela," in Leacock, *The Culture of Poverty*, 101–109. Valentine, *Culture and Poverty*, 70.

6. Joseph T. Howell, *Hard Living on Clay Street* (Garden City, N.Y.: Anchor Books, 1973).

7. Lillian Breslow Rubin, *Worlds of Pain: Life in the Working-Class Family* (New York: Basic Books, 1976).

8. Rubin, *Worlds of Pain*, 210.

9. See Lourdes Arizpe, "Mujeres migrantes y economía campesina: Análisis de una cohorte migratória a la ciudad de México, 1940–1970," *America Indígena* 38(2):305–327; "Relay Migration and the Survival of the Peasant Household," in Helen Icken Safa, ed., *Towards a Political Economy of Urbanization in Third World Countries* (Delhi: Oxford University Press, 1982), 19–41. Brígida García and Orlandina de Oliveira, "Reflexiones teórico-metodológicas sobre el estudio de las relaciones entre el trabajo de la mujer y la fecundidad en la ciudad de México," *Investigación Demográfica en México* (México, D.F.: CONACYT, 1978), 277–293. Brígida García et al., *Hogares y trabajadores en la ciudad de México* (Mexico, D.F.: El Colegio de México/UNAM, 1982). Larissa Adler Lomnitz *Networks and Marginality: Life in a Mexican Shantytown* (New York: Academic Press, 1977). Humberto Muñoz et al., *Migración y desigualdad social en la ciudad de México* (México, D.F.: El Colegio de México/UNAM, 1977).

10. For studies of poor city dwellers in Latin America, see Jorge Balan et al., *Men in a Developing Society: Social and Geographical Mobility in Monterrey, Mexico* (Austin: University of Texas Press, 1973). Wayne A. Cornelius and F. M. Trueblood, eds., *Urbanization and Inequality*, Latin American Urban Research vol. 5. (Los Angeles: 1975). Sage,

For Mexico City, Lomnitz, *Networks and Marginality*. For Ciudad Guyana, Venezuela, Lisa Redfield Peattie, *The View from the Barrio* (Ann Arbor: University of Michigan Press, 1968). Janice E. Perlman, *Myth of Marginality: Urban Poverty and Politics in Rio de Janeiro* (Berkeley and Los Angeles, University of California Press, 1976). Bryan Roberts, *Organizing Strangers: Poor Families in Guatemala City* (Austin: University of Texas Press, 1973). John F. C. Turner, *Housing by People* (London: Marion Boyar, 1976).

11. Instituto Nacional de Estadísticas Geografía e Informática, *Estadísticas Históricas de México*, Tomo I (México, D.F.: INAH SEP, 1990).

12. Consejo Nacional de Población, México, *México demográfico* (México, D.F., 1982).

13. Leopoldo Nuñez Fernández, "México: Las encuestas nacionales en la estimación de los niveles de fecundidad," in Beatriz Figueroa Campos, ed., *La fecundidad en México: Cambios y perspectivas* (México, D.F.: El Colegio de México, 1989), 90–120.

14. Francisco Alba and Joseph E. Potter, "Population and Development in Mexico Since 1940: An Interpretation," *Population and Development Review* 12:47–70.

15. Peter Laslett, *The World We Have Lost* (London: Methuen, 1965).

16. See Jorge Balan, "Migrant-Native Socioeconomic Differences in Latin American Cities: A Structural Analysis," *Latin American Research Review* 4(1); Glenn H. Beyer, *The Urban Explosion in Latin America: A Continent in Process of Modernization* (Ithaca: Cornell University Press, 1967).

17. Orlandina de Oliveira, "Migración y absorción de mano de obra en la ciudad de México: 1930–1970," Centro de Estudios Sociológicos no. 14 (México, D.F.: El Colegio de México).

18. Victor Urquidi, "The Underdeveloped City," in J. C. Hardoy, ed., *Urbanization in Latin America: Approaches and Issues* (Garden City, N.Y.: Anchor Books, 1975), 339–366.

19. Balan et al., *Men in a Developing Society*, 22.

20. Anibal Quijano, "Redefinición de la dependencia y proceso de marginalización en America Latina," in Francisco C. Weffort and Anibal Quijano, eds., *Populismo, marginalidad y dependencia* (San José, Costa Rica: Editorial Universitaria Centro-Americano, 1973), 171–329.

21. de Oliveira, "Migración y absorción."

22. See Muñoz et al., *Migración y desigualidad*. José Nun, "Subrepoblación relativa, ejército industrial de reserva y masa marginal," *Revista Latinamericana de Sociología* 4(2): 178–237. Lisa Redfield Peattie, "The Concept of 'Marginality' As Applied to Squatter Settlements," *Latin American Research* 4, eds. Wayne A. Cornelius and Felicity M. Trueblood (Beverly Hills and London: Sage, 1974), 101–109.

23. Arizpe, "Mujeres migrantes."

24. Peattie, *The View from the Barrio*, 119.

25. Arizpe, "Mujeres migrantes." Esther Corona, "Impresiones sobre una sexualidad," *FEM* 4(6). Douglas Butterworth and John K. Chance, *Latin American Urbanization* (Cambridge: Cambridge University Press, 1981), 123. Lomnitz, *Networks and Marginality*, 16. Henry A. Selby, "The Study of Social Origins in Traditional Mesoamerica," in Hugo Nutini, Pedro Carrasco, and James M. Taggert, eds., *Essays on Mexican Kinship*, (Pittsburgh: University of Pittsburgh Press, 1976), 29–41. Henry A. Selby et al., *The*

Mexican Urban Household: Organizing for Self-Defense (Austin: University of Texas Press, 1990), 121.

26. Brígida García, "La participación de la población en la actividad economica," *Demografía y Economía* 9(1):18. Larissa Adler Lomnitz, "Migration and Network in Latin America," in Alejandro Portes and Harley Browning, *Current Perspectives in Latin American Urban Research* (Austin: University of Texas, Institute of Latin American Studies), 130–150. Sarah Radcliffe, "Gender Relations, Peasant Livelihood Strategies and Migration: A Case Study from Cuzco, Peru," *Bulletin of Latin American Research* 5(2):29–47. Helen Safa, "Female Employment in the Puerto Rican Working Class," in June Nash and Helen Safa, eds., *Women and Change in Latin America* (South Hadley, Mass.: Bergen and Garvey, 1986).

27. Lomnitz, "Migration and Network in Latin America," 133–150.

28. Andrew H. Whiteford, *Two Cities in Latin America* (New York: Anchor Books, 1964), 138.

29. García et al., *Hogares y trabajadores*.

30. Francisco Alba, *The Population of Mexico: Trends, Issues and Policies* (New Brunswick: Transaction Books, 1982).

31. Dirección General de Planificación Familiar, Secretaria de Salud, México, *Encuesta nacional sobre fecundidad y salud, 1987*.

32. For discussions of the effect on family life of income maintenance programs in Britain, see Laslett, *The World We Have Lost*, 218–220. Peter Townsend, *The Family Life of Old People* (London: Routledge & Kegan Paul, 1957). Michael Young and Peter Wilmott, *Family and Kinship in East London* (London: Routledge & Kegan Paul, 1957).

33. Sylvia Chant, *Women and Survival in Mexican Cities* (Manchester: Manchester University Press, 1991), 183.

34. Victor Urquidi, 1967. "El crecimiento demográfico y el desarollo económico latinoamericano," *Demografía y Economía* 1(1).

35. Brígida García, "Anticoncepción en el México rural, 1969," *Demografía y Economía* 10(3):297–351.

36. Consejo Nacional de Población, México, *México demográfico* (México, D.F.

37. Viviane Marquez, "Política de planificación familiar en México: Un proceso institucionalizado?" *Revista Mexicana de Sociología* 46:285–310.

38. Cheryl English Martin, *Rural Society in Colonial Morelos* (Albuquerque: University of New Mexico Press, 1985), 23–45.

39. Laura R. Helguera et al., *Los campesinos de la tierra de Zapata: Adaptación, cambio y rebelión* (México, D.F.: Centro de Investigaciones Superiores, Instituto Nacional de Antropología e Historia, 1974).

40. Roberto L. Chavez and M. Isabel Vargas, *Urban Dwelling Environments: Cuernavaca, Mexico*. Cambridge: MIT School of Architecture and Planning, 1976), 12–17.

41. Robert A. LeVine et al., "Women's Schooling and Child Care in the Demographic Transition: A Mexican Case Study," *Population and Development Review* 17(3): 459–496.

42. Helen Ware, "Effects of Maternal Education, Women's Roles and Child Care on Child Mortality," *Population and Development Review*, Supplement to Vol. 10, 191–214. John Cleland and J. Hobcraft, *Reproductive Change in Developing Countries: Insights from*

the *World Fertility Survey* (New York: Oxford University Press, 1985). John Cleland and Jerome van Ginneken, "Maternal Education and Child Survival in Developing Countries: The Search for Pathways of Influence," *Social Science and Medicine* 27:1357–1368.
    43. García et al., *Hogares y trabajadores*, 59.

Chapter 1. Niñez: Childhood from the 1920s to the 1970s

    1. Jim Tuck, *The Holy War in Los Altos: A Regional Analysis of Mexico's Cristero Rebellion* (Tucson: University of Arizona Press, 1982), 29.
    2. See Ernest Gruening, *Mexico and Its Heritage* (New York: The Century Co., 1928), 162. John Womack, Jr., *Zapata and the Mexican Revolution* (New York: Knopf, 1969), 376.
    3. John M. Ingham, *Mary, Michael and Lucifer: Folk Catholicism in Central Mexico* (Austin: University of Texas Press, 1986), 60.
    4. Robert C. Hunt, "Components of Relationships in the Family: A Mexican Village," in Francis Hsu, *Kinship and Culture* (Chicago: Aldine, 1971), 106–143.
    5. Silvia Marina Arrom, *The Women of Mexico City, 1790–1857* (Palo Alto: Stanford University Press, 1985), 20.
    6. Henry A. Selby, Arthur D. Murphy, and Stephen A. Lorenzen, *The Mexican Urban Household: Organizing for Self-Defense* (Austin: University of Texas Press, 1990), 117.
    7. Jim Tuck, *The War in Los Altos*, 187.

Chapter 2. Ya Soy Señorita: Adolescence and Courtship

    1. J. M. Stycos, *Familia y fecundidad en Puerto Rico* (México, D.F.: Fondo de Cultura Económica, 1958).
    2. Carrie B. Douglas, "Toro muerto, vaca es: An interpretation of the Spanish bullfight," *American Ethnologist* 11(2):242–258.
    3. James M. Taggert, "Gender, Segregation and Cultural Constructions of Sexuality in Two Hispanic Societies," *American Ethnologist* 19(1):75–96.
    4. Noemi Quezada, "La sexualidad en México, "*Anales de Antropología* 16:233–244.
    5. Julieta Quilodrán, "Tipos de uniones maritales in México," Ponencia presentada en la Reunión Nacional sobre la Investigación Demográfica en México (México, D.F.: CONACYT).
    6. Ana Lau Jaiven, *La nueva olla del feminismo en México: Conciencia y acción de la lucha de las mujeres* (México, D.F.: Fasiculos Planeta, S.A. de C.V., 1987), 67.
    7. Julieta Quilodrán, *Niveles de fecundidad y patrones de nupcialidad en México* (México, D.F.: El Colegio de México, 1991).
    8. Consejo Nacional de Población, México, *El programa nacional de educación sexual* (México, D.F., 1979).
    9. Esther Corona, "Impresiones sobre una sexualidad," FEM 4(6).

10. Sarah LeVine and Clara Sunderland Correa, "Are Teenage Mothers Different?" Paper presented at the First International Meeting on the Sexual and Reproductive Health of Adolescents, Oaxtepec, Mexico. December 1985.

11. Stephen Gudeman, "Compadrazgo as a Reflection of the Natural and Spiritual Person," *Proceedings of the Royal Anthropological Institute*, 45–71.

12. Tracy Bachrach Ehlers, *Silent Looms: Women and Production in a Guatemalan Town* (Boulder: Westview Press, 1990), 133–135.

Chapter 3. *La Vida de Casada: Expectations and Realities of Marriage*

1. For commentaries on male and female in Mexico, see: Rogélio Díaz-Guerrero, "Neurosis and the Mexican Family Structure," *American Journal of Psychiatry* 112: 411–419; *Estudios de psicología del mexicano* (México, D.F.: Antigua Librería Robredo, 1961); "La mujer y las premisas histórico-socioculturales de la familia mexicana," *Revista Latina de Psicología* 6:7–16. Robert N. Mollinger, "Creative Writers on Personality: Octavio Paz and Carlos Fuentes on the Mexican National Character *Psychoanalytic Review* 71(2):305–317. June Nash and Helen Safa, eds., Introduction to *Sex and Class in Latin America* (New York: Praeger, 1976). Octavio Paz, *El laberinto de la soledad* (México, D.F.: Cuadernos, Mexicanos, 1950). S. Ramos, *Profile of Man and Culture in Mexico*, trans. P. G. Earle (Austin: University of Texas Press, 1962). Eric Wolf, *Sons of the Shaking Earth* (Chicago: University of Chicago Press, 1959).

2. Ann Pescatello, *Power and Pawn: The Female in Iberian Families, Societies and Cultures* (Westport, Conn.: Greenwood Press, 1976).

3. Elena Buenaventura-Posso and Susan Brown, "Westernization and the Bari of Colombia," in Eduardo Archetti et al., eds., *Sociology of Developing Societies* (Basingstoke: Macmillan, 1987), 321–328. Alison MacEwen Scott, "Industrialisation, Gender Segregation and Stratification Theory," in Rosemary Crompton and Michael Mann, eds., *Gender and Stratification* (Cambridge: Polity Press, 1986), 154–189.

4. See Tessa Cubitt, *Latin American Society* (London: Longmans, 1988), 103.

5. Erich Fromm and Michael Maccoby, *Social Character in a Mexican Village: A Sociopsychoanalytic Study* (Englewood Cliffs, N.J.: Prentice Hall, 1970).

6. Lola Romanucci-Ross, *Conflict, Violence and Morality in a Mexican Village*. Palo Alto: National Press Books, 1973), 51.

7. Selby, "The Study of Social Origins," 29–41.

8. Chant, *Women and Survival in Mexican Cities*, 13. Brígida García et al., "Familia y trabajo en México y Brasil," *Estudios Sociológicos* 1(3):487–507.

9. Richard W. Cuthbert and Joe B. Stevens, "Documentation: The Net Economic Incentive for Illegal Mexican Migration: A Case Study," *International Migration Review* 15(3):543–550.

10. Mercédes González de la Rocha, *Recursos de la pobreza: Familias de bajos ingresos en Guadalajara* (Guadalajara: El Colegio de Jalisco, 1986), 27.

11. González de la Rocha, *Recursos de la pobreza*, 126.

12. Alberto Alvarez Gutierrez, "Como se sienten los mexicanos?" in Alberto Her-

nández Medina and Luis Narro Rodríguez, eds., *Como somos los mexicanos?* (México, D.F.: Centro de Estudios Educativos, 1987), 41–92.

13. Octavio Giraldo, "El machismo como fenómeno psicocultural," *Revista Latinamericana de Psicología* 4(3):295–309.

14. Oscar Lewis, "Husbands and Wives in a Mexican Village: Study in Role Conflict," *American Anthropologist* 51(4):602–610.

15. Romanucci-Ross, *Conflict.*

16. Ingham, *Mary, Michael and Lucifer*, 56–62.

17. María Roldán, "Pautas de control del circúito monetario domésticas y formas de conciencia entre trajabadoras industriales domiciliarias en la ciudad de México." Ponencia presentada en la Reunión de Investigación sobre La Mujer e Investigación Feminista, Montevideo, Uruguay, GRECMU, 1984.

18. María del Carmen Elu de Leñero, 1969. *¿Hacia dónde va la mujer mexicana?* (México, D.F.: Instituto Mexicano de Estudios Sociales), 161.

19. Arrom, *The Women of Mexico City, 1790–1857*, 64.

20. Evelyn P. Stevens, "Marianismo: The Other Face of Machismo in Latin America," in Ann Pescatello, ed., *Female and Male in Latin America: Essays* (Pittsburgh: University of Pittsburgh Press, 1973).

21. Jaquette, "Literary Archetypes and Female Role Alternatives: The Woman and the Novel in Latin America," in Pescatello, ed., *Female and Male in Latin America: Essays.*

22. Susan C. Bourque and Kay Barbara Warren, *Women of the Andes: Patriarchy and Social Change in Two Peruvian Towns* (Ann Arbor: University of Michigan Press, 1981).

23. Ehlers, *Silent Looms*, 134.

24. Tracy Ehlers, "Debunking Marianismo: Economic Vulnerability and Survival Strategies Among Guatemalan Wives," *Ethnology* 30(1):1–12.

25. See George M. Foster, *Empire's Children: The People of Tzintzuntzán* (Washington, D.C.: Smithsonian Institution, 1948). Hugo G. Nutini, "Polygyny in a Tlaxcalan Community," *Ethnology* 4:123–148.

26. Luis Leñero Otero, "Valores familiares y dramaturgía social," in Hernández Medina and Narro Rodríguez, *¿Como somo los mexicanos?*

27. Jorge Gissi, "Mythology about Women with Special Reference to Chile," in Nash and Safa, eds., *Sex and Class in Latin America.*

28. See Sylvia Chant and Peter Ward, "Family Structure and Low-Income Housing Policy," *Third World Planning Review* 9(1):5–19; and Caroline Moser, "The Impact of Recession and Structural Adjustment Policies at the Micro-Level: Low-Income Women and Their Households in Guayaquil, Equador," *Invisible Adjustment* 2 (New York: UNICEF Americas and Caribbean Regional Office, 1989), 137–162.

29. Selby, "The Study of Social Origins."

30. García et al., "Hogares y trabajadores."

31. Chant and Ward, "Family Structure." Mercédes González de la Rocha, "Economic Crisis, Domestic Reorganization and Women's Work in Guadalajara, Mexico, "*Bulletin of Latin American Research* 7(2):207–223.

32. Marianne Schmink, "Women in the Urban Economy in Latin America," *Work-*

ing Paper No. 1, Population Council, New York. Marta Tienda and Sylvia Ortega, "Las familias ancabezadas por mujeres y la formación de nucleos extensos." Estudios pobre la mujer I. (México, D.F.: SPP), 319–344.

33. Romanucci-Ross, *Conflict*, 46.

34. Russell W. Coberley, "Maternal and Marital Dyads in a Mexican Town," *Ethnology* 19(4):447–457.

35. Lewis, *Five Families*, 17–18.

36. Arizpe, "Relay Migration," 80.

37. For social networks in urban Mexico, see Lomnitz, *Networks and Marginality*, 4. Carlos Vélez-Ibáñez, *Rituals of Marginality: Politics, Process and Culture Change in Urban Central Mexico, 1969–1974* (Berkeley and Los Angeles: University of California Press, 1983), 10–16.

38. Elizabeth Bott, *Family and Social Networks* (London: Tavistock, 1957).

39. Peter Marris, *Family and Social Change in an African City.* (London: Routledge & Kegan Paul, 1961).

40. Bryan Roberts, *Organizing Strangers: Poor Families in Guatemala City* (Austin: University of Texas Press, 1973).

41. Carlos Vélez-Ibáñez, *Bonds of Mutual Trust: The Cultural Systems of Rotating Credit Associations among Urban Mexicans and Chicanos* (New Brunswick, N.J.: Rutgers University Press, 1983), 19.

42. Young and Willmott, *Family and Kinship in East London.*

43. Hill Gates, *Chinese Working-Class Lives* (Ithaca: Cornell University Press, 1987).

44. Larissa Lomnitz and Marisol Pérez-Lizaur, "Dynastic Growth and Survival Strategies: The Solidarity of Mexican Grand Families," in Raymond T. Smith, ed., *Kinship Ideology and Practice in Latin America* (Chapel Hill: University of North Carolina Press, 1984), 183–195. Larissa Adler Lomnitz, Posición de la mujer en la gran familia: Unidad basica de solidaridad en America Latina," in *La mujer en el sector popular urbano: America Latina y el Caribe* (Santiago, Chile: Naciones Unidas, 1984).

45. R. S. Bryce-Laporte, "Urban Relocation and Family Adaptation in Puerto Rico: A Case Study in Urban Ethnography," in William Mangin, ed. *Peasants in Cities* (Boston: Houghton Mifflin, 1970), 85–97.

46. Douglas Butterworth, "Two Small Groups: A Comparison of Migrants and Non-Migrants in Mexico City," *Urban Anthropology* 1:29–50.

47. Lomnitz, *Networks and Marginality.*

48. Susan Eckstein, *The Poverty of Revolution* (Princeton: Princeton University Press, 1977).

49. See George M. Foster, "Confradía and Compadrazgo in Spain and Spanish America," *Southwestern Journal of Anthropology* 9:1–18. Connie Horstmann and Donald V. Kurtz, "Compadrazgo and Adaptation in Sixteenth-Century Central Mexico," *Journal of Anthropological Research* 35(3):361–373.

50. Sidney W. Mintz and Eric R. Wolf, "An Analysis of Ritual Co-parenthood (Compadrazgo)," *Southwestern Journal of Anthropology* 6(4):341–369.

51. George M. Foster, "Godparents and Social Networks in Tzintzuntzán," *Southwestern Journal of Anthropology* 25:261–278.

52. Gudeman, "Compadrazgo."

53. Guillermo de la Peña, A Legacy of Promises: Agriculture, Politics, and Ritual in the Morelos Highlands of Mexico (Austin: University of Texas Press, 1981), 202.

54. Gloria González Sálazar, "Participation of Women in the Mexican Labor Force," in Nash and Safa, eds., Sex and Class in Latin America, 183–201.

55. Nash and Safa, eds., Sex and Class in Latin America, introduction: xiii.

56. Chant, Women and Survival, 16.

57. Peattie, The View from the Barrio, 123.

58. Elu de Leñero, "Women's Work and Fertility," 46–68.

59. González de la Rocha, Recursos de la pobreza, 121.

60. Graciela Rodríguez de Arizmendi et al., "Algunos factores psicológicos que afectan el cambio del papel y estatus de la mujer en México," Acta Psicológica 1(1):43–52.

61. Julia Tunon Pablos, Mujeres en México: Una historia olvidada (México, D.F.: Planeta, 1987), 160.

62. Nora Lustig and Teresa Rendón, "Condición de actividad y posición ocupacional de la mujer y caracteristicas socioeconómicas de la familia en México," in Lourdes Arizpe, ed., La mujer y el desarrollo II: La mujer y la unidad doméstica, antología (México, D.F.: SEP Diana, 1982), 43–86.

63. Elizabeth Jelin, "La mujer y el mercado de trabajo," Estudios Cedes 1(6).

64. Brígida García and Orlandina de Oliveira, "Dinámica Poblacional de México: Tendencias recientes," Revista Mexicana de Sociología 47:189–205.

65. Chant, Women and Survival, 179–197.

66. See Moser, "Impact of Recession," for Ecuador. Marianne Schmink, "Women and Urban Industrial Development in Brazil," in Nash and Safa, eds., Women and Change in Latin America, 136–164.

67. Cecilia Blondet, "Nuevas formas de hacer política: Las amas de casa populares," Alapanchis 21(25):196–207.

68. Verena Stolke, "The Exploitation of Family Morality: Labor Systems and Family Structure in São Paulo Coffee Plantations, 1850–1979," in Smith, ed., Kinship, 264–296.

69. Catharine Boyle, "Images of Women in Contemporary Chilean Theatre," Bulletin of Latin American Research 5(2):81–96.

70. Vélez-Ibáñez, Bonds of Mutual Trust, 31.

71. Elu de Leñero, ¿Hacia dónde va la mijer mexicana?

72. Glen Elder, "Democratic Parent-Youth Relations in Cross-National Perspective," Social Science Quarterly 49(2):216–228.

Chapter 4. Con Todos Estos Chamacos: Child Rearing in the City

1. INEGI, Estadísticas.

2. Lucille C. Atkins et al., "Neonatal Behavior and Maternal Perceptions of Urban Mexican Infants," in J. Kevin Nugent, Barry M. Lester, and T. Berry Brazelton, eds., The Cultural Context of Infancy, 2: Multicultural and Interdisciplinary Approach to Parent-Infant Relations (Norwood, N.J.: Ablex, 1991), 201–238.

3. Richard Currier, "The Hot and Cold Syndrome and Symbolic Balance in Mexican and Spanish American Folk Medicine," *Ethnology* 5:251–263.

4. Barry M. Popkin et al., "Breast-Feeding Patterns in Low-Income Countries," *Science* (December) 218.

5. Rodólfo Tuiran y Elsa López, "Prácticas anticonceptivas y clases sociales en México: La experiencia reciente," Ponencia presentada en el seminario, La fecundidad en México: Cambio y perspectivas (México, D.F.: El Colegio de México, 1984.)

6. Carlos Welti, "La investigación del efecto de la anticoncepción sobre la fecundidad," in Beatriz Figeroa Campos, ed., *Fecundidad en México*, 317–348.

7. See "Confradía and Compradrozyo"; "Disease Etiologies in Non-Western Medical Systems," *American Anthropologist* 78(4):773–782. Horacio Fabrega, Jr., "On the Specificity of Folk Illnesses," *Southwestern Journal of Anthropology* 26:305–314; "Illness Episodes, Illness Severity and Treatment in a Pluralistic Setting," *Social Science and Medicine* 13b:41–52. Horacio Fabrega, Jr., and Peter Manning, "An Integrated Theory of Disease: Ladino-Mestizo Views of Disease in the Chiapas Highlands," *Psychosomatic Medicine* 35:223–239. John M. Ingham, "On Mexican Folk Medicine," *American Anthropologist* 72:76–87.

8. Currier, "The Hot and Cold Syndrome."

9. Foster, "Confradía and Compadrazgo."

10. Arthur Rubel et al., *Susto, a Folk Illness.* (Chicago: University of Chicago Press, 1985).

11. Kaja Finkler, *Spiritualist Healers in Mexico: Success and Failures of Alternative Therapeutics* (New York:Praeger, 1985), 10.

12. Michael Kearney, "Spiritualist Healing in Mexico," in Peter Morley and Roy Wallis, eds., *Culture and Curing: Anthropological Perspectives on Traditional Medical Beliefs and Practices* (Pittsburgh: University of Pittsburgh Press, 1978), 19–39.

13. For pilgrimage in Mexico, see Eric Wolf, "The Virgin of Guadalupe: A Mexican National Symbol," *Journal of American Folklore* 71:34–39; Victor Turner and Edie Turner, *Image and Pilgrimage in Christian Culture* (Oxford: Blackwell, 1975).

14. Estatado de Morelos, INEGI, 1983.

15. Frances Rothstein, "Capitalist Industrialization and the Increasing Cost of Children, in Nash and Safa, eds., *Sex and Class in Latin America*.

Chapter 5. Se Acaba la Lucha: Widowhood and Old Age

1. World Development Report, 1991. World Bank.

2. Oliveira, "Migración y absorción de mano de obra en la ciudad de México: 1930–1970." Coberley, "Maternal and Marital Dyads."

3. Lomnitz, *Networks and Marginality*, 123.

4. Mariclaire Acosta, 1973. "Los estéreotipos de la mujer mexicana en las fotonovelas," *Diágolos* 19(5):29–31.

5. Gates, *Chinese Working-Class Lives*, 154.

6. Sally Falk Moore, "Old Age in a Life-Time Social Arena: Some Chagga of

Kilimanjaro in 1974," in Barbara Myerhoff and Andrei Simic, eds., *Life's Career—Aging: Cultural Variations in Growing Old* (Beverly Hills: Sage, 1978).

7. M. C. Goldstein et al., "Social and Economic Forces Affecting Intergenerational Relations in Extended Families in a Third World Country: A Cautionary Tale from South Asia," *Journal of Gerontology* 38:716–724.

8. Carlos Vélez-Ibáñez, "Youth and Aging in Central Mexico: One Day in the Life of Four Families of Migrants," in Barbara Myerhoff and Andrei Simic, eds., *Life's Career—Aging*, 107–162.

Chapter 6. ¿Cumplir o Exigir? Urban Women in the 1990s

1. UNICEF, *The State of the World's Children* (Oxford: Oxford University Press, 1991).

2. Martha Judith Sánchez Gómez, "Consideraciones teórico-metodológicas en el estudio del trabajo doméstico en México," in de Oliveira, ed., *Trabajo, poder y sexualidad*.

3. Elliott Liebow, *Tally's Corner: A Study of Negro Streetcorner Men* (Boston: Little, Brown, 1967), 135–136.

4. Howell, *Hard Living on Clay Street*.

5. Janet M. Fitchen, *Poverty in Rural America: A Case Study* (Boulder: Westview Press, 1981); *Endangered Species, Enduring Places* (Boulder: Westview Press, 1991).

6. See Lynn A. Bolles, "Economic Crisis and Female-Headed Households in Urban Jamaica," in Nash and Safa, eds., *Sex and Class in Latin America*, 65–83. M. G. Smith, *West Indian Family Structure*, American Ethnological Society Monographs (Seattle: University of Washington Press, 1962). Raymond T. Smith, *The Negro Family in British Guiana* (London: Routledge & Kegan Paul, 1956).

7. Peattie, *The View from the Barrio*, 45.

8. Quilodrán, "Niveles de fecundidad y patrones de nupcialidad en México."

9. Selby et al., The Mexican Urban Household: Organizing for Self-Defense. Austin: University of Texas Press, 1990, 93.

Bibliography

Acosta, Mariclaire. 1973. Los estéreotipos de la mujer mexicana en las fotonovelas. *Diálogos* 19(5):29–31.

Alba, Francisco. 1982. *The Population of Mexico: Trends, Issues and Policies.* New Brunswick, N.J.: Transaction Books.

Alba, Francisco, and Joseph E. Potter. 1986. Population and Development in Mexico Since 1940: An Interpretation. *Population and Development Review* 12:47–70.

Álvarez, Alfredo Juán. 1979. *La mujer joven en México.* México, D.F.: Ediciones el Caballito.

Álvarez Gutiérrez, Alberto. 1987. ¿Cómo se sienten los mexicanos? In *¿Cómo somos los mexicanos?* edited by Alberto Hernández Medina and Luis Narro Rodríguez, 41–92. México, D.F.: Centro de Estudios Educativos CREA.

Arizpe, Lourdes. 1978. Mujeres migrantes y economía campesina: Análisis de una cohorte migratória a la ciudad de México, 1940–1970. *America Indígena* 38(2): 305–327.

Arizpe, Lourdes. 1982. Relay Migration and the Survival of the Peasant Household. In *Towards a Political Economy of Urbanization in Third World Countries,* edited by Helen Icken Safa, 19–41. Delhi: Oxford University Press.

Arizpe, Lourdes. 1989. *La mujer en el desarrollo de México y de America Latina.* México, D.F.: UNAM/CRIM.

Arrom, Silvia Marina. 1985. *The Women of Mexico City, 1790–1857.* Palo Alto: Stanford University Press.

Atkins, Lucille C., María del Carmen Olvera, Martha Givaudan, and Gerarda Landeros. 1991. Neonatal Behavior and Maternal Perceptions of Urban Mexican Infants. In *The Cultural Context of Infancy. Vol 2. Multicultural and Interdisciplinary Approaches to Parent-Infant Relations,* edited by J. Kevin Nugent, Barry M. Lester, and T. Berry Brazelton, 201–238. Norwood, N.J.: Ablex.

Balan, Jorge. 1969. Migrant-Native Socioeconomic Differences in Latin American Cities: A Structural Analysis. *Latin American Research Review* 4(1).

Balan, Jorge, Harley L. Browning, and Elizabeth Jelin. 1973. *Men in a Developing Society: Social and Geographical Mobility in Monterrey, Mexico.* Austin: University of Texas Press.

Beyer, Glenn H., ed. 1967. *The Urban Explosion in Latin America: A Continent in Process of Modernization.* Ithaca: Cornell University Press.

Blondet, Cecilia. 1985. Nuevas formas de hacer política: Las amas de casa populares. *Alapanchis* 21(25):196–207.

Bolles, A. Lynn. 1986. Economic Crisis and Female-Headed Households in Urban Jamaica. In *Women and Change in Latin America,* edited by June Nash and Helen Safa, 65–83. South Hadley, Mass.: Bergen and Garvey.

Bibliography

Bott, Elizabeth. 1957. *Family and Social Networks*. London: Tavistock.

Bourque, Susan C., and Kay Barbara Warren. 1981. *Women of the Andes: Patriarchy and Social Change in Two Peruvian Towns*. Ann Arbor: University of Michigan Press.

Boyle, Catharine. 1986. Images of Women in Contemporary Chilean Theatre. *Bulletin of Latin American Research* 5(2):81–96.

Brydon, Lynne, and Sylvia Chant. 1989. *Women in the Third World: Gender Issues in Rural and Urban Areas*. Aldershot: Edward Elgar.

Buenaventura-Posso, Elena, and Susan Brown. 1987. Westernization and the Bari of Colombia. In *Sociology of Developing Societies*, edited by Eduardo Archetti et al., 321–328. Basingstoke: Macmillan.

Butterworth, Douglas. 1972. Two Small Groups: A Comparison of Migrants and Non-Migrants in Mexico City. *Urban Anthropology* 1:29–50.

Butterworth, Douglas, and John K. Chance. 1982. *Latin American Urbanization*. Cambridge: Cambridge University Press.

Chant, Sylvia. 1985. Single Parent Families: Choice or Constraint? *Development and Change* 16:635–656.

Chant, Sylvia, and Peter Ward. 1987. Family Structure and Low-Income Housing Policy. *Third World Planning Review* 9(1):5–19.

Chant, Sylvia. 1991. *Women and Survival in Mexican Cities*. Manchester: Manchester University Press.

Chavez, Roberto L., and M. Isabel Vargas. 1976. *Urban Dwelling Environments: Cuernavaca, Mexico*. Cambridge: MIT School of Architecture and Planning.

Cleland, John, and J. Hobcraft. 1985. *Reproductive Change in Developing Countries: Insights from the World Fertility Survey*. New York: Oxford University Press.

Cleland, John, and Jerome van Ginneken. 1988. Maternal Education and Child Survival in Developing Countries: The Search for Pathways of Influence. *Social Science and Medicine* 27:1357–1368.

Coberley, Russell W. 1980. Maternal and Marital Dyads in a Mexican Town. *Ethnology* 19(4):447–457.

Consejo Nacional de Población, Mexico. 1979. *El Programa Nacional de Educación Sexual*. México, D.F.

Consejo Nacional de Población, Mexico. 1982. *México demográfico*. México, D.F.

Cornelius, Wayne A., and F. M. Trueblood, eds. 1975. *Urbanization and Inequality*. Latin American Research, vol. 5. Los Angeles: Sage.

Corona, Esther. 1989. Impresiones sobre una sexualidad. *FEM* 4(6).

Cubitt, Tessa. 1988. *Latin American Society*. London: Longmans.

Currier, Richard. 1966. The Hot and Cold Syndrome and Symbolic Balance in Mexican and Spanish American Folk Medicine. *Ethnology* 5:251–263.

Cuthbert, Richard W., and Joe B. Stevens. 1980. Documentation: The Net Economic Incentive for Illegal Mexican Migration, A Case Study. *International Migration Review* 15(3):543–550.

de la Peña, Guillermo. 1981. *A Legacy of Promises: Agriculture, Politics, and Ritual in the Morelos Highlands of Mexico*. Austin: University of Texas Press.

de la Peña, Guillermo. 1984. Ideology and Practice in Southern Jalisco: Peasant,

Bibliography

Rancheros and Urban Entrepreneurs. In *Kinship and Practice in Latin America*, edited by R. T. Smith. Chapel Hill: University of North Carolina Press.

de Oliveira, Orlandina. 1976. Migración y absorción de mano de obra en la ciudad de México: 1930-1970. Centro de Estudios Sociológicos, no. 14. México, D.F.: El Colegio de México.

Díaz Guerrero, Rogélio. 1955. Neurosis and the Mexican Family Structure. *American Journal of Psychiatry* 112:411-419.

Díaz Guerrero, Rogélio. 1974. La mujer y las premisas histórico-socioculturales de la familia mexicana. *Revista latina de psicología* 6:7-16.

Dirección General de Planificación Familiar, Secretaria de Salud, México. 1988. *Encuesta nacional sobre fecundidad y salud, 1987*.

Douglas, Carrie B. 1984. Toro muerto, vaca es: An Interpretation of the Spanish Bullfight. *American Ethnologist* 11(2):242-258.

Eckstein, Susan. 1977. *The Poverty of Revolution*. Princeton: Princeton University Press.

Ehlers, Tracy Bachrach. 1990. *Silent Looms: Women and Production in a Guatemalan Town*. Boulder: Westview.

Ehlers, Tracy Bachrach. 1991. Debunking Marianismo: Economic Vulnerability and Survival Strategies among Guatemalan Wives. *Ethnology* 30(1):1-12.

Elder, Glen. 1968. Democratic Parent-Youth Relations in Cross-National Perspective. *Social Science Quarterly* 49(2):216-228.

Elu de Leñero, María del Carmen. 1969. ¿Hacia dónde va la mujer mexicana? México, D.F.: Instituto Mexicano de Estudios Sociales, A.C.

Elu de Leñero, María del Carmen. 1976. Women's Work and Fertility. In *Sex and Class in Latin America*, edited by June Nash and Helen Safa, 46-48. New York: Praeger.

Fabrega, Horacio, Jr. 1970. On the Specificity of Folk Illnesses. *Southwestern Journal of Anthropology* 26:305-314.

Fabrega, Horacio, Jr. 1979. Illness Episodes, Illness Severity and Treatment Options in a Pluralistic Setting. *Social Science and Medicine* 13b:41-52.

Fabrega, Horacio, Jr., and Petter Manning. 1973. An Integrated Theory of Disease: Ladino-Mestizo View of Disease in the Chiapas Highlands. *Psychosomatic Medicine* 35:223-239.

Finkler, Kaja. 1985. *Spiritualist Healers in Mexico: Successes and Failures of Alternative Therapeutics*. New York: Praeger.

Fitchen, Janet M. 1981. *Poverty in Rural America: A Case Study*. Boulder: Westview Press.

Fitchen, Janet M. 1991. *Endangered Species, Enduring Places*. Boulder: Westview.

Foster, George M. 1948. *Empire's Children: The People of Tzintzuntzán*. Publications of the Institute of Social Relations. Washington, D.C.: Smithsonian Institution.

Foster, George M. 1953. Cofradía and Compadrazgo in Spain and Spanish America. *Southwestern Journal of Anthropology* 9:1-18.

Foster, George M. 1969. Godparents and Social Networks in Tzintzuntzán. *Southwestern Journal of Anthropology* 25:261-278.

Foster, George M. 1976. Disease Etiologies in Non-Western Medical Systems. *American Anthropologist* 78(4):773-782.

Bibliography

Fromm, Erich, and Michael Maccoby. 1970. *Social Character in a Mexican Village: A Sociopsychoanalytic Study.* Englewood Cliffs, N.J.: Prentice-Hall.

García, Brígida. 1975. La participación de la población en la actividad económica. *Demografía y Economía* 9(1). México, D.F.: El Colegio de México, CEED.

García, Brígida. 1976. Anticoncepción en el México rural, 1969. *Demografía y Economía* 19(3):297-351.

García, Brígida, and Orlandina de Oliveira. 1978. Reflexiones teórico-metodológicas sobre el estudio de las relaciones entre el trabajo de la mujer y la fecundidad en la ciudad de México. *Investigación Demográfica en México.* México, D.F.: CONACYT, Programa Nacional Indicativo de Investigación Demográfica, 277-293.

García, Brígida, and Orlandina de Oliveira. 1985. Dinámica poblacional de México: Tendencias recientes. *Revista Mexicana de Sociología* 47:189-205.

García, Brígida, Humberto Muñoz, and Orlandina de Oliveira. 1982. *Hogares y trabajadores en la ciudad de México.* México, D.F.: El Colegio de México/UNAM.

García, Brígida, Humberto Muñoz, and Orlandina de Oliveira. 1983. Familia y trabajo en México y Brasil. *Estudios Sociológicos* 1(3):487-507. México, D.F.: El Colegio de México.

Gates, Hill. 1987. *Chinese Working-Class Lives.* Ithaca: Cornell University Press.

Giraldo, Octavio. 1972. El machismo como fenómeno psicocultural. *Revista Latinoamericana de Psicología* 4(3):295-309.

Gissi, Jorge. 1976. Mythology about Women with Special Reference to Chile. In *Sex and Class in Latin America,* edited by June Nash and Helen Safa, 30-45. New York: Praeger.

Goldstein, M. C., S. Schuler, and J. L. Ross. 1983. Social and Economic Forces Affecting Intergenerational Relations in Extended Families in a Third World Country: A Cautionary Tale from South Asia. *Journal of Gerontology* 38:716-724.

Gonzáles de la Rocha, Mercédes. 1986. *Recursos de la pobreza: Familias de bajos ingresos en Guadalajara.* Guadalajara: El Colegio de Jalisco and CIESAS.

Gonzáles de la Rocha, Mercédes. 1988. Economic Crisis, Domestic Reorganization and Women's Work in Guadalajara, Mexico. *Bulletin of Latin American Research* 7(2): 207-223.

González Sálazar, Gloria. 1976. Participation of Women in the Mexican Labor Force. In *Sex and Class in Latin America,* edited by June Nash and Helen Safa. New York: Praeger.

Gruening, Ernest. 1928. *Mexico and Its Heritage.* New York: The Century Company.

Gudeman, Stephen. 1972. Compadrazgo as a Reflection of the Natural and Spiritual Person. *Proceedings of the Royal Anthropological Institute:* 45-71.

Helguera, Laura R., Lopez M. Sinecio, and Ramon Ramírez M. 1974. *Los campesinos de la tierra de Zapata: Adaptación, cambio y rebelión.* México, D.F.: Centro de Investigaciones Superiores, Instituto Nacional de Antropología e Historia.

Horstmann, Connie, and Donald V. Kurtz. 1979. Compadrazgo and Adaptation in Sixteenth-Century Central Mexico. *Journal of Anthropological Research* 35(3):361-373.

Howell, Joseph T. 1973. *Hard Living on Clay Street.* Garden City, N.Y.: Anchor Books.

Hunt, Robert C. 1971. Components of Relationships in the Family: A Mexican Village. In *Kinship and Culture,* edited by Francis Hsu, 106-143.

Bibliography

Ingham, John M. 1970. On Mexican Folk Medicine. *American Anthropologist* 72: 76–87.

Ingham, John M. 1986. *Mary, Michael and Lucifer: Folk Catholicism in Central Mexico.* Austin: University of Texas Press.

Instituto Nacional de Estadísticas Geografía e Informática. 1990. *Estadísticas Históricas de México.* Tomo I. México, D.F.: INAH SEP

Instituto Nacional de Estadísticas Geografía e Informática. *X Censo General de Población y Vivienda 1980. Estado de Morelos 3.* Tomo 17. México, D.F.: INEGI.

Instituto Nacional de Estadísticas Geografía e Informática. *XI Censo General de Población y Vivienda, 1990.* México, D.F.: INEGI.

Jaquette, Jane S. 1973. Literary Archetypes and Female Role Alternatives: The Woman and the Novel in Latin America. In *Female and Male in Latin America: Essays,* edited by Ann Pescatello, 3–28. Pittsburgh: University of Pittsburgh Press.

Jelin, Elizabeth. 1978. La mujer y el mercado de trabajo. *Estudios Cedes* 1:6.

Jiménez Ornelas, Rene. 1988. Marginalidad y mortalidad. *Revista Mexicana de Sociología* 50(4):171–186.

Kearney, Michael. 1978. Spiritualist Healing in Mexico. In *Culture and Curing: Anthropological Perspectives on Traditional Medical Beliefs and Practices,* edited by Peter Morley and Roy Wallis, 19–39. Pittsburgh: University of Pittsburgh Press.

Kurtz, Donald. 1973. The Rotating Credit Association: An Adaptation to Poverty. *Human Organization* 32(1):49–71.

Laslett, Peter. 1965. *The World We Have Lost.* London: Methuen.

Lau Jaiven, Ana. 1987. *La nueva olla del feminismo en México: Conciencia y acción de lucha de las mujeres.* México, D.F.: Fasiculos Planeta, S.A. de C.V.

Leacock, Eleanor Burke, ed. 1971. *The Culture of Poverty: A Critique.* New York: Simon and Schuster.

Leeds, Anthony. 1971. The Concept of the "Culture of Poverty": Conceptual, Logical and Empirical Problems, with Perspectives from Brazil and Peru. In *The Culture of Poverty: A Critique,* edited by Eleanor Burke Leacock, 226–284. New York: Simon and Schuster.

Leñero Otero, Luis. 1987. Valores familiares y dramaturgía social. In *¿Cómo son los mexicanos?* edited by Alberto Hernández Medina and Luis Narro Rodríguez. México, D.F.: Centro de Estudios Educativos A.C.

LeVine, Robert A., Sarah LeVine, Amy Richman, F. Medardo Tapia Uribe, Clara Sunderland Correa, and Patrice M. Miller. 1991. Women's Schooling and Child Care in the Demographic Transition: A Mexican Case Study. *Population and Development Review* 17(3):459–496.

LeVine, Sarah. 1986. Parent-Child Relations and Economic Survival in Old Age in Urban Mexico. *Journal of Cross-Cultural Gerontology* 1(3):223–227.

LeVine, Sarah, and Clara Sunderland Correa. 1985. Are Teenage Mothers Different? Paper presented at the First International Meeting on the Sexual and Reproductive Health of Adolescents, Oaxtepec, Mexico.

LeVine, Sarah, Clara Sunderland Correa, and Medardo Tapia Uribe. 1986. The Marital Morality of Mexican Women: An Urban Study. *Journal of Anthropological Research* 42:183–202.

Bibliography

Lewis, Oscar. 1949. Husbands and Wives in a Mexican Village: Study in Role Conflict. *American Anthropologist* 51(4):602–610.

Lewis, Oscar. 1951. *Life in a Mexican Village: Tepoztlán Revisited.* Urbana: University of Illinois Press.

Lewis, Oscar. 1959. *Five Families.* New York: Basic Books.

Lewis, Oscar. 1960. *Tepoztlán: Village in Mexico.* New York: Holt, Rinehart and Winston.

Lewis, Oscar. 1961. *The Children of Sánchez: Autobiography of a Mexican Family.* New York: Random House.

Lewis, Oscar. 1966a. *La Vida: A Puerto Rican Family in the Culture of Poverty—San Juan and New York.* New York: Random House.

Lewis, Oscar. 1966b. "The Culture of Poverty." *Scientific American* 215:19–25.

Lewis, Oscar. 1968. *A Study of Slum Culture: Backgrounds for La Vida.* New York: Random House.

Liebow, Elliott. 1967. *Tally's Corner: A Study of Negro Streetcorner Men.* Boston: Little Brown.

Lomnitz, Larissa Adler. 1977a. *Networks and Marginality: Life in a Mexican Shantytown.* New York: Academic Press.

Lomnitz, Larissa Adler. 1977b. Migration and Network in Latin America. In *Current Perspectives in Latin American Urban Research,* edited by Alejandro Portes and Harley Browning, 133–150. Institute of Latin American Studies. Austin: University of Texas Press.

Lomnitz, Larissa Adler. 1984. Posición de la mujer en la gran familia: Unidad básica de solaridad en America Latina. In *La Mujer en el sector popular urbano: America Latina y el Caribe.* Santiago, Chile: Naciones Unidas.

Lomnitz, Larissa Adler, and Marisol Pérez-Lizaur. 1984. Dynastic Growth and Survival Strategies: The Solidarity of Mexican Grand Families. In *Kinship Ideology and Practice in Latin America,* edited by R. Smith, 183–195. Chapel Hill: University of North Carolina Press.

Lustig, Nora, and Teresa Rendón. 1982. Condición de actividad y posición ocupacional de la mujer y características socioeconómicas de la familia en México. In *La Mujer y el desarrollo II; La mujer y la unidad doméstica: Antología,* edited by Lourdes Arizpe. México, D.F.: SEP Diana.

Marquez, Viviane B. 1984. Política de planificación familiar en México: Un proceso institucionalizado? *Revista Mexicana de Sociología* 46:285–310.

Marris, Peter. 1961. *Family and Social Change in an African City.* London: Routledge and Kegan Paul.

Martin, Cheryl English. 1985. *Rural Society in Colonial Morelos.* Albuquerque: University of New Mexico Press.

Meyer, Jean. 1977. *Los Cristeros.* México, D.F.: El Colegio de México.

Mintz, Sidney W., and Eric R. Wolf. 1950. An Analysis of Ritual Co-parenthood (Compadrazgo). *Southwestern Journal of Anthropology* 6(4)341–369.

Mollinger, Robert N. 1984. Creative Writers on Personality: Octavio Paz and Carlos Fuentes on the Mexican National Character. *Psychoanalytic Review* 71(2):305–317.

Moore, Sally Falk. 1978. Old Age in a Lifetime Social Arena: Some Chagga of Kiliman-

Bibliography

jaro in 1974. In *Life's Career—Aging: Cultural Variations in Growing Old*, edited by Barbara Myerhoff and Andrei Simic, 23–76. Beverly Hills: Sage.

Moser, Caroline. 1989. The Impact of Recession and Structural Adjustment Policies at the Micro-Level: Low-Income Women and Their Households in Guayaquil, Ecuador. In *Invisible Adjustment 2*, 137–162. New York: UNICEF Americas and Caribbean Regional Office.

Muñoz, Humberto, Orlandina de Oliveira, and Claudio Stern. 1977. *Migración y desigualdad social en la ciudad de México*. México, D.F.: El Colegio de México/UNAM Instituto de Investigaciones Sociales.

Nagel, J. 1978. Mexico's Population Policy Turnaround. *Population Bulletin* 33(5):1–40.

Nash, June, and Helen Safa, eds. 1976. Introduction to *Sex and Class in Latin America*. New York: Praeger.

Nolasco, Margarita. 1978. La Familia Mexicana. *FEM* 2(7):14–19.

Nun, José. 1969. Sobrepoblación relativa, ejército industrial de reserva y masa marginal. *Revista Latinoamericana de Sociología* 4(2):178–237.

Nuñez Fernández, Leopoldo. 1989. México: Las encuestas nacionales en la estimación de los niveles de fecundidad. In *La fecundidad en México: Cambios y perspectivas*, edited by Beatriz Figueroa Campos, 90–120. México, D.F.: El Colegio de México.

Nutini, Hugo G. 1965. Polygyny in a Tlaxcalán Community. *Ethnology* 4:123–148.

Oliviera, Mercedes. 1976. The Barrios of San Andrés, Cholula. In *Essays on Mexican Kinship*, edited by Hugo G. Nutini, Pedro Carrasco, and James M. Taggert, 65–92. Pittsburgh: University of Pittsburgh Press.

Paz, Octavio. 1950. *El laberinto de la soledad*. Mexico City: Cuadernos Mexicanos.

Peattie, Lisa Redfield. 1968. *The View from the Barrio*. Ann Arbor: University of Michigan Press.

Peattie, Lisa Redfield. 1971. The Structural Parameters of Emerging Life Styles in Venezuela. In *The Culture of Poverty: A Critique*, edited by Eleanor Burke Leacock, 285–298. New York: Simon and Schuster.

Peattie, Lisa Redfield. 1974. The Concept of "Marginality" as Applied to Squatter Settlements. *Latin American Urban Research 4*, edited by Wayne A. Cornelius and Felicity M. Trueblood, 101–109. Beverly Hills and London: Sage.

Perlman, Janice E. 1976. *Myth of Marginality: Urban Poverty and Politics in Rio de Janeiro*. Berkeley and Los Angeles, University of California Press.

Pescatello, Ann. 1976. *Power and Pawn: The Female in Iberian Families, Societies and Cultures*. Westport, Conn.: Greenwood Press.

Popkin, Barry M., Richard E. Bilsbrow, and John Akin. 1982. Breast-Feeding Patterns in Low-Income Countries. *Science* (December):218.

Quezada, Noemi. 1979. La sexualidad en México. *Anales de Antropología* 16:233–244.

Quijano, Anibal. 1973. Redefinición de la dependencia y proceso de marginalización en America Latina. In *Populismo, marginalidad y dependencia*, edited by Francisco C. Weffort and Anibal Quijano, 171–329. San José, Costa Rica: Editorial Universitaria Centro-Americano.

Quilodrán, Julieta. 1980. Tipos de uniones maritales en México. Ponencia presentada en la Segunda Reunión Nacional sobre la Investigación Demográfica en México. México, D.F.: CONACYT.

Quilodrán, Julieta. 1991. Niveles de fecundidad y patrones de nupcialidad en México. México, D.F.: El Colegio de México.

Radcliffe, Sarah. 1986. Gender Relations, Peasant Livelihood Strategies and Migration: A Case Study from Cuzco, Peru. *Bulletin of Latin American Research* 5(2):29–47.

Ramírez, Santiago. 1968. El mexicano: La psicología de sus motivaciones. *Monografías Psicoanalíticos.* Asociación Psicoanalítica Mexicana. Mexico City: MexPax.

Ramos, S. 1962. *Profile of Man and Culture in Mexico,* trans. P. G. Earle. Austin: University of Texas Press.

Roberts, Bryan. 1973. *Organizing Strangers: Poor Families in Guatemala City.* Austin: University of Texas Press.

Rodríguez de Arizmendi, Graciela, Eduardo Almeida, Dolores Mercado, and Marcela Rivero Weber. 1981. Algunos factores psicológicos que afectan el cambio del papel y estatus de la mujer en México. *Acta Psicológica* 1(1):43–52.

Roldán, María. 1984. Pautas de control del circúito monetario domésticas y formas de conciencia entre trabajadoras industriales domiciliarias en la ciudad de México. Ponencia presentada en la Reunión de Investigación sobre La Mujer e Investigación Feminista. Montevideo, Uruguay: GRECMU.

Romanucci-Ross, Lola. 1973. *Conflict, Violence and Morality in a Mexican Village.* Palo Alto: National Press Books.

Rothstein, Frances. 1986. Capitalist Industrialization and the Increasing Cost of Children. In *Women and Change in Latin America,* edited by June Nash and Helen Safa. South Hadley, Mass.: Bergen and Garvey.

Rubel, Arthur, Carl O'Nell, and R. Collado Ardon. 1985. *Susto: A Folk Illness.* Chicago: University of Chicago Press.

Rubin, Lillian Breslow. 1976. *Worlds of Pain: Life in the Working-Class Family.* New York: Basic Books.

Safa, Helen. 1986. Female Employment in the Puerto Rican Working Class. In *Women and Change in Latin America,* edited by June Nash and Helen Safa, 84–105. South Hadley, Mass.: Bergen and Garvey.

Sánchez Gómez, Martha Judith. 1989. Consideraciones teórico-metodológicas en el estudio del trabajo doméstico en México. In *Trabajo, poder y sexualidad,* edited by Orlandina de Oliveira. México, D.F.: El Colegio de México.

Schmink, Marianne. 1982. Women in the Urban Economy in Latin America. Working Paper #1, Population Council, New York.

Schmink, Marianne. 1986. Women and Urban Industrial Development in Brazil. In *Women and Change in Latin America,* edited by June Nash and Helen Safa, 136–164. South Hadley, Mass.: Bergen and Garvey.

Scott, Alison MacEwen. 1986. Industrialization, Gender Segregation and Stratification Theory. In *Gender and Stratification,* edited by Rosemary Crompton and Michael Mann, 154–189. Cambridge: Polity Press.

Selby, Henry A. 1976. The Study of Social Origins in Traditional Mesoamerica. In *Essays on Mexican Kinship,* edited by Hugo Nutini, Pedro Carrasco, and James M. Taggert, 29–41. Pittsburgh: University of Pittsburgh Press.

Bibliography

Selby, Henry A., Arthur D. Murphy, and Stephen A. Lorenzen. 1990. *The Mexican Urban Household: Organizing for Self-Defense.* Austin: University of Texas Press.

Smith, M. G. 1962. *West Indian Family Structure.* American Ethnological Society Monographs. Seattle: University of Washington Press.

Smith, Raymond T. 1956. *The Negro Family in British Guiana.* London: Routledge and Kegan Paul.

Stevens, Evelyn P. 1973. Marianismo: The Other Face of Machismo in Latin America. In *Female and Male in Latin America: Essays,* edited by Ann Pescatello, 89–102. Pittsburgh: University of Pittsburgh Press.

Stolke, Verena. 1984. The Exploitation of Family Morality: Labor Systems and Family Structure in São Paulo Coffee Plantations, 1850–1979. In *Kinship Ideology and Practice in Latin America,* edited by Raymond T. Smith, 264–296. Chapel Hill: University of North Carolina Press.

Stycos, J. M. 1958. *Familia y fecundidad en Puerto Rico.* México, D.F.: Fondo de Cultura Económica.

Taggert, James M. 1992. Gender, Segregation and Cultural Constructions of Sexuality in Two Hispanic Societies. *American Ethnologist* 19(1):75–96.

Tienda, Marta, and Sylvia Ortega. 1982. Las familias encabezadas por mujeres y la formación de nucleos extensos. Estudios sobre la mujer I. *El Empleo y la Mujer,* 319–344. México, D.F.: SPP.

Townsend, Peter. 1957. *The Family Life of Old People.* London: Routledge and Kegan Paul.

Tuck, Jim. 1982. *The Holy War in Los Altos: A Regional Analysis of Mexico's Cristero Rebellion.* Tucson: University of Arizona Press.

Tuiran, Rodólfo, and Elsa López. 1984. Prácticas anticonceptivas y clases sociales en México: La experiencia reciente. Ponencia presentada en el seminario, *La fecundidad en México: cambios y perspectivas.* México, D.F.: El Colegio de México.

Tunon Pablos, Julia. 1987. *Mujeres en México: Una historia olvidada.* México, D.F.: Planeta.

Turner, Victor, and Edie Turner. 1975. *Image and Pilgrimage in Christian Culture.* Oxford: Blackwell.

Turner, John F. C. 1976. *Housing by People.* London: Marion Boyar.

UNICEF. 1991. *The State of the World's Children.* Oxford: Oxford University Press.

Urquidi, Victor. 1967. El crecimiento demográfico y el desarollo económico latinoamericano. *Demografía y Economía* 1(1).

Urquidi, Victor. 1975. The Underdeveloped City. In *Urbanization in Latin America: Approaches and Issues,* edited by J. C. Hardoy, 339–366. Garden City, N.Y.: Anchor Books.

Valentine, Charles. 1968. *Culture and Poverty: Critique and Counter-Proposals.* Chicago: University of Chicago Press.

Vélez Ibáñez, Carlos G. 1978. Youth and Aging in Central Mexico: One Day in the Life of Four Families of Migrants. *Life's Career—Aging: Cultural Variations on Growing Old,* edited by Barbara G. Myerhoff and Andrei Simic, 107–162. Beverly Hills: Sage.

Vélez Ibáñez, Carlos G. 1983a. *Bonds of Mutual Trust: The Cultural Systems of Rotating Credit Associations among Urban Mexicans and Chicanos.* New Brunswick, N.J.: Rutgers University Press.

Bibliography

Vélez Ibáñez, Carlos G. 1983b. *Rituals of Marginality: Politics, Process, and Culture Change in Urban Central Mexico, 1969–1974*. Berkeley and Los Angeles: University of California Press.

Ware, Helen. 1984. Effects of Maternal Education, Women's Roles and Child Care on Child Mortality. *Population and Development Review* [supplement to vol. 10]:191–214.

Weffort, Francisco C., and Anibal Quijano, eds. 1973. *Populismo, marginalidad y dependencia*. San Jose, Costa Rica: Editorial Universitaria Centro-Americano.

Welti, Carlos. 1989. La investigación del efecto de la anticoncepción sobre la fecundidad. In *Fecundidad en México: Cambios y perspectivas*, edited by Beatriz Figueroa Campos, México, D.F.: El Colegio de México.

Whetten, Nathan L. 1948. *Rural México*. Chicago: University of Chicago Press.

Whiteford, Andrew H. 1964. *Two Cities in Latin America*. New York: Anchor Books.

Wolf, Eric. 1959. *Sons of the Shaking Earth*. Chicago: University of Chicago Press.

Wolf, Eric. 1966. Kinship, Friendship and Patron-Client Relationships in Complex Societies. In *The Social Anthropology of Complex Societies*, edited by M. Bantan. London: Tavistock.

Wolf, Eric. 1978. The Virgin of Guadalupe: A Mexican National Symbol. *Journal of American Folklore* 71:34–39.

Womack, John, Jr. 1968. *Zapata and the Mexican Revolution*. New York: Knopf.

Young, Michael, and Peter Willmott. 1957. *Family and Kinship in East London*. London: Routledge and Kegan Paul.

Index

Abduction, 56–57, 70–71
Abortion, 66, 152, 153
Abram (Eloisa's son), 76, 157–58, 159
Adolescence, 21–22, 52–78
Adoption, 67, 173
Afuera: defined, 84; world of, 84–85, 200, 203
Agriculture, 7
Ahijado, 103
Aire, el, 144, 145, 155
Alcoholics Anonymous, 86, 196
Alcoholism. *See* Drinking
Alfonso (Inés's son), 115, 126
Alfredo (Luz María's mother's lover), 45–49
Amando (Lourdes's first husband), 25
Amelia (Soledad's mother), 100–101
Andrés (Inés's son), 159, 163
Angel (Lourdes's son), 142–43
Anticlericalism, 57. *See also* Catholic Church;
    Constitution of 1917
Antonio (Inés's husband), 24, 59, 82, 101, 112,
    119–26, 138, 181–82, 206
Arizpe, Lourdes, 97
Arnaldo (Inocencia's lover), 132–35
Arrom, Silvia, 89
Arturo (Lourdes's son), 188
Arturo (Margarita's brother), 42, 43, 44
Arturo (Ofelia's husband), 27, 126–30
Atkins, Lucille, 145
Augustín (Padre), 107–8
Avila Camacho, Manuel, 39, 120
Aztec empire, 11, 14

Baptism, 102, 103, 162, 171
Battered wives. *See* Domestic violence
Beatriz (Verónica's daughter), 55, 174, 175
Bible study groups, 107–8
Birth: age of mother at first, 140. *See also*
    Childbearing
Birth control, 76; absence of, 6, 120, 123, 151,
    167; views of, 10–11, 45, 151–53; lack of
    candor about, 65, 66; knowledge of, 93,
137, 173, 176; and breast-feeding, 147. *See
    also* Abortion; Family planning; Family
    size; Population growth; Sterilization
Birthdays, 161–63
Birth rates, 6, 11
Blás (Catalina's suitor), 70–71
Bottle-feeding. *See* Breast-feeding vs. bottle-
    feeding
Bourque, Susan, 89
Boyle, Catharine, 113
Brazil, 11, 110
Breast-feeding vs. bottle-feeding, 145–48, 167, 176
Butterworth, Douglas, 9

California, 206; economic advantages in,
    29–31, 81, 84, 114–15. *See also* Los Ange-
    les; San Francisco
Calles, Plutarco Elias, 30, 57
Canijos, defined, 94
Cárdenas, Lázaro, 39, 65, 120
Carlos (Soledad's grandson), 170, 171, 172, 207
Carlota (Inocencia's daughter), 130, 134–36,
    181
Catalina, 105; description of, 25, 207; child-
    hood of, 31, 36, 37, 39, 50, 158, 161; adoles-
    cence of, 70–74; marriage of, 82, 102, 137;
    on religion, 107–8; childbearing of, 142,
    144, 151; mother of, 158; as widow, 181; as
    mother, 182. *See also* Joaquín
Catholic Church: in 1917 Constitution, 30;
    ceremonies associated with, 102; and Los
    Robles respondents, 106–8; and Spir-
    itualist Church, 156–57. *See also* Anti-
    clericalism; Godparents
Celia, 122
Cerrada del Condor (Mexico City), 100
César (Irene's son), 152
Chant, Sylvia, 94, 95, 110, 112, 200
Chicago (IL), 180, 182, 206
Child abuse. *See* Child rearing; Domestic vio-
    lence; Sexual abuse

231

Index

Childbearing, 23, 140–60, 176
Childhood, 21, 28–51, 195–96
Child rearing: changes in, 18, 23, 145–77. See
 also Education
Children: adult, as safety net, 23, 63, 178–85;
 household responsibilities of, 37–38, 161,
 174, 198; need of, for fathers, 86; legiti-
 macy of, 91, 134; in female-headed house-
 holds, 95; and women's employment, 110–
 11; problems of raising, in USA, 115, 206.
 See also Childbearing; Child rearing; Fam-
 ily size; Fathers; Infants; Employment op-
 portunities; Household responsibilities;
 Mother(s)
Children of Sánchez, The (Lewis), 3–4, 201
China, 193
Chucho (Gloria's husband), 73–74
Chucho (Matilda's son), 106
Ciudad Guayana (Venezuela), 7, 98
Coberley, Russell, 96
Code of honor. See Male honor
Colombia, 11
Colonia: defined, 15
Colonias populares. See Squatters
Comedor popular, 110
Compadrazgo (fictive kinship), 101, 162, 171; as
 safety net, 10, 67, 102–6
Compadres: defined, 103–4. See also *Compadrazgo*
CONAPO (Consejo Nacional de Población),
 11
Concha (Estela and Inés's sister), 104
Confirmation, 102, 162, 171
Consejo Nacional de Población (CONAPO),
 11
Consensual unions, 56, 125, 129, 172
Constitution of 1917 (Mexico), 9; on religion,
 30, 39; on education, 38, 39
Contraception. See Birth control; Family plan-
 ning; Sterilization
Corona, Esther, 66
Cortés, Hernán, 11, 14, 15
Courtship, 21–22; before 1940, 55–59, 119–20,
 168; after 1940, 59–62, 77, 84–85. See also
 Engagement
Coyote, el: defined, 114
Creci. See Lucrecia
Credit associations, 115, 119
Crisis, la: in Cuernavaca, 5, 21; origins of, 10;
 and women's employment, 23, 112–13,

139, 200–201; effects of, on marriage, 69,
 139, on men's employment, 83–84, on
 domestic violence, 86–87, 93–94
Cristero War, 30, 31, 57
Cristina (Catalina's daughter), 181
Cuarentena, 144, 151
Cuates: defined, 93; violence by, 203
Cuernavaca: as site of study, 5, 18–19; urban-
 ization of, 6; history of, 11, 14–17; age at
 marriage in, 64–65; women's employment
 in, 113–14, 200. See also Los Robles; Work-
 ing class life
"Culture of poverty" concept, 4
Currier, Richard, 146

de la Peña, Guillermo, 87–88, 104
Depression: economic. See crisis, la
Díaz, Porfirio, 7, 14
Diego, Juan, 157
DIF (Department of Family Services), 129
Divorce, 67, 92, 95–96, 125, 134, 136
Doble jornada (double work load), 83, 110, 139,
 200, 201
Domestic violence, 3, 22, 84–87, 88, 136,
 195–96, 203; and gender roles, 35, 93–94;
 in Ofelia's family, 35, 128; in Eloisa's fam-
 ily, 36, 76–77; in Luz María's family, 46–47,
 85–86, 87; in Irene's family, 88; women's
 resistance to, 97–98, 110, 138, 187; in
 Arturo's family, 127, 128; in Soledad's fam-
 ily, 167–68, 170; in Lourdes's family, 186,
 187. See also sexual abuse
Double standard (of marital fidelity), 87–94.
 See also Promiscuity
Douglas, Carrie, 53–54
Drinking, 3, 22, 84–87, 136, 183, 196–97, 203;
 in Soledad's family, 31, 168, 183; in Ofelia's
 family, 35; in Catalina's family, 36, 70; in
 Eloisa's family, 76–77; in Julia's family, 119;
 in Lourdes's family, 183, 186–87

Echeverría, Luis, 11
Eckstein, Susan, 102
Economy. See *Crisis, la*
Edmundo (Margarita's husband), 24, 56–57,
 60, 80–81, 112, 144
Eduardo (Lourdes's son), 187–88
Education: and social mobility, 9, 41–42, 59,
 164; and fertility of Mexican women,

Index

García, Brígida, 19, 95
Gates, Hill, 193
Gender roles: in the Sánchez family, 3; in Mexican families, 22–23, 63–64, 89–90, 93–94; during *la crisis*, 139. *See also* Husbands; Machismo; Marianismo; Marriage: division of labor in; Wives
General Law of Population, 11
Generations: changes in relations between, 54, 183; lack of gap between, among Mexican men, 138. *See also* Gran familia
Giraldo, Octavio, 54, 87
Gissi, Jorge, 94
Gloria (Catalina's daughter), 61, 73–74, 108
Gloria (Doña), 156
Godparents, 23, 102–6, 158, 162, 171. *See also* Compadrazgo; Madrina de boda; Padrino de boda
Goldstein, Marvin, 193
González de la Rocha, Mercédes, 86–87, 95, 109, 110, 113, 200
González Sálazar, Gloria, 108
Graduations, 162–63
Grandmother(s): role of, 34, 180–81, 193; Luz María's, 46, 86, 181; Inés and Estela's, 59, 144; Catalina's, 70; Eloisa's, 74–76; Soledad's, 167
Gran familia, 99–100, 194
Great Britain, 98, 99; urbanization in, 6–7, 9–10
Great Depression, 30–31. *See also* Crisis, la
Guadalajara, 30; studies of, 86–87, 110, 113, 200
Guatemala, 67, 69, 90, 98, 198
Gudeman, Stephen, 103
Guillermo (Rocío's lover), 92–93

Hard Living on Clay Street (Howell), 4
Health care: improvements in Mexican, 5, 6, 193, 197–98; medicalization of, 18, 23, 140–41, 153–54, 176; Luz María's, 48; folk remedies for, 153–58; and urbanization, 202. *See also* Health insurance; Hospitals
Health insurance, 8, 140–41
Héctor (Luz María's son), 44, 45, 159, 164
Hembrismo, 79–80. *See also* Marianismo
Herlinda (Lourdes's sister), 187
Hospitals: childbirth in, 142–43, 167
Household(s): variations in, in Los Robles, 19;

female-headed, 19, 95; role of elderly women in, 23,181, 182, 189, 190; married, 82–84; matrifocal, 203–4. *See also* Family relations; *Gran familia*; Kin; *Otra mujer, La*; Safety net; Single adults; Single mothers; Wives
Household responsibilities, 37–38; Margarita's childhood, 44; Luz María's childhood, 47–48; of contemporary adolescents, 63
Housing: acquisition of, 83, 84. *See also* Household(s)
Houston (TX), 180, 206
Howell, Joseph, 4, 203
Hugo (Rosa's husband), 26–27, 108, 208
Hunt, Robert, 37
Husbands: and family size, 65, 152, 197; obligations of, 79–81, 90, 96; relations of, with family members, 96–97, 136; reactions of, to wives' employment, 113, 201; and birth of their children, 142, 144, 145; sleeping arrangements of infants, wife, and, 150, 176; and *cuarentena*, 151; financial condition of Los Robles, 183. *See also* Children; Fathers; Machismo; Men; Promiscuity

Immunization, 153–54
IMSS (Instituto Mexicano de Seguro Social), 141, 143
Indigenous Mexican societies, 79–80
Industrialization: in Mexico, 6–7
Inequality: in Mexico, 8, 9–10
Inés, 81, 115; description of, 24, 207; childhood of, 29–31, 34, 39; adolescence of, 52–53, 57, 59; marriage of, 82, 101, 119–26, 138; on religion, 106; employment of, 112, 113, 125; childbearing of, 144; child rearing by, 146, 150, 158, 159, 162–63, 182; as grandmother, 181–82. *See also* Antonio
Infants: sleeping arrangements for, 145, 149–51, 176. *See also* Children; Mortality rates: infant
Infidelity. *See* Promiscuity
Ingham, John M., 35, 88, 151, 156
Inocencia: description of, 25, 206; childhood of, 32–33, 34, 37, 50; as single mother, 130–36, 182; as grandmother, 181
Instituto de Seguridad y Servicios Sociales de los Trabajores del Estado (ISSSTE), 141, 143, 174

Index

Occupations. *See* Employment opportunities; Men

Octavio (Luz María's husband), 27, 44–45, 55, 66, 85–86, 87, 114, 145

Ofelia, 81; description of, 27, 206; childhood of, 32, 34; adolescence of, 61–62, 140; marriage of, 82, 126–30, 138; religion of, 106; childbearing of, 152; as mother, 161. *See also* Arturo

Oficios, 8, 82

Orange County (CA), 29–31

Ornelas, Jiménez, 154

Otra mujer, la, 35, 137; situation of, 91; Antonio's, 121–24, 206; Arturo's father's, 127; Jorge's, 167; Rubén's, 172; and widowhood, 181–82. *See also* Promiscuity

Padrino de boda, 56, 57, 58, 67. *See also* Godparents

Pancho (Julia's consensual husband), 26, 119

Parteras (midwives), 141–43, 167

Partido Revolucionario Institutional (PRI), 9, 99; and *la crisis*, 10

Passion: male vs. female, 53–54

Pati (Rocío's daughter), 93, 161, 185, 188–89

Peattie, Lisa, 7, 98, 109, 204

Pedro (Matilde's husband), 25–26, 62, 82, 95, 152

Pensions: in Mexico, 23, 179, 193

Pérez-Lizaur, Marisol, 99, 100

Philandering. *See* Promiscuity

Pilgrimages, 157–58

Polygyny, 92

Population growth: in Mexico, 6; and urbanization, 7; Echeverría on, 11; in Cuernavaca, 15. *See also* Birth control; Birth rates; Family planning; Family size

Pregnancy, 140–45. *See also* Childbearing

Prenatal care, 143, 197

Presentación, 162

PRI (Partido Revolucionario Institutional), 9, 10, 99

Primary school completion, 9, 59, 163

Promiscuity: by males, 3, 35, 50, 87–90, 121–30, 136, 137, 195–96, 203, theories about, 80, 127, types of, 90–91; lack of, by females, 87–88, 122–23, 128, 174, exceptions to, 189. *See also* Double standard; *Otra mujer, la*

Prostitutes, 123

Protestant denominations, 106, 107

Public education. *See* Education; Educational opportunities; SEP

Puerto Vallarta (Mexico), 110

Querétaro (Mexico), 8, 18, 110, 112, 200

Quilodrán, Julieta, 204

Quinceaños, 60–61, 64, 76, 132

Ramírez, Santiago, 80

Rape. *See* Sexual abuse

Raul (Nina's lover), 125

Regla, La. See Menstruation

Religion, 106–8, 128. *See also* Catholic Church; Faith

Revolution of 1910, 6, 14–15, 31; effects of, on Los Robles women, 21, 29, 31, 32–33, 42–43, 50, 112

Ricardo, 130, 134, 136

Roberto (Ofelia's son), 126, 127, 130, 140, 161

Rocío (Lourdes's daughter), 25, 92–93, 146, 161–62, 185, 187, 188–89, 207. *See also* Pati

Rodrigo (Catalina's son), 181, 182

Rodríguez de Arizmendi, Graciela, 109

Rogelio (Judith's lover), 132, 133

Roldán, María, 88

Romanucci-Ross, Lola, 88, 96, 97

Rosa, 196; description of, 26–27, 208; childhood of, 37; as aerobics instructor, 84, 208; marriage of, 97, 108; as mother, 164. *See also* Hugo

Rosalía (Soledad's granddaughter), 171, 207

Rothstein, Frances, 164

Rubel, Arthur, 155

Rubén (Verónica's husband), 26, 172–74

Rubin, Lillian, 4–5, 196

Rural Mexico: resistance to family planning campaign in, 11; migrants' nostalgia for, 32; urbanites' views of, 33

Rural stagnation: and urbanization, 7, 15

Safa, Helen, 109

Safety net, 10; adult children as, 23, 63, 178–85

Salinas, Carlos, 201

Salomon (Margarita's son), 206

Salvador (Inés's son), 123–24

Sánchez, Consuelo, 3–4, 50, 201

Sánchez, Jesús (father), 50, 80, 92, 201

Index

difficulties of raising children in, 115, 206; importation of birth control from, 151; infant mortality in, 198. *See also* California; Washington, D.C.

Urbanization: effects of, on Mexican women, 3, 176, 201–4, on men, 201–4; in Mexico, 6–7. *See also* Educational opportunities; Family planning; Health care; Industrialization; Migrants; Rural stagnation

Urquidi, Víctor, 7, 10

Vecindades: defined, 15; described, 16–17

Vélez-Ibáñez, Carlos, 98, 115, 194

Venezuela, 7, 98, 109, 204

Vera (Catalina's cousin), 71–72

Verónica: description of, 26, 206; adolescence of, 54–56; marriage of, 82, 173, 175; as mother, 164, 172–76. *See also* Rubén

Víctor (Irene's husband), 26, 61, 88

Victoria (Soledad's daughter), 169–71

Violence: street, against males, 203. *See also* Domestic violence; Machismo

Virginity (female), 46, 56, 59, 67, 72; and male honor, 52–54, 77. *See also* Promiscuity: lack of, by females; Seclusion

Virgin of Guadalupe, 30, 76, 157

Wages: women's, 109; docking of men's, to support their families, 129; inadequacy of men's, 208

Walking: by infants, 149

War(s). *See* Cristero War; Revolution of 1910

Ward, Peter, 94, 95

Warren, Kay, 90

Washington, D.C., 4

Water: in Los Robles, 17

Weaning. *See* Breast-feeding vs. bottle-feeding

Welfare. *See* Safety net

Whitehead, Andrew, 8

Widows: social customs concerning, 43; support for, 178–85

Wife battering. *See* Domestic violence

Wives: relations of, with their mothers and mothers-in-law, 82–83, 86, 99–101, 127, 145; of polygynists, 91–92; behavior of, 94. *See also* Otra mujer, la; Seclusion; Women

Wolf, Eric, 103

Women: generational differences between Mexican, 3, 20, 21–24; childhoods of, 21, 28–51, 195–96; adolescences of, 21–22, 52–78; and courtship, 21–22, 55–67; economic position of elderly, 23, 178–94; childbearing by, 23, 140–45, 197–98, 201–5; child rearing by, 23, 140–77, 198; marriages of, 79–139; sources of self-respect for, 87, 89, 97, 196–98, 201; legal status of, 108–9; life expectancy of, 178; effects of urbanization on, 201–2. *See also* Employment opportunities; Marriage; Mother(s); Sexual relations; Single women; Spiritual superiority; Wages; Wives

Women's Liberation, 23, 137–38

"Women's Schooling, Fertility and Maternal Behavior" (study), 17–20

Working class life: international studies of, 3–5; in Cuernavaca, 5–6; stratification in, 8–9; in Los Robles, 16–17; changes in, 195–96. *See also* Social mobility

World Fertility Study, 64, 147

Worlds of Pain (Rubin), 4–5

Yael (Carlota's daughter), 134

Yolanda (Catalina's daughter), 73

Zapata, Emiliano, 14, 200

Life Course Studies
David L. Featherman
David I. Kertzer
    General Editors

Nancy W. Denney
Thomas J. Espenshade
Dennis P. Hogan
Jennie Keith
Maris A. Vinovskis
    Associate General Editors

Family and the Female Life Course:
The Women of Verviers, Belgium, 1849–1880
George Alter

Political Attitudes over the Life Span:
The Bennington Woman after Fifty Years
Duane F. Alwin, Ronald L. Cohen,
and Theodore M. Newcomb

The Ageless Self: Sources of Meaning in Late Life
Sharon R. Kaufman

The Healer's Tale: Transforming Medicine and Culture
Sharon R. Kaufman

Family, Political Economy, and Demographic Change:
The Transformation of Life in Casalecchio, Italy, 1861–1921
David I. Kertzer and Dennis P. Hogan

Dolor y Alegría: Woman and Social Change in Urban Mexico
Sarah LeVine,
in collaboration with
Clara Sunderland Correa